THE RUSSIAN PIANO SCHOOL

THE RUSSIAN PIANO SCHOOL

Russian Pianists and Moscow Conservatoire Professors on the Art of the Piano

TRANSLATED AND EDITED BY CHRISTOPHER BARNES

KAHN & AVERILL
LONDON

Published by Kahn & Averill
2-10 Plantation Road
Amersham, Buckinghamshire, HP6 6HJ
United Kingdom

www.kahnandaverill.co.uk

First published in Great Britain in 2007 Kahn & Averill

Translation © 2007 Christopher Barnes

'Advice from a Pianist and Teacher', 'Three Answers to Questions about Beethoven's Appasionata', 'Work on Beethoven's Sonata in A Major Opus 101', 'Notes on Chopin's Ballade in F Minor', 'Chopin's Fourth Ballade in F Minor' © Publishing House Muzyka, Moscow

A CIP record of this book is available from the British Library

Cover and book design by Simon Stern

Printed in Great Britain by Halstan UK
2-10 Plantation Road
Amersham, Buckinghamshire, HP6 6HJ
United Kingdom

www.halstan.co.uk

ISBN 978-1-871-08288-3

CONTENTS

INTRODUCTION   IX

A NOTE ON THE AUTHORS   XXII

PART ONE TECHNIQUE AND ARTISTRY

SAMUIL FEINBERG The Road to Artistry   3

ALEXANDER GOLDENWEISER Advice from a Pianist and Teacher   53

LEV OBORIN Some Principles of Pianoforte Technique   68

KONSTANTIN IGUMNOV Some Remarks on Technique   78

GRIGORII GINZBURG Notes on Mastery of the Piano   84

PART TWO LESSONS AND MASTERCLASSES

SAMUIL FEINBERG Beethoven's Appassionata: A Performer's Commentary   97

SVIATOSLAV RICHTER Three Answers to Questions about Beethoven's
   Sonata Appassionata   107

HEINRICH NEUHAUS Work on Beethoven's Sonata in A major Opus 101   110

MARIA ESHCHENKO Chopin Études (based on classes with Samuil Feinberg)   129

YAKOV FLIER Reflections on Chopin's Fourth Ballade   146

ALEXANDER GOLDENWEISER Notes on Chopin's Ballade in F minor   158

KONSTANTIN IGUMNOV *Chopin's Fourth Ballade in F minor*   165

NINA LELCHUK AND ELENA DOLINSKAYA *Lessons with Yakov Flier*
  (on Liszt's Mephisto Waltz No 1 and Prokofiev's Sonata No 3)   172

OLGA STUPAKOVA AND GENRIETTA MIRVIS *Yakov Zak as Teacher*
  (on Liszt's Sonata, Schumann's Études Symphoniques,
  and Rakhmaninov's Paganini Rhapsody)   201

BIBLIOGRAPHY   225

INDEX OF PIANISTS, COMPOSERS, AND WORKS   227

INDEX OF PIANO PLAYING TERMS   234

I dedicate this book to Svetlana, my wife, musician, counsellor and friend, with love and gratitude.

INTRODUCTION

This book is intended not only for piano teachers, performers and students. It should also interest any amateur pianist concerned to reach beyond the first foothills of the pianistic Parnassus, and in fact anyone with an interest in Russian musical culture. It offers some new insights into the Russian school of pianism, which first coalesced in the 1860s around the conservatoires of St Petersburg and Moscow, although it is Moscow that has more recently predominated as a musical centre and has produced a greater number of the modern world's supreme piano teaching and performing talents.

Along with conductors like Rozhdestvensky, Kondrashin, or Mravinsky, the cellist Rostropovich, or violinists such as David Oistrakh and Leonid Kogan, the finest representatives of Russian pianism have for decades made an unforgettable impression on international audiences. Yet while the artistry of Richter, Gilels, Ashkenazy, or recently emergent masters such as Mikhail Pletnev, Arcadi Volodos or Evgeny Kissin, clearly transcends any process of formal teaching, the perennial ability of Russian pianists to take leading prizes in international competitions, and of their mentors to attract pupils and disciples from around the world, has inevitably led to the Russian piano school – and notably the Moscow Conservatoire – being recognized as the hearth and home of all that is best in modern piano playing. This is of course not to deny the importance of some other European conservatoires and North American centres of pianoforte culture such as the Juilliard School or Curtis Institute – yet even here some of the twentieth century's best and most stimulating teachers, such as Josef and Rosina Lhevinne, Isabelle Vengerova, and Josef Hofmann (a protégé of Anton Rubinstein), originated from the Russian school.

The nineteenth and early twentieth century saw the appearance in Western Europe of a multitude of piano manuals and methods that concentrated in the main on a physiological approach to piano technique rather than all-round coverage of the whole art and culture of piano playing. At the same time, although the fostering and training of fine talent was preserved and continued by many individuals such as – at various times – Moscheles, Leschetizky, Teichmüller, Busoni, or Edwin Fischer, and in various cities such as Berlin, St Petersburg, Vienna, London and Paris, characteristically some of the finest virtuoso performers of both earlier and modern times were unforthcoming, in print at least, on many questions of their art. It is true, there has always been a steady flow of useful manuals such as György Sandor's *On Piano Playing*, Walter Gieseking and Karl Leimer's *Piano Technique*, Josef Lhevinne's *Basic Principles of Pianoforte Playing*, or Josef Hofmann's *Piano Playing with Questions Answered*. However, there is a body of writing on virtually every aspect of piano playing and representing the fruit of over a hundred years of accumulated experience by Russian teachers, which vastly exceeds the totality of anything available in English or other languages. Yet mainly due to distance and to language barriers, most of this literature has remained untranslated and unavailable to non-Russian readers. Similarly, although since the later twentieth century many Russian performers and teachers reside and work in Western Europe and America, the record of that rich experience enjoyed by those who actually taught or studied at the Moscow Conservatoire still remains accessible only indirectly. Some privileged insights were offered by Heinrich Neuhaus' book, *The Art of Piano Playing*, published in 1958 and later translated into German, English, and other languages, but the writings of other distinguished Russian performers and teachers published over the last half century or so remain little known. It is the purpose of this book partially to lift the veil on an artistic and technical teaching process that has produced some of the world's finest modern pianists.

Presented here is the work of various generations of modern Russian pianism. The 'elders' are represented by Alexander Goldenweiser (1875-1961), his pupil Samuil Feinberg (1890-1962), Heinrich Neuhaus (1888-1964), and Konstantin Igumnov (1873-1948). As inheritors and custodians of a rich nineteenth-century tradition, these men were the mainstays of the early Soviet school of pianism. The next generation consisted largely of their pupils, who came to prominence as performers and teachers in the mid twentieth century: Yakov Flier and Lev Oborin both studied with Igumnov, Grigory Ginzburg with Goldenweiser, while Yakov Zak and Sviatoslav

Richter were pupils of Heinrich Neuhaus (spelt and known as 'Genrikh Neigauz' in Russian).

It should be emphasized that apart from the occasional writings of Lhevinne and Neuhaus mentioned above, the present small volume is, in effect, a first presentation of its subject in English. The contents are of necessity highly selective. Some of the inclusions may seem debatable, and many omissions might perhaps be covered in later publications. The inclusion of Richter, for instance, is slightly anomalous in that he studied but never taught at the Moscow Conservatoire, although he informally assisted some younger artists, such as Andrei Gavrilov. On the regular professorial staff, Feinberg, Goldenweiser and Neuhaus were fairly prolific writers on matters musical – Igumnov and others less so, while the teaching of such masters as Flier and Zak has been preserved thanks to the notes and records of devoted pupils. But apart from the present contributors, there have been many others, going back to Safonov, Medtner, or Felix Blumenfeld, as well as artists and teachers of the more recent past, such as Gilels or Yakov Milstein, whose contribution to the art of piano playing and teaching still awaits an English readers' attention, at least on the printed page.

It should also be stressed that this book is not in itself a systematic, structured course in piano playing, although within its pages virtually all the major technical and interpretative problems are addressed. Those in search of information on particular works, composers, or technical aspects, such as octave playing, double notes, use of pedal, et cetera, can locate all relevant passages by using the subject indexes provided at the end.

Part one of the book presents a sampling of writings that best illustrate the philosophy and methods of leading representatives of the Moscow school. Some of what they have to say is of course echoed in the best of European and North American piano teaching, but inevitably the accents fall differently. There is much new and valuable advice and information on technique and various aids to trouble-shooting (such as Feinberg's 'mirror' exercises for left and right hand), as well as insight into tone production and control, and the building of a complete artistic performance that leads beyond any mere technically accurate reading of the text.

The second part of this book provides a privileged view of events in the classrooms of the Moscow Conservatoire and of teaching by Flier, Goldenweiser, Neuhaus and others. The Moscow teaching repertoire embraces virtually the complete history of pianoforte literature from J.S. Bach and Scarlatti to

Prokofiev, Shostakovich, Stravinsky and contemporary Russian, European and American music. The amplitude of syllabus depends partly of course on the gifts of the particular student, and on the taste of individual teachers. The Russian piano school has produced figures such as Feinberg and Gilels, whose Bach playing was no less impressive than their Romantic and modern virtuoso repertoire, and transcripts of lessons by Oborin and Goldenweiser on the Baroque are just as revealing as their presentation of later works. However, in the present short volume, rather than cast the net too broadly, we have selected and provided more detailed commentary on that repertory in which Russian pianists have specially excelled. Part two thus offers a series of approaches to specific works by Beethoven, Chopin, Liszt, Rakhmaninov and Prokofiev. Feinberg and Sviatoslav Richter discuss Beethoven's *Appassionata*, while Heinrich Neuhaus comments on a student performance of the late A major Sonata, opus 101. Maria Eshchenko, one of Feinberg's pupils, summarizes his discussion of a selection of Chopin Etudes, and three prominent teacher-performers offer their views on the Chopin Fourth Ballade in F minor. The final two chapters present records of coaching on a series of Romantic and modern works by two of the great virtuosi and teachers of the mid-twentieth century, Yakov Flier and Yakov Zak.

It is worthwhile bearing in mind that, despite the fame and achievement of what might be termed the 'Moscow piano school', Conservatoire professors were as much individuals in their teaching style as in their personal playing, and despite substantial agreement on the essentials of technique, there was never a single monolithic and unchanging 'method'. Igumnov in fact talks about how some of Goldenweiser's and his own approaches have changed over time (pp.67-71). Readers may thus detect some slight variance in the recommendations of various authors, as well as subjective idiosyncrasy in matters of interpretation. Thus, for instance, Yakov Flier talks of the penultimate episode of Liszt's first *Mephisto Waltz* as suggesting a 'state of bemusement in the wake of disaster' (p 164), whereas the extracts from Lenau's *Faust* with which Liszt prefaced his score confirm the composer's known intention that this was a representation of the lovers listening to a nightingale in the woods. However, annotation of all such passages has not been provided in the text, and no attempt has been made to provide detailed critical commentaries that compare or 'unify' the wisdom of the various contributors – all this would be part of a lengthier study in a different book. It might, nevertheless, be in place to point out that many of these great teachers and executants were not always total masters of musicology, or of the history of their instrument and its repertoire, and there are a few slightly misleading statements in some of their contributions. Thus, for instance, Samuel Feinberg seems mistaken in suggesting (p 20) that Mozart's piano had only half the compass of the modern grand. Also, Mozart's instrument did not lack dampers, as Grigorii Ginzburg implies (p 76), although they were certainly lighter than those on modern instruments. At another point, one wonders whether Svyatoslav Richter was merely being polite, or whether he shared his interviewer Dmitrii Blagoi's belief (pp 92-3) that Beethoven's *Appassionata* was a reflection of reading Shakespeare's *The Tempest*. In fact, as we know, Beethoven's famous interpretative clue given to Schindler, referred not to the *Appassionata* but to the D minor Sonata, opus 31 No 2. Modern students and players of both these sonatas may well also find that Feinberg's 'Performer's Commentary' takes insufficient account (p 91) of the difference between Beethoven's pianos and modern instrument, and of the development of piano pedaling. Such scholarly oversights, however, seem to be far outweighed by the valuable substance of what these authors have to say.

When reading the articles that follow, it may be of help to view them in context as part of the history of Russian piano teaching and playing over the last 150 years. According to the Russian pianist Alexander Siloti, who studied with Franz Liszt in Weimar in the early 1880s, Liszt 'never missed an opportunity of insisting that Germany and France had had their say in music, and that everything new must perforce come from Russia'.[1] Liszt's words were recorded à propos of the imminent visit to Weimar of Borodin and Glazunov, and evidently referred mainly to the realm of musical composition. However, they could well have been said with even greater relevance to the world of Russian pianism. Indeed, Liszt's remark had an almost prophetic significance. It was more or less at that time, in the late nineteenth century, that the European tide of pianistic talent had been noticeably reversed: after a predominance of foreign pianists and teachers in St Petersburg and Moscow, native Russian pianists in the wake of Anton Rubinstein were beginning to emerge and make an increasing impact on an astounded Western public. Symptomatic was the comment of Emil von Sauer – although traditionally recognized as a Liszt pupil, he in fact maintained that by the mid 1880s Liszt had been too old to teach him very much, and that he owed most to his two years of study, in 1879-81, with Nikolai Rubinstein in Moscow.[2]

An identifiably Russian school of pianism was in fact somewhat late in emerging, although some native talent was apparent from the outset – the first recorded concert by a Russian pianist was given in Moscow by Daniil Kashin in the year 1790. But most of the early pioneers of piano playing in Russia were foreigners, some of them short-term visitors, others permanent residents. Among them was the composer and pianist Johann Hässler (1747-1822), a grand-pupil of J.S. Bach who came to Russia in 1792 and lived there until his death in Moscow in 1822. Another was the German virtuoso pianist-composer and teacher Daniel Steibelt (1765-1863), a figure of slightly vacuous flamboyance who settled in Russia in 1809; however, alongside several now forgotten concertos, he composed études which until the early twentieth century ranked alongside those of Cramer and Clementi, as well as many lyrical salon pieces that reflected his particular style of playing. The most influential figure, though, was the Irish born pianist-composer John Field, a Clementi pupil who came to Russia in 1802 and stayed for thirty years. The acknowledged 'inventor' of the Nocturne and a formative influence on Chopin, he won fame with his concertos and solo piano compositions, playing a major role in the emergence of Russian pianism, with future celebrities including the composer Glinka among his pupils. His style of playing was lyrically poetic and marked by innovative pedalling that matched the texture of his own writing and the glistening jeu perlé of his finger-work. Further major stimuli to native Russian pianism were the concert tours by prominent western Europeans, notably by Hummel, a pupil of both Mozart and Salieri, who played in Russia in 1822. Later, in mid century, Sigismund Thalberg appeared in Russia in 1839, followed by Liszt in 1842 and 1843, and Clara Schumann in 1844 and 1864. Meanwhile, young Russian pianists improved their talent at major music centres abroad; among them was Anton Gerke (later the piano teacher of Mussorgsky and Tchaikovsky) who studied under Kalkbrenner at the Paris Conservatoire and later with Ries in Hamburg, while other young talents went to Leipzig and Vienna.

Liszt's performances in St Petersburg and Moscow in the 1840s had the same galvanizing effect as they had on audiences elsewhere. After the essentially lyrical romanticism of earlier virtuosi, his playing marked the triumph of a new declamatory and elemental sense of drama, as well as taking piano technique to new heights of perfection. However, Russia very shortly produced probably the only nineteenth-century pianist who could rival Liszt, and who by his playing and related musical activities did more than anyone else to establish a Russian national piano tradition.

Born in 1829, Anton Rubinstein was Liszt's junior by eighteen years. Taught initially by his mother and then by Alexander Villoing in Moscow, he in 1840 embarked on the first of many triumphant concert tours and prolonged sojourns abroad. Although Franz Liszt declined to accept him as a pupil, Rubinstein gained much from long years of cordial relations with the Hungarian master. Apart from a youthful cult of several Lisztian mannerisms at the keyboard, more significantly, he employed an obviously 'modern' technical approach similar to that of Liszt, in which tone production relied not just on the digital strength and dexterity practised by earlier generations, but was supported by the full weight of arm, shoulder and torso. Probably this was largely thanks to Villoing (see Igumnov's comments below). But Rubinstein's artistry went beyond what any teacher could impart: his playing was characterized by rhetorical and dramatic power, spontaneity, an unprecedented range of tone colour and dynamics, and also by a mastery of sustained melodic phrase and intonation that owed much to the example of some great singers of the day. Also, while Liszt in private knew and played virtually everything written for piano, his public repertoire almost excluded Bach and the Vienna classics and embraced a limited choice even of works by Beethoven and Schumann. By contrast Anton Rubinstein eventually crowned his career with a series of concerts in major cities of Europe and the USA that illustrated the entire history of piano music from the Baroque to contemporary Russian composers. Rubinstein's example left its imprint on the next few generations of performers everywhere, but nowhere more than in his native land.

Apart from his additional extensive activities as conductor and composer, Rubinstein effectively transformed the nation's musical life and subsequent history by setting up the Russian Music Society in 1859, and by founding the St Petersburg Conservatoire three years later, acting as professor and director until 1865 and again from 1887 to 1891. Despite opposition at court and among St Petersburg's 'Mighty Handful' of composers, who cherished the 'national idea' in Russian music along with an irrational fear of academicism, and hopelessly underrated the importance of systematic professional training, the St Petersburg Conservatoire flourished. Rubinstein personally taught pianoforte, composition, orchestral and ensemble playing, while several other fine teachers engaged for the piano faculty included Theodor Leschetizky (a Polish born Czerny pupil whose Russian students included Esipova, Gabrilowitsch, and Safonov), Anton Gerke (the 'pre-Lisztian' pupil of John Field, Kalkbrenner, Moscheles and Ries, and whose students included Mussorgsky, Stasov, and Tchaikovsky), and Alexander Dreyschock (Czech born virtuoso, trained by Tomáschek, and famed specially for his left-hand technique). These were later joined in 1888 by the elderly German Adolf Henselt, a pupil of Hummel who had lived and taught in St Petersburg since 1838.

In 1866 a similar conservatoire was founded in Moscow on the initiative of Anton Rubinstein's younger brother Nikolai, who remained as its director until his death in 1881. While less internationally famed, Nikolai Rubinstein was by all accounts quite the equal of his elder brother as pianist and pedagogue. Alongside Tchaikovsky who joined the Moscow staff as professor of composition and orchestration, the impressive piano faculty was headed by Nikolai Rubinstein and included the German Liszt pupil Karl Klindworth, Anton Door, a Viennese pupil of Czerny, and the young Hungarian Rafael Joseffy, a pupil of Tausig, Moscheles and Liszt. Later, in 1871, these men were joined by Nikolai Zverev. A pupil of Dubuque and Henselt, but unmotivated towards a concert career, Zverev became one of Moscow's most prominent piano teachers and leading specialist of the Conservatoire's preparatory division. Over the next two decades his finest pupils, whom he personally accommodated and partially financed, included Rachmaninov, Scriabin, Igumnov, Lhevinne, and Alexander Siloti.

After Nikolai Rubinstein's death in 1881, advanced classes in the Moscow piano faculty were taken over by two new major figures. Paul (or Pavel) Pabst, a former pupil of Door, went on to produce a constellation of brilliant graduates, including Igumnov, Goldenweiser, Karl Kipp, and Sergei Liapunov, of whom the first three became founding fathers of the Soviet school of piano playing. Nikolai Rubinstein's other major successor was Vasilii Safonov, who nurtured a series of pianistic giants including Scriabin, Nikolai Medtner, and Josef and Rosina Lhevinne, and was later for a few years director of the Moscow Conservatoire. In the 1890s, along with Pabst and Safonov, Busoni, Siloti and Scriabin also served on the Moscow piano faculty staff, although too briefly to leave any permanent personal legacy.

As a performer, Pabst was most at home in Beethoven, Liszt, Schumann, and Tchaikovsky, and his broad and exacting teaching syllabus centred round these figures. Like Pabst, Safonov too was rigorously demanding in technical matters, requiring assiduous study of scales, exercises, and studies by Czerny, Hanon, Kullak, Reinecke and others. Like all his colleagues, he also insisted on absolute observance of the musical text, cultivating rich tone production, smooth and relaxed movement at the keyboard, and rejected any notion of finger dexterity in isolation from the player's total physique. Difficult passages were to be practised pianissimo, without pedal, and at reduced tempo. Also characteristic of Safonov and of the entire Russian school of piano playing, as it emerged by the late nineteenth century and continues to this day, was a concern that pupils should correctly grasp and convey the entire 'content', 'artistic image', and the spirit and style of all works performed.

Initially the Moscow Conservatoire course for instrumentalists lasted six years, then in 1879 it was extended to nine for pianists, violinists and cellists, with junior and senior divisions. As in St Petersburg, graduates received the title of 'free artist' (a translation of the German *freischaffender Künstler*), which meant recognition of their membership in an officially acknowledged profession. Apart from some features unique to the Moscow Conservatoire programme, such as the teaching of Russian Orthodox Church music, special aspects of the piano programme were designed by Nikolai Rubinstein and included intensive technical training at junior level, special attention to touch and tone production, exclusion from the syllabus of 'salon' style pieces, and concentration on three types of work: (a) classical (Beethoven, Schumann, Mendelssohn, Hummel, Bach, etc), (b) virtuoso (Liszt, Litolff, Hummel, Kullak, Weber, etc), and (c) 'genre' types of composition, such as the Mendelssohn *Songs Without Words*, nocturnes by Field and Chopin, Schubert-Liszt transcriptions, and so on. For piano specialists there was also tuition in ensemble playing, accompaniment, sight-reading of piano and orchestral scores, and transposition. With some variations, these principles and provisions have remained in force until the present day – with an obvious subsequent extension of repertoire to include all major piano music of the later nineteenth and twentieth century. Moreover there was one further overriding principle established at the outset by Nikolai Rubinstein and consistently honoured by the Moscow Conservatoire. This, in the founder's own words, was an obligation to train not merely instrumentalists, but to prepare 'musicians in the broadest sense of this word',[3] that is, to produce not mere fleet-fingered technicians, but accomplished artists with a rigorous intellectual understanding of their art, a cultivated sense of taste, style, and artistic imagination, a trained musical erudition, as well as a knowledge of musical history and of related artistic subjects.

Various changes in organization and syllabus after the Revolution of 1917 and during the Soviet period served to refine and extend the Moscow Conservatoire's activities. The basic course of study for students settled at five years, with further three-year graduate studies and assistantships for the most talented. A special group for gifted children set up in association with the Conservatoire in 1931 was five years later constituted as the Central Music School under the direction of Goldenweiser and provided complete primary and secondary education with intensive musical training, some of it given by actual conservatoire professors. This structure was also replicated at other Russian musical centres, and has continued to channel a steady stream of expertly prepared students into conservatoire programmes. In consequence there have been hardly any Soviet prizewinners in international competitions over the last half-century who did not commence their studies at one of the country's special music schools. By the late twentieth century there were well over three thousand such music schools, over a thousand music colleges, and twenty-four conservatoires throughout the Soviet Union.

Yet despite the unprecedented spread of musical enlightenment in Russia, there has been a long-standing tendency for the finest teaching and performing talents to gravitate towards Moscow, with other centres (including even Leningrad-St Petersburg) assuming a secondary, provincial status. Moscow's being the Soviet capital, and the wartime blockade of Leningrad were further contributory factors to a migration that in fact began early in the century. Thus, for instance, Felix Blumenfeld as well as his nephew Heinrich Neuhaus came to Moscow Conservatoire professorships in 1922, after previous appointments in Kiev; Maria Yudina came to Moscow in 1936 after earlier working in Leningrad and Tiflis; Sofronitsky never returned to Leningrad after his evacuation and relocation in Moscow in 1942; and world-ranking musicians such as Oistrakh, Gilels, Sviatoslav Richter and Yakov Zak came from Odessa in the 1930s as a matter of course to complete their training at the Moscow Conservatoire.

While the excellent organization of piano and other instrumental tuition in Russia has not affected the birthrate of true musical genius, it has ensured a cultural background against which genuine talent rarely goes unrecognized. It has also ensured an unsurpassed level of technical mastery among performers, even in cases where original creative fires have burned less brightly. However, technique is not in itself a touchstone of artistry, and there has been a consistent refusal at the Moscow Conservatoire and other centres of excellence to recognize a distinction between true artistry and its physical embodiment. As Heinrich Neuhaus recalled in his well-known manual, 'I am constantly reminding my students that the word 'technique' comes from the Greek word τεχνη, and "tekhne" meant "Art" itself.'[4]

Inevitably, in the century since Pabst and Safonov taught in Moscow, piano technique has itself significantly expanded, partly in response to new approaches required in performing music by many modern composers. However, essentially there has been an extension and refinement, and not a repudiation, of earlier principles of performance. The writings in this book variously reiterate the unfading importance of listening minutely to one's own playing, intellectually and emotionally comprehending every work one plays, the essentials of pedalling, legato and cantabile playing, of 'supported' tone production and what Heinrich Neuhaus called the 'total use of all the body's natural anatomical movements' as a prerequisite for mastering the complete literature of the instrument. And while leaving these technical foundations in place, the changes introduced by various of the authors below include the discovery of more efficacious fingerings and techniques of practising: the abandonment of mechanical repetition of such as Hanon's exercises (once described by Rakhmaninov as a *sine qua non* of his own training) in favour of more fruitful purpose-designed exercises, a reluctance to countenance tucking under of the thumbs over large distances, and the design of more dramatic, expressive fingering.

During the mid twentieth century, Neuhaus, Goldenweiser, and Igumnov were doyens and central pillars of the Moscow Conservatoire piano department, and between them, directly or indirectly, they shaped and polished almost all the major Russian stars of the last half-century; via pupils they have passed on their legacy to subsequent generations. Pianistic generations overlap of course, and Goldenweiser's own teaching career spanned six decades. At the risk of scattering a plethora of names, the following deserve mention as the principle successors to the Soviet period 'founders': Dmitrii Bashkirov, Samuil Feinberg, Grigorii Ginzburg, Tatiana Nikolayeva, composer Dmitrii Kabalevsky and organist Leonid Roizman all studied with Goldenweiser and in turn became professors at the Moscow Conservatoire; Goldenweiser's other celebrated pupils also included Lazar Berman, Arnold Kaplan, Dmitrii Paperno, and Roza Tamarkina. Igumnov was the teacher of Nikolai Orlov, Bella Davidovich, Maria Grinberg, Yakov Flier, Yakov Milstein, Lev Oborin, Naum Starkman, of whom the last four eventually joined the Moscow piano faculty staff. Neuhaus at various times taught his own son, Stanislav Neuhaus, Leonid Brumberg, Evgeny Malinin, Sviatoslav Richter, Yakov Zak, Emil Gilels, Alexei Lyubimov, Alexei Nasedkin, Evgenii Mogilevsky, Vladimir Krainev, Vera Gornostayeva, Igor Zhukov, and Alexander Slobodyanik, six of whom later took up conservatoire teaching positions. To generate a complete list of further pianistic progeny from the above would be an invidious and lengthy operation, but it would involve naming many artists presently at the pinnacle of their careers, including such as Vladimir Ashkenazy, Vladimir Krainev, Radu Lupu, Alexander Toradze, Ivo Pogorelich, and many others.

At the dawn of the twenty-first century, and particularly after a cultural diaspora that began with the exodus of Russia's Jewish population in the 1970s, followed by the break-up of the Soviet Union in 1991, many artists and teachers from Russia have been spending extended periods, or become permanently resident, in Western Europe and North America. We are fortunate in the musical and artistic enrichment that their presence has brought. The musical and pedagogic offerings that follow are intended as a supplement to that cultural bequest. It is hoped this book may assist some of today's students, teachers and performers in appreciating some features of the Russian piano tradition, and in applying them in their own artistic explorations.

In preparing this volume a special part was played by my wife Svetlana, who, as a violinist graduate and pupil of Tsyganov and Fichtenholz, shared with me her invaluable inside knowledge and experience of study at the Moscow Conservatoire and the Russian musical profession. I am also grateful to Lev Grigoryevich Ginzburg, whom I met through Leonid Maximenkov, and who, as the son of one of the contributors and an expert on the history of Russian pianism, offered valuable advice. I also owe an earlier but longstanding debt of gratitude to various piano teachers who directly or indirectly afforded me a sense of living contact with the Russian piano school tradition, notably: Phyllis Palmer, a pupil of Nikolai Medtner, the late Wight Henderson, pupil of Emil Sauer and grand-pupil of Nikolai Rubinstein, and Colin Kingsley of the Music Department of Edinburgh University.

CHRISTOPHER BARNES
Toronto 2007

NOTES

1) Alexander Siloti, 'My Memories of Liszt' in *Remembering Franz Liszt*, introduction by Mark N. Grant, New York: Limelight Editions, 1986, p 367.

2) Harold C. Schonberg, *The Great Pianists*, London: Gollancz, 1978, p 200.

3) L. Barenboim, *Nikolai Grigor'evich Rubinshtein: Istoriya, zhizn' i deyatel'nost'*, Moscow: 'Muzyka', 1982, p 105.

4) G. Neigauz, *Ob iskusstve fortep'yannoi igry. Zapiski pedagoga*, Moscow, 1958, p 7.

A NOTE ON THE AUTHORS

SAMUIL FEINBERG (1890-1962)

Studied with Goldenweiser at Moscow Conservatoire, later pianoforte professor there 1922-62. Began touring abroad in 1912. His playing showed fine balance of emotion and intellect, and he was equally at home in Bach, the Vienna classics, Beethoven, Chopin, Schumann, and Russian composers. He showed a particular affinity for Scriabin, who was a partial influence on his own original piano compositions. In addition, Feinberg produced piano arrangements of music by Bach, Vivaldi, Borodin, Tchaikovsky and others, cadenzas for Beethoven and Mozart concertos, as well as a monograph and various articles on the art of the piano.

YAKOV FLIER (1912-77)

Graduated in 1937 from Igumnov's class at Moscow Conservatoire, and international concert appearances began in 1935. First prizes at the second All-Union Performing Musicians' Competition (1935) and the International Competition in Vienna (1936). Appointed to Moscow Conservatoire staff in 1937; his pupils include Rodion Shchedrin, Viktoria Postnikova, and Mikhail Pletnev. An essentially romantic player, he was at his best in concertos and large-scale works of the 19th and early 20th century repertoire (Chopin, Liszt, Tchaikovsky, Rakhmaninov), and became one of the best-known Russian pianists of his time.

GRIGORII GINZBURG (1904-61)

Studied at Moscow Conservatoire under Goldenweiser. Prizewinner at First Chopin Competition in Warsaw, 1927, and performed abroad regularly from 1923. Taught at Moscow Conservatoire 1919-59 with Akselrod and Dorensky among his pupils. A virtuoso player of great lyric refinement (in the Igumnov mould), he excelled especially in Liszt and other 19th century composers. He composed effective piano arrangements of works by various composers.

ALEXANDER GOLDENWEISER (1875-1961)
Pupil of Siloti and Pabst at Moscow Conservatoire, where he was later professor 1906-61; his art was shaped also by personal contacts with Rakhmaninov, Scriabin and Medtner. A devoted and sensitive interpreter of a wide range of composers, his playing was marked by deep intellectual understanding. In over fifty years as teacher, he produced many fine pupils, including Ginzburg, Feinberg, Dmitrii Bashkirov, Lazar Berman, Oxana Yablonskaya, and Tatiana Nikolaeva. As musical scholar, he also produced editions of Bach, Mozart, Beethoven. Schumann, Liszt and Tchaikovsky.

KONSTANTIN IGUMNOV (1873-1948)
Pupil of Zverev, Pabst, and Siloti at Moscow Conservatoire, and prizewinner in the Rubinstein Competition in Berlin (1895). He was professor at Moscow Conservatoire from 1899 and for several years headed the piano department. He was a player of sensitive, elegant, lyric refinement, with a special attunement to Tchaikovsky. His pupils included Oborin, Flier, Maria Grinberg, Bella Davidovich, and Naum Shtarkman.

HEINRICH NEUHAUS [GENRIKH NEIGAUZ] (1888-1964)
Pupil of Blumenfeld, and of Godowsky in Vienna. He taught at Kiev Conservatoire before coming to Moscow, where he was one of the city's most celebrated and productive teachers, and his own solo career and artistry partly suffered as a result. His greatest pupils were Gilels and Richter, but he produced a galaxy of other fine pupils. His own playing had a refined romanticism; he was particularly outstanding in Scriabin and Chopin.

LEV OBORIN (1907-1974)
Pupil of Igumnov, and first winner of the Warsaw Chopin Competition in 1927. He was appointed to the Moscow Conservatoire staff in 1928, where his many noted pupils included Vladimir Ashkenazy. At home in the classical repertoire, he was at his best in the Romantics, but also a noted performer of Soviet music, and gave the premiere of Khachaturyan's piano concerto. Apart from solo recital and concerto work, he was a fine ensem-

ble player, a regular duo partner with David Oistrakh, and formed a trio with Oistrakh and the cellist Knushevitsky.

SVYATOSLAV RICHTER (1915-97)
Partly self-taught, repetiteur at Odessa Opera, before going to study with Neuhaus in Moscow in 1937. He emerged as a leading soloist in the war years. He gave the premiere of Prokofiev's 7th Sonata, was dedicatee of his 9th Sonata, and earned a Stalin Prize in 1949. He began appearing in Western Europe and the USA only in the 1960s. A supreme virtuoso, with fine romantic intellect, he was unsurpassed in most of his extensive repertoire, high points of which included his Haydn, Schumann, Rakhmaninov, Prokofiev, and Debussy.

YAKOV ZAK (1913-76)
Studied in Odessa and later with Neuhaus at the Moscow Conservatoire, taking first prize in the Warsaw Chopin Competition in 1937. He taught at Moscow Conservatoire from 1935, where his pupils included Nikolai Petrov, Yury Egorov and Alexander Toradze. An 'objective' rather than romantic performer, his playing was marked by refined virtuosity and a strong sense of form and structure. He toured widely in Europe, North and South America.

PART ONE

Technique and Artistry

SAMUIL FEINBERG

The Road to Artistry

This composite essay is based on transcripts of lectures by Samuil Feinberg given at various times at the Moscow Conservatoire, supplemented by fragments from various other verbatim records, conversations, and observations preserved in Feinberg's notebooks. In reworking these notes and records for publication, the editors have aimed to preserve every nuance of Feinberg's ideas, as well as his speech style and the humour that was typical of him. This accounts for an occasional improvisatory quality in the following pages.

L. FEINBERG

PIANOFORTE TONE

Over long years of playing the piano, all pianists get so used to producing music from their instrument that they tend to forget all about the complex mechanism linking the piano keys to the hammers that strike the strings. With well-practised hand movements, honed and polished to perfection, it appears to them as they play that they are producing sound directly from the keyboard itself. There is no doubt in the pianist's mind that the piano has an extraordinarily rich variety of sonority and timbre. Indeed, the instrument's tonal palette is exceptionally broad, and depending on his individual gifts and artistic personality, every pianist should be able to produce and create his own particular world of sonority and tone colour.

We can readily distinguish fine performers by the quality of their *legato*, their beautiful touch, and their singing tone and sound colouration. Beneath the hands of each pianist, the instrument acquires its own particular sonority, despite the fact that experts in acoustics are sceptical about any player's ability to impart any personal quality or unique tone colour to the sound of the piano. Indeed, when we strike an individual key, the nature of the sound produced depends directly on the force with which the note is struck – more precisely, on the speed with which the hammer hits the string. Furthermore, it is not hard to convince ourselves that by ear alone we cannot distinguish whether the key is pressed down by a finger, by a wad of cotton wool, or – with the same intensity – by a piece of metal.

According to their type of tone production, we can divide string instruments as a whole into various natural groups. On guitar and harp the tone is produced directly by the finger tips acting on the string; a violinist or cellist's right hand and arm movements are transferred to the string via the bow, while the keys of the piano are linked up to the strings by a complex system of levers, springs, and rods that simultaneously activate the hammers and raise the dampers. Yet it is quite clear to any unbiased listener that the tonal range available on the piano is far broader than that offered by the harp or the guitar.

How is it that piano playing taken as a whole is so rich in shades of colour whereas the timbre of a single note is strictly limited? One can perform a simple experiment familiar to the majority of pianists. You open the lid of the piano and depress the right-hand pedal, then sing some distinct note or even pronounce some vowel sound. The strings of the instrument will resonate and reproduce not only the note you sing but also echo the quality of that particular vowel. The piano can imitate the voice of the violin on any note struck by the bow, and also copy the sound of the clarinet. This means that all timbres, tone colours, and shades of sound are potentially present in the string sound of the piano.

It does not of course follow from this that we can play a chord on the grand piano that sounds exactly like the violin, or that the piano can sing with a human voice. But it is possible for an experienced performer to play a melody so expressively that it will sound as if sung, alternatively he can convey the illusion of violin pizzicato with a series of detached chords.

Enriched by the broad possibilities of instrumental technique, the timbre of the piano can hint and convey every shade of orchestral sonority, choral sound, and even the intonations of speech. Largely for this reason pianoforte arrangements are a highly convenient way of acquainting oneself with much symphonic music, opera, and oratorio.

One need play just two notes of a melody, or a single chord, in order to impart a particular tone colour to the sound of the piano. Indeed, the playing of a single melody is sometimes sufficient for us to identify a great virtuoso as accurately as we would a violinist or a singer. A pianist's playing is described by various epithets characterizing the particular sound of the instrument beneath his fingers. One speaks of his colourful sound, orchestral variety of timbre, his singing quality, gentle touch, powerful forte, and so on. Indeed, a pianist has so many possibilities for producing totally different sonorities and a great variety of tone colours that in this respect he has at his disposal a richer tonal palette than performers on any other instrument.

The tone of a grand piano made by Bechstein differs greatly from that of a Steinway and other instruments. Yet no matter which of these instrument he plays, we can always still recognize playing by a pianist of powerful personality.

Piano tone colour thus depends not on a single note, but on the combination and interrelation of notes. First of all, the perfect mechanism of the modern piano allows the pianist great variation in strength of touch – from extreme *pianissimo* to the most shattering *fortissimo*. The performer enjoys complete control over the strength of each note. Moreover, while any single note played on the piano cannot be given a particular tone colour, any chord will already be governed by the pianist's own choice of timbre, depending on the varying strength of the notes in the chord.

Furthermore, if a single chord can be coloured in a particular way, then even more so can a melody, or series of consecutive notes, have its own characteristic tone colour. The overtones of successive notes interweave in the acoustic resonance of the piano and create the most subtle and unique combinations of timbre...

To the above we should also add the role of the pedal, a device whose complete mastery is an indispensable component of the pianist's art. The link between pedal and dampers is simpler and more direct than that between the piano keys and hammers, and with the help of the pedal a pianist can achieve the most varied expressivity of tone.

It should also be said that the pianist's colouristic possibilities are broad, indeed inexhaustible, because the piano's sonority has the ability to stimulate the listener's musical imagination. The complex texture of piano writing provides scope for the most varied notions of timbre. It is known that a listener immersed in appreciating some polyphony can mentally distinguish one voice from another, and in the subtle nuances of the listener's imagination the piano can exercise the same power and persuasiveness as it begins to sound like an orchestra, a chorus, or a single human voice. I would describe this characteristic of piano sound as a capacity to create a form of 'concrete illusion', and in handling his instrument's various registers the experienced pianist should strive to act on the musical imagination of his listeners and to carry them with him.

The sound quality of an instrument depends of course on what makes the sound and how. To take an image from everyday life, if someone tells you some good news, the speaker's voice will usually sound pleasant. But if that same voice announces bad tidings, it will probably strike you as less agreeable. In the same way, when a pianist plays logically, phrases well, and has a perfect mastery of polyphony, and when his playing is well fleshed out emotionally, then the actual sound of the instrument will seem better than when played by a weaker pianist.

Sometimes, though, we might encounter a quite different state of affairs. Suppose that a splendid pianist has the misfortune to play on a very inferior piano. The interference caused by this will no doubt be extremely bothersome, and listeners will be distressed despite the varied and surprising tones that a great virtuoso can coax from a poor instrument.

I do not recall ever having heard a human voice with more beautiful timbre than that of Chaliapin. Yet some specialists maintain that though Chaliapin was a remarkable artist and performer, he was inferior to some other singers both in the power of his voice and beauty of its timbre. But Chaliapin as an artist always struck me by his ability to enunciate words, and by the profound meaning with which he filled each phrase, and for that reason it seemed to me there could never be a more splendid voice than his.

In the same way, the pianist should strive, as it were, to surpass the limitations of his instrument. If we forever feel ourselves bound by considerations of mere piano sound, we shall deprive ourselves of a whole range of tonal possibilities and emotional nuances. In fact, once we decide that because of the piano's complex mechanism direct contact with the string is unachievable, and that piano tone is something inert, unyielding and limited by its very nature, we shall find it hard to strive for and achieve any true songfulness or fine cantilena in our playing. This would, however, be a cruel miscalculation on our part.

Fortunately, pianists are in fact inclined to forget about the piano's mechanical complexity, just as any human being usually forgets about the activity of the various organs making up his body. Indeed, if as he played a pianist did concentrate on the function of the dampers, wippens, hammers, jacks, et cetera making up the piano action, this would indicate a peculiar and unhealthy attitude toward his own artistry.

TONE PRODUCTION, MOVEMENT AND GESTURE

In what ways can a young pianist work so as to achieve a mastery of piano sound and produce a beautiful, singing tone? In the first place, the combination of his own natural gifts is important: he must have a good general musicality, a fine ear, and a love of music. But apart from any inborn talent, which must of course be nurtured in every way possible, I believe the most important thing is an ability to coordinate correctly and accurately those movements that are involved in piano tone production.

In order to achieve a beautiful sound, a pianist must have the capacity to control it. But in order to control this sound, he must also know how to hear it. Teachers often tell pupils about the need to listen to one's own playing. I would also add that a student must not only listen to himself, but also *hear* himself. How often does it happen that a pianist who listens attentively to his own playing fails to recognize his performance when recorded on tape! This means that the pianist had not actually *heard* his own playing. It turns out that one can listen to oneself and still fail to hear how one actually sounds.

What is it that prevents a pianist from properly hearing his own performance, from outside as it were? I think it would probably be correct to say that the main fault lies in an excess of movement.

Essential in playing the piano are a certain degree of restraint, achieving tone production by the simplest, most efficient means, and the elimination of all superfluous gestures such as swinging the head and body, flapping the elbows, excessive tension in the legs, or marking time with one's feet. All such superfluous movement and unwanted tension are in fact a form of self-hypnosis by which the pianist compensates for various emotional and technical shortcomings in his playing. Thanks to these movements, the pianist hears his own playing not as it really sounds but as he would like, and intends, it to sound.

When sustaining a long note, a relatively inexperienced amateur often continues holding down the key while vibrating his hand. This induces in the player an illusion that the sound too is vibrating. Try out this experiment, and it will probably seem to you that the note is indeed wavering very slightly, especially if you inject a certain measure of feeling into this experience.

While amateur players go in for superfluous movements as if striving to make up for shortcomings in their own playing, even some experienced professionals sometimes involuntarily indulge in superfluous gesture. The actual sound then appears to them different from how it is in reality. By these unnecessary movements performers thus indulge in a form of autosuggestion and thereby prevent themselves from hearing objectively the sounds that their hands are producing.

As a teacher, I would say that it is useful for a young pianist to achieve sufficient physical restraint and concentration so that he, as it were, feels the sound of the instrument beneath his own fingertips. This of course only a form of image, but it captures the type of correct attitude toward the sounds that we are trying to produce.

It is worth recalling the enormous stress that the drama producer Stanislavsky placed on an actor's ability to free his body of excess tension. This is a by no means easy thing to do. Even when lying and relaxing on a couch, one finds that some superfluous tension usually remains in certain muscles. But the aim should be to concentrate attention on total relaxation so as to completely switch off one's entire muscular system.

A pianist, too, can teach himself to eliminate all superfluous gesture, concentrating total attention on the sound and mentally projecting the sensation of that sound into the tips of his fingers. One should keep returning systematically to this form of exercise even at slow tempo. Achieving perfection and precision of contact with the keys can gradually free the pianist of all unnecessary and excessive movement.

At this point let us distinguish between two concepts – those of movement and of gesture.

By 'movement' we should understand that purposeful and useful motion involved in depressing the key, and which is essential in order to produce any musical sound or series of sounds. This is distinct from 'gesture', which we might describe as that part of the motion that is designed to express the performer's own mood, feeling, and emotion.

I say that 'part of the motion' because both goals – depression of the key and the external expression of feeling – are fused together and are invariably present in every movement made by the performer. The only important thing is which of the two goals predominates, and to what extent any gesture is consciously organized.

The motion of the finger that depresses the key by eight to ten millimeters is not always a directly downward movement. Generally speaking, the action of the pianist's hand and arm is a highly complex combination of motions, consisting of movements of the fingers, wrist, elbow, forearm, and the whole torso. In former times, it was precise and accurate finger movements that were cultivated first and foremost. It should be borne in mind that on the organ or harpsichord the strength of the sound does not depend on the strength of the stroke that depresses the key. This feature was reflected in the texture of works written at that time, and for a long time afterwards it influenced the character of writing for the pianoforte. For this reason piano performance style was for a long time bound up with the development of pure finger technique.

However, Beethoven and the Romantics who came after him introduced to the repertoire of favourite devices new effects such as the use of broader chords, passagework, and figuration that required freer and more gliding movements from the pianist. This Romantic development later reached its culmination, and possibly its completion, in the piano style of Scriabin. Subsequently there was a tendency to return to neoclassicism – this is partly true of such remarkable modern composers as Prokofiev and Medtner.

The path of development from Mozart to Scriabin can perhaps be some-what arbitrarily described as the gradual development of sliding, or gliding, hand and arm movements in place of the vertical finger stroke. This is not to deny, of course, that any modern pianist still continues to appreciate the value of pure finger technique.

One nevertheless occasionally comes across theoreticians who still main-tain that a gliding motion is less efficient than a direct vertical keystroke. Here, though, one should keep in mind various further considerations. First of all, a gliding motion inevitably arises due to the broader distribution of romantic figurations, which in turn are bound up with different approaches to the use of pedal from those typical of classical style playing.

A gliding motion also, as it were, joins up and unites a whole series of widely distributed notes, and from this viewpoint this form of hand motion is thus highly expedient and efficient. Apart from which, a transverse gliding motion of the hand assists in regulating the strength of the keystroke with particular accuracy. When the finger depresses a key directly, the strength of the stroke depends on a very small segment of its trajectory, i.e. on the speed of the last few millimeters. With gliding hand motion these few millimeters form part of a longer transverse arc along which the fingertip moves. In this way it becomes easier to achieve absolute accuracy of key pressure.

In addition, it is essential to consider one further point – namely that an arching movement of the hand often emerges as more emotionally expressive.

At this point we can address the question of the dual role played by gesture. We have already agreed that gesture expresses the feeling and mood of the performer. But this element of hand and arm movement that is permeated by emotion may be directed toward the feelings or even the subconscious of the pianist himself, or else, conversely, it may openly and consciously help to convey the performer's inner experiences to the audience.

In the first case the gesture is something superfluous and usually has a harmful effect on the performance, since, as I said already, it is meant to compensate the pianist for shortcomings in his own playing. In this case the gesture corresponds to something that cannot actually be heard. And even if the performer fails to notice his own self-deception, the audience will not always be inclined to pardon excessive gesticulations that bear no relation to the actual sounds that they hear.

In the second case everything depends on the tactfulness and taste of the pianist. If his gestures really do correspond to the music he plays, and if they truthfully and graphically reflects his own feelings, then such expressive or decorative movement cannot be ruled out as a fault. It should certainly not be thought that a performer who makes slight movements of the head or of the elbow as he plays is in some way defective. In this respect one should not be a total ascetic.

Frequently an experienced concertgoer tries to find a seat in the concert hall from where he can easily watch the movement of the pianist's hands. For such a listener every gesture by the performer, the expression on his face, and his whole appearance may add something to the interpretation. Yet at the same time another, no less musical listener may close his eyes so as to concentrate fully on the music and remain alone, as it were, in his own world of sound.

Sometimes, especially at the start of a performance, a pianist may resort to certain gestures, which, although not totally necessary, are nevertheless helpful since they assist in setting the mood of the performer himself.

All this notwithstanding, we might – perhaps somewhat arbitrarily – divide all pianists into two categories: those who do their utmost to avoid superfluous gesticulation and confine themselves only to the most efficacious movements, and those who regularly go in for decorative and demonstrative gestures and try to express the aesthetic experience graphically via certain additional movements. And if our taste as well as theoretical considerations prompt us to favour the first category, nevertheless there is no denying that many illustrious virtuosi have regularly resorted to a great variety of superficially expressive gestures.

I need hardly say that we are not likely to encounter either the first or the second category of pianists 'in pure form'. In his overall treatment of the instrument and in his whole appearance a pianist is bound to express his feelings and experiences. The audience is even affected by the way a pianist crosses the platform and seats himself at the instrument, and how he sustains the pause before beginning to play. Even those fifteen seconds of total stillness before the artist begins his performance are a form of gesture, designed to summon listeners to concentrate their attention, like a conductor's raised baton before the first beat.

A desire to eschew superfluous gesture at all costs is thus a form of purism that does not always benefit the performer, since it may cause a certain constraint and a sense of loss of freedom. Gesturing, after all, is sometimes designed not just to evoke and shape the mood of the pianist himself, but also to liberate him from inhibition and excessive emotional tension.

In addition, if a pianist allows his listeners to sense his artistic self-discipline and limits himself to a minimum of useful expressive movement, then even the slightest gesture reflecting the performer's mood – a slight flourish on lifting a hand from the keys, or a barely noticeable sway of the body – will be registered and felt by the audience. In such cases the slightest hint of expressive gesture is bound to be picked up by listeners. An audience is extraordinarily quick to notice such things, especially against an otherwise austere background of concentration and restraint by the soloist. Indeed, these small marks of genuine feeling produce a much greater impression on the listener than the entire well-known repertoire of ornamental gestures, such as chords played with a sweep and airy flight of the hands, absent gaze, or inspired staring into space with body flung back and arms extended, and so forth.

It has to be said that performers often underestimate the musical sensitivity of their audience. It is true, an audience consisting of seventy-five percent students and amateurs may be corrupted by its own juvenile or dilettante habits of interpretation (different categories). Nevertheless, the majority of listeners are musical people who for one reason or another, sometimes by pure chance, failed to reach a professional standard themselves, and this type of audience often parts with preconceived opinions more readily than a more highly qualified one.

A performer therefore makes a great mistake if he deliberately eliminates every fine nuance and sophisticated device from his playing on the assumption that these will not be perceived by the audience. It is also important to distinguish a genuine deep-seated effect on an audience from mere short-term external success, which can prove an impediment to proper recognition in the long term.

Returning to the question of excessive movement, it is often the case that a teacher has to wrestle with a gifted student's tendency to over-expressive gesture. But just as often he finds himself having to free students up from excessive constraint, cramped muscles, and unwanted tension or stiffness of the wrist, elbow or shoulder. These are frequently the consequence of incorrect training of the hand, the relics of adolescent inhibition, and sometimes the result of slightly mistaken theoretical views.

LEGATO, NON LEGATO, FORTE AND PIANO

The question of *legato* and *non legato* playing is a an extremely complex one. It is closely bound up with the other important problem of how to impart a singing quality to a melody, and how to achieve a true cantilena on the piano.

Many prejudices exist, based on a pseudo-scientific approach to the question of piano tone. Most of them arise from a disregard for the psychology of musical perception and specifically the particular features of piano sound. For instance, one quite often hears statements that on the piano a longer note has to be played louder than a short one. At first sight such an idea might seem obvious and incontrovertible, yet the practicalities of musical performance often contradict it. The character of piano sound is fundamentally different from that of the violin. Playing a note with his bow, a violinist can sustain the sound evenly, or increase or reduce it at will. A note played on the piano loses a significant part of its strength immediately it is struck, and thereafter the sound gradually fades away altogether. So in order to understand properly how piano playing is perceived, one must remember that in his imagination the listener constantly needs to compensate for this peculiarity of piano sonority. The step-like change between successive notes of a group that is peculiar to piano playing is hardly noticed by an audience provided that the pianist skillfully coordinates the strength of consecutive sounds. But what exactly is involved in such coordination? What does the singing quality of a piano melody depend on?

Of course, the harder we strike the key, the longer the sound will last. However, the duration of the sound is not proportional to the strength of the keystroke. If we strike a note with five times the normal force, its duration is barely doubled. This disproportion is due to the fact that a loud note on the piano very quickly spends the greater part of its strength. So that the louder a note is played on the piano the more steeply its strength fades away during the first second. The listener notices this rapid fading of a loud note, and it can thus seem to him that a sound played more softly in fact lasts longer, because the fading of a soft or *mezzo forte* note occurs less abruptly.

An appreciation of these features of piano sound is essential in order to master the art of cantilena playing. The performer always intuitively takes account of this, and an experienced and gifted pianist senses the strength needed to play any series of consecutive notes in a melody.

However, since various theoretical views encroach on this aspect of performance, and any young pianist is likely to hear differing ideas, opinions, and advice, it is essential that some preconceptions be dispelled. For instance, I am not maintaining that long notes should always be played quieter than short notes. But I can cite a number of instances where a long note seems longer precisely because it is played more softly.

It quite often happens that after a series of short chords one needs to play a chord that is meant to last longer, and one is prompted to play this chord somewhat more gently. This prompting is based on an absolutely correct artistic intuition. The rapid fading of a series of short loud chords seems natural. But if one plays a long chord with even greater strength, the listener is bound to notice the rapid fall-off in sonority, and the long chord will thus seem to him just as short as the preceding ones. But if one plays the longer chord somewhat more softly, it is then easier to sense the gently fading sound and even to prolong its effect in one's imagination. Take, for instance, the following passage from Chopin's Scherzo No 4, opus 20:

Here the chords written in half- and dotted half-notes are usually played more softly than the successions of *staccato*. Why? Because it is essential to show the calm and steady sonority of these chords, framed by the other precise and rapid flights of figuration. One could quote many similar such examples

If I want to link a close succession of two chords, I can trace the fading sound of the first of them and connect it with a second chord of weaker strength. But how to proceed when playing a melody consisting of long notes, when one note has almost ceased to sound altogether by the time I strike the next note?

One frequently encounters a suggestion that the strength of each note of a melody should be made to match the volume level surviving from the previous note. In this way, some theoreticians claim, one can achieve a true cantilena on the piano, with a smooth and even flow of sound. However, this view is founded on an obvious misunderstanding. A complete correspondence in volume between each note and the lingering echo of the previous one would doom any melody to die away almost immediately in a rapid *diminuendo*. In fact, any melody played in this manner could only last for a matter of seconds – no longer, in fact, than the duration of one single note!

We also need to remember that the sound of the piano's upper register fades more quickly than the vibration of the bass strings, which are thicker and under less tension. This is why the upper notes on the piano do not require any dampers. Does this mean, though, that we ought to play a melody in the upper register at a particular speed in order to achieve a singing effect? Obviously not.

Thus, in playing a melody properly and striving for a true *cantabile*, we should go by the initial strength of sonority in a consecutive series of notes, and we must correlate the strength of each note with the initial, and not the final, volume level of its predecessor.

If we play a scale slowly, then in dynamic terms an obvious step-wise series of notes will emerge. And if some acoustic apparatus is used to outline the dynamic curve, a zigzag line will appear, marked by a series of sharp, almost vertical upward jerks each time the next string is struck, followed by a rapidly falling arc as each sound fades away. Yet if we play an impeccably even scale, it will seem to us that each note flows into the next evenly and smoothly. This means that the usual work of our imagination has come into play, correcting the step-like quality of the series of notes and, as it were, smoothing out the sharp undulations in sonority.

The evenness and smoothness of a scale played on the piano is thus illusory. One's ear gets accustomed to judging what it hears by the strength of the consecutive hammer strokes. As he plays a melody, the pianist intuitively appeals to the musical imagination of his listeners. This inevitable work of the imagination is no doubt subject to certain laws, but so far this has not been adequately studied.

It is thus far from easy to deduce any norms for melodious playing or to define any rules for achieving a cantilena. The pianist is forced to stimulate the musical imagination of his audience. He has to be able so to distribute the strength of the notes forming a melody that an illusion of songfulness is created. And we should not be afraid of this expression, since the notion of illusion is bound up with the very principle of piano sound – a 'concrete illusion' of the type already mentioned.

I should also remind readers once again: the illusionistic nature of pianoforte tone opens up broad perspectives of sonority that are inaccessible on any other instrument. The piano can in fact convey every aspect and nuance of orchestral sound.

One of the most reliable means of achieving a singing quality in performance lies in the use of tangible expressive movements of the hand. Every movement the performer makes relies on a complex interaction of related forces. Everything in piano technique is so closely interrelated that melodious playing depends on efficacious movement, and expressivity depends on its plastic physical embodiment.

Thus a pianist's work on tangible physical movement can lead him to achieve a cantilena tone. But one could equally maintain, conversely, that the effort to achieve a beautiful tone and cantilena stimulates efficacious movement and the physical embodiment of technical devices. This is one further reason why even when playing purely technical exercises it is essential to cultivate a free and expressive movement of the hands and arms and to concern oneself with the beauty of the sound. Hence the question of *piano* and *forte* playing arises in terms of the technical processes involved in producing them.

How does one achieve a beautiful, powerful tone? It is evident that whatever the methods and exercises recommended, they must correspond to the character of pianoforte sound. Let me dwell on just one or two points in connection with this. After playing a loud chord, some pianists believe it correct to leave their hands forcibly pressed down on the keys. It strikes me that this contradicts the very principle of tone production on the piano. First and foremost, it clearly involves an excessive waste of energy, since after the notes have been struck any further pressure on the keys is pointless: very light pressure is quite sufficient to keep the keys depressed and the chord sounding. Both physically and in its underlying idea, this mannerism contradicts the way in which piano tone is produced – it is comparable to an orchestral percussionist loudly clashing the cymbals and then keeping them tightly pressed together. A pianist who insists on pressing down hard on the keys after a *fortissimo* chord also forces the piano mechanism and places a quite unnecessary strain on it. Apart from which, as a rule, modern pianists usually use the sustaining pedal to pick up each powerful chord. Such fruitless doubling of effort can therefore hardly be regarded as a useful activity.

One also often sees pianists playing chords with an excessive flourish, raising their arms above their head and letting them crash down onto the keyboard. Two reasons are usually given in support of this. It is claimed that a broad sweep of the arm is needed to impart extra power to the chord. Furthermore, it is pointed out that a flourish of the arm looks impressive to an audience, and by this gesture which graphically demonstrates the power of his playing, the performer can make an even stronger impact on his listeners.

Certainly, a powerful tone does depend on the speed of the pianist's hand at the instant it strikes the keyboard, and of course a sweep of the arm is needed to achieve this speed and power. But in fact eight to twelve inches at the most is more than adequate to achieve this. It is essential to bear in mind that speed of movement and thus the power of the down-stroke are also bound up with the need for accuracy and confidence. If a pianist is convinced that his downward keystroke is absolutely on target and that he will not miss or inadvertently strike a single wrong note, then he may permit his hands to crash down onto the keys with maximum speed and power. But a performer who lifts his hands too high automatically deprives himself of this certainty. Then, at the last decisive moment he intuitively exercises some slight caution and discretion and thereby deprives this gesture of the total freedom and strength that it requires.

Not infrequently a pianist who is used to decorative hand flourishes finds that in performing leaps and skips he is forced at the last moment to slightly reduce speed in order not to make a mistake. Thus we often observe that much greater power usually results from restrained, efficient and controlled arm movements than from the use of other flourishing gestures.

As for the graphic effectiveness of more exaggerated flourishes, it should be remembered that these are more likely to impress only less sophisticated listeners. Apart from which, if a technical hitch does occur, the audience will notice and will be especially scornful at the contrast between this ostentatious display of daring and its negative results. However, if a pianist still wants to go in for broad gestures in order to release his emotion and convey this to the audience, surely it is better to make these gestures after the chord in question, rather than before it? This way the safety of the chord is guaranteed as it remains held on the pedal, and freedom of movement is also demonstrated.

The piano possesses deep and powerful bass notes, and some composers make special use of the lowest octave on the keyboard. The lowest notes on the grand piano are ideal for suggesting the tolling of great bells, whereas the orchestra has no powerful instruments in this register. Double basses and contrabassoon are incapable of a *fortissimo*, and even in Wagner's *Parsifal* the bells sound closer to the middle of the register. The orchestra's most powerful resources are the horns, trombones and trumpets, and they all sound in the range of the middle three octaves. On the piano, too, the most powerful sonority largely depends on the middle register. This should have a full-bodied and powerful tone, and then a beautiful sonority will result, approximating closely to that of the orchestra.

A pianist should have the ability to concentrate all his willpower and strength on the powerful keystrokes required at the culmination or the concluding moment of a piece. However, he should not too often approach the extreme limits of tonal intensity and power. Monotonously loud playing loses in brilliance and expressiveness. In piano performance, as in any art, the laws of contrast play a fundamental role. A wise and subtle distribution of dynamics, a considered and properly felt plan of contrasting episodes, a succession of rising and falling sonority, can assist not only the artistic level of performance but also protect the pianist from excessive expenditure of energy. And in all of this, artistry is of prime importance.

The pianist must distinguish between absolute and relative strength of sound. He should seek the foundation for an impressive and beautiful *forte* in a profound *piano*. In order to achieve vivid and powerful tone, a broad range of dynamics and intelligent distribution of contrast are more important than athletic muscles.

The sound of the grand piano as it reaches the back of the concert hall is many times weaker than for a listener sitting in the front row. In this instance an acoustic measuring device would probably register at least a tenfold diminution in volume level. But a listener in the hall would tend not to notice any excessive difference. Again, a certain adaptation of the ear comes into play. For a listener in the back row, a beautiful *forte* retains its powerful effect although in actual fact it sounds much feebler than to those sitting closer to the platform. This means that relative volume levels, changes in dynamic scheme, contrasts and juxtapositions, play a greater role than any absolute measurement of loudness.

When working on the singing tone of a melody or cantilena, we more often find ourselves dealing with *piano* and *mezzo forte* level playing rather than full *forte*. Because of the very nature of its sonority, it is easier to achieve a cantilena on the piano on a *diminuendo* rather than on a *crescendo* passage. Truly melodious playing is thus built on a controlled accumulation of tone and its gradual dispersal. But here, as elsewhere, one should avoid preconceived ideas and dogmas. Taste, creative initiative and subtle artistic feeling should always be the decisive factor.

When practising at *piano* level, one should not lose sight of the need to develop not just a singing tone, but also a really soft *pianissimo*. It is essential to be able to sustain a long, even sonority at low volume, as though the sound is muted or muffled. At the same time no single note should stick out, and none should fail to sound. To achieve this the hand should be rid of every last trace of tension or nervousness. All the fingers should sense their own equal importance and total assurance in contact with the keys. Playing of such exercises should be marked by freedom from any superfluous effort, and by calm, concentrated attention.

A profound and sustained *piano* has no less an effect on the audience than a powerful *forte*. Furthermore it induces a quietness and concentration in the listener. It is essential to work on playing quietly not only at a slow tempo but also at speed, which is much harder. One of the pinnacles of pianistic artistry consists of rapid passagework or complex figuration played at *pianissimo* level.

Let me pause again on one further point. You might ask a young pianist whose playing often sounds relatively well in the concert hall to play you the same pieces in a smaller room where every sound can be clearly heard. You will find that most pianists fall into two categories: some of them *can* play in a smaller room, while the playing of others loses all its artistic charm in this setting. An inexperienced pianist rarely has such mastery of the instrument that his tone retains its quality in ordinary room conditions. While it is often claimed that one must be able to play in large halls, my own wish would be slightly different: many pianists who gear themselves up only to performing on a large stage would do well to learn also how to play with perfection and beauty in a domestic setting.

If one can play well in a room, then one can hope to play with immaculate tone control on the platform. But even a decent performance in a large hall far from guarantees good tone production in room conditions. A performance on stage that seems fairly accomplished may quickly reveal its defects in a smaller space.

ON TALENT AND VIRTUE

When people talk about a pianist, violinist, or even a singer, and maintain that he or she is a good musician, this description unfortunately is not always tantamount to genuine praise. Listening to the 'music of these words', one frequently detects a negative element: someone is maybe a pianist, but without the makings of a virtuoso, or they may be a singer who nevertheless lacks a remarkable voice. Of course, such distrust of the term 'good musician' is maybe not entirely normal or natural. However, I would like there to be some true causal link between such phrases as 'good pianist', 'good performer', 'good musician', and even especially the term 'good person'.

A person is a good musician not only because he or she is musically gifted, but also because their inner world is a rich and interesting one. They play, or conduct, or compose well because they are good musicians, valuable persons, emotionally rich, intellectually developed, and because their whole personality is remarkable and interesting.

The relationship between humanity and art is something that has concerned many thinkers and poets. One recalls that one of Pushkin's remarkable so-called *Little Tragedies*, 'Mozart and Salieri', is devoted to this question. [1]

From the text of the play, we learn that ever since his childhood Salieri displayed exceptional musical talent, and devoted immense effort to achieving the highest level of artistry. Yet he accuses heaven and fate of injustice:

Where is the justice when a sacred gift,
When immortal genius does not reward
An ardent love, self-sacrifice,
Labour, diligence and prayers,
But shines instead upon a madman,

An idle reveller?... O Mozart, Mozart!

But there is one thing Salieri cannot understand: the fact that as a person he is immeasurably inferior to Mozart. Salieri's soul is that of a base, secretive, envious and even criminal being. Mozart, though, is profoundly gifted. He is kindly and trusting, a man of radiant spirit, open to genuine inspiration. Salieri poisons Mozart, but in doing so he also kills himself, both as a person and as musician. Fate was not mistaken in rewarding Mozart with genius and rejecting Salieri's talents:

> *... And yet could he be right,*
> *And am I not a genius? Genius and villainy*
> *Are two things incompatible.*

This is the final conclusion that Pushkin reaches and one to which he leads Salieri too.

The plot of Pushkin's tragedy is often regarded mainly as a conflict between mere craftsmanship and genuine talent, between mediocrity and genius. The result of this, the moral lesson of the drama, so brief yet full of sublime thought, is often relegated to the background. It seems to me that each of us should absorb the idea contained in Pushkin's work. Then maybe we shall cease to misconstrue what it means to be a 'good musician'.

ON PRACTISING

I have rarely come across very diligent pianists in recent times. How many of us can say with hand on heart that we work on our piano playing with sufficient dedication? In their memoirs of Rakhmaninov, the Skalon sisters recall that as a young pianist when living on their estate, he worked for three or four hours a day at one and the same étude by Schloezer, trying to achieve an absolutely perfect performance.[2] One knows of a whole series of similar instances where great pianists of the past have shown quite extraordinary diligence. Many of them would select some difficult work, such as the finale of Chopin's B flat minor Sonata, and work at it with extraordinary perseverance for three to six hours a day.

I am far from believing that this particular kind of work is entirely useful. Possibly Rakhmaninov as a youth did not really need to spend so many hours a day on Schloezer's rather mediocre study. Quite probably the brilliant composer and pianist did more for his future artistry in the hours that he devoted to free artistic improvisation. But I am more impressed by the moral example of this case – by the exceptional demands that Rakhmaninov made of himself, by his deep devotion to his art, and by his persistent striving towards the highest summits of pianistic mastery.

It is characteristic that although young Rakhmaninov's teacher strictly forbade him to indulge in improvisation, he was unable to stifle either his creative urge or, at the same time, his striving for total mastery of his instrument.

How should one work on a new piece?

When setting out to learn a new work, one should never think of the first stage as a tedious exercise that has to be overcome with great effort. On the contrary, getting to know a new composition may well emerge as the most absorbing part of a pianist's work. Every performer should develop and cultivate an ability to find his way around a new score. A young pianist is usually equipped already with a certain repertoire of technical habits and with some ability to overcome various difficulties. For this reason it would therefore be wrong to regard a new work as some impenetrable fortress that can only be seized by laborious assault.

One rarely sees young pianists open up some new music on the stand and simply try to play the new piece as well as their skills and accumulated experience allow. Usually they bypass any artistic opportunity and immediately embark on the tedious and inefficient process of memorizing separate fragments and working out some hastily invented exercises.

For some reason, a number of pianists are also convinced that playing loudly assists in memorizing more quickly and thoroughly. It seems to me quite the contrary, however, and that sounds that are too loud 'knock out' the memory. (I was reminded of this expression by a trumpet player who once told me, 'we trumpeters can only play from music because the high volume level knocks out your memory.' I am not sure whether all trumpeters would agree with their colleague, but I do believe that for pianists 'hammering out' the notes is more likely to hinder memorization than assist it.)

In this regard it is a good idea to ask oneself the question: what exactly do I have to learn by heart? Do I have to memorize the entire work of music, or else should I gradually stitch together the pieces made up of several variants, various crudely hewn fragments, and episodes with no beginning or ending?

When approaching a new piece, if a pianist first tries to play various passages using artificial exercises, he will be left without any view of the total work of art to be memorized. But if you need to learn the work in question by heart, in order to do so you first need to be able to play it. And the first thing required of you is to try – so far as technical ability allows – to play the new piece from the music. And from the very outset it is important to approach the new work with a lively aesthetic sense, treating it as an artistic whole. You have to form a clear idea of how the work is constructed. And once you have learnt to play it correctly from the music, then you will be better placed to memorize it. You will notice that it is easier to memorize ideas that make musical sense when performed on the instrument, rather than a series of unmusical fragments and exercises into which you tried to divide the piece in the initial stages of practice.

Summarizing, one can therefore state as follows: first play and only then practise. On no account practise first before you play the piece. As a teacher, I am often confronted by students asking: Now that you have assigned me such and such a work, how do I go about learning it? The answer is that one should not start by learning it. First of all you should try to play through the piece decently.

It is true that if a teacher gives such advice, he can expect that after one or two lessons the student will come and say that things are not working out. The teacher is then entitled to ask: What exactly isn't working out? And his task is then to advise the young pianist how to master the difficult passages and to suggest various helpful exercises.

Teachers often require a pupil first of all to play pieces by heart. This method is regarded as training the memory. I am not entirely in agreement with this. I would be prepared to say that sometimes students memorize badly because they play too much without the music. The more thoroughly a pianist wants to familiarize himself with a work, the more intently he should study the printed text. And it is not all that simple to read what is written there in the music. Josef Hofmann once said he would undertake to prove to any pianist that he played not more than what was there in the text, but less. Such an assertion might at first seem rather strange. Many pianists consider that they display their own individuality precisely when they go beyond the musical text. For them the printed music serves as a fulcrum and as a starting point for their own individual artistry. But here they make a serious mistake, since every composer, and especially a great one, is quite capable of incorporating all the essentials of his music in the actual text. But to read and understand everything essential about the music is so hard that by no means every performer is capable of doing so. A pianist's individuality is expressed not in what he does over and beyond the printed score, but chiefly in how attentively he can read the actual musical text and how deeply he can understand and reveal this to his listeners.

But what exactly does 'reading the musical text' mean? Many people might think that I regard the composer's markings as being of primary importance – those governing tempo, expression, and other nuances. But in fact I am referring only to the actual notes themselves. This musical notation in itself tells a pianist so much that if he is capable of assimilating it, then all the composer's other indications regarding performance become self-evident.

I once asked one of our leading pianists the following question: 'Supposing that in his First Ballade Chopin had failed to place a single expression or tempo marking, would pianists perform the work any differently, or would this not affect their performance?' The pianist thought for a moment and then answered: 'No, it wouldn't affect the performance.' This means that interpretation of the First Ballade hardly depends on the additional marking put in by Chopin, but only on the notes themselves, which any true performer can read, hear, and make perfect sense of.

Of course, some composers' markings are integrally bound up with the printed music – for instance, indications such as *doppio movimento, tempo primo*, et cetera. But I am talking about markings that relate only to the actual performance and execution, and this accounts for the vast majority of such markings. To use a comparison that might help to clarify this point, I would regard the actual musical text as the legacy bequeathed to us by the composer, whereas his performance markings could be likened merely to a form of 'covering letter', as it were, that accompanies the will.

We should treat the great composers with reverence, we should treasure every word that comes down to us from that distant age when their creative genius was alive, and we should closely examine the meaning of their personal instructions. At the head of the last movement of the *Appassionata*, for instance, Beethoven writes '*Allegro ma non troppo*'. And as we carefully try to fathom every word of this, we might wonder what is the most important thing to observe. What is more significant – '*ma non troppo*', or '*Allegro*'? I am the last person to belittle the importance of a composer's indications, yet, as I said, they are only a form of accompanying letter to the text. Beethoven's music itself says so much that a pianist who recalls all the time he plays that the opening of the *Appassionata* is marked 'Allegro assai' might tend to approach this marvellous work with less freedom and profundity than a player who gets carried away and forgets all about the tempo markings. Sometimes, too, performance indications run so much counter to our own genuine feelings, that we might decide not to heed them – or in an extreme case we might even abandon work on the piece altogether. Even in Beethoven, whose expression marks are extremely valuable, subtle and meaningful, one comes across *sforzando* markings that one is sometimes bound to ignore.

Very often, too, we are inclined to treat a composer's markings too literally. For instance, in Schumann a *sforzando* is more an indication of some internal harmonic significance, or else it marks a melodic break, rather than simply calling for stronger pressure on the piano keys. Schumann merely wants to point out that some particular note has a special meaning, but how to bring this out will depend on the individual performer. A single note or chord can be emphasized in various ways, including even a sudden reduction of dynamics or a slowing of the tempo.

I would also stress, however, that under no circumstances should one regard performance markings as mere obstacles to a free and emotionally satisfactory performance. While listening to some pupils' otherwise good playing, I have sometimes observed that certain blemishes in their performance are caused by a too superficial understanding of the composer's indications. The markings are interpreted too literally, without understanding the artistic reasoning underlying them.

The age when it was the done thing for pianists to play with the music in front of them had its advantages. Of course, in many respects it makes sense for a virtuoso performer to play from memory. First of all there is the matter of pure technical convenience: if the pianist's gaze is not constantly distracted by the music, he is free to concentrate on what his hands are doing. Also, the keyboard on a modern grand piano is twice as wide as in Mozart's day, and it has become difficult to perform accurately without looking at the bass notes while at the same playing some complex and rapid figuration further up the keyboard. Yet what a rich repertoire the performer had in the classical era! He had to spend much less time on learning each new piece, and the reading of music and playing at sight was cultivated much more at that time.

If students approach a work incorrectly and attempt at all costs to learn the notes by heart from the outset, before 'performing' the piece, this sometimes leads nowadays to young pianists losing altogether the ability to play from the music. I find there are occasions when students have not yet learned a piece thoroughly, and I tell them they should by all means play from the music, and I then discover that not only does the music not help them, but they are actually unable to play from it.

In times gone by people used to go in more for private music making. But nowadays our students do too little study of musical literature using the score. They do not develop an ability to read at sight, and we do little to correct this. Yet by failing to develop his sight-reading, a pianist hinders himself from acquiring a broad general knowledge of musical literature and thus makes any approach to new works more difficult for himself. All that I have said can be summed up in one short phrase: A good musician should both love music and love to make music.

How should one go about learning difficult passages? I believe this problem needs discussing in more detail. There is a certain attitude towards the playing of exercises that could be described as superstitious or even 'mystical'. Time periods and numbers start to acquire a mysterious power over the student, and he begins to believe in some miraculous result that can be achieved if over a period he spends a certain number of hours per day playing through certain exercises.

There was a time when every exercise book contained a foreword that made such promises. Nowadays, students are not forced to play through Hanon, although in our day we spent hundreds of hours systematically ploughing through the exercises in that celebrated volume. The introduction to Hanon's collection announced that if a pianist daily played through all the exercises, taking two or three hours over this, he would eventually achieve ultimate perfection. Indeed, the final exercise in particular – in *tremolo* playing – was likely to set any listener trembling! [3]

Put more simply, one can say that every exercise should bring some tangible benefit. And the number of hours spent at the instrument is of some importance if progress is to be made. This is especially important for beginners. For this reason at an early stage pupils are made to spend a certain number of hours playing the usual exercises, scales and arpeggios. But more advanced young players will inevitably question the aim of all this. The road leading to fairly quick mastery of a certain number of basic technical habits is not always going to lead to the highest pinnacles of artistry. Indeed, some practice methods that prove beneficial at an intermediate stage may eventually become an obstacle to achieving perfection.

The young pianist who tends to listen to various advice, not always from the most qualified sources, would do well to ponder this dilemma. For a pianist striving to perfect his mastery of the instrument, it is natural to seek for a universal panacea that will rid his playing of every flaw in a short space of time. But in doing so, he may fall into a double trap. On the one hand, in every method suggested to him there is some benefit to be gained. There will always be some area of technique – sometimes quite a small one – in which a certain practice method may prove useful. The harm only occurs when this is allowed to acquire some sort of universal significance. Unfortunately, though, this happens all too often.

On the other hand, by seeking advice 'on the side' some students frequently adopt training methods that while promoting technical progress at the same time may free them of all tension when practising. There is thus a tendency for students to try and replace artistic concentration with thoughtless, mechanical forms of exercise.

The danger is that each new method that adds something to what has already been achieved may indeed move the pianist ahead a certain way in the first instance. And this raises hopes that usually prove unfounded. In the final analysis, the majority of such 'universal methods' lead nowhere. Progress usually ceases once the student casts aside his previous habitual exercises. A period of even greater persistence then begins, usually culminating in a student's disappointment both with the remarkable new method and with his own artistic abilities.

After some familiarity with the preconceptions and artificial training methods that were especially current in the nineteenth century, one invariably concludes that great pianists of the past achieved the peak of artistic perfection not thanks to these methods, but despite them. I know of one such method of developing finger technique that involved placing a glass of water on the back of the hand, and the student was supposed to practise without spilling a single drop of liquid. Try and perform this exercise and it will become clear to what excesses these various 'theories' and 'secrets of the art' could lead!

The story of the glass of water may nowadays raise a smile. But just consider how many not only fruitless, but actually harmful experiments were designed to artificially improve finger extension. One such exercise involved placing corks between the fingers while practising, bending the thumb back toward the forearm, and playing an extended chord and pressing down on the keyboard with all one's strength. One is bound to say that such artificial teaching methods are based on terrible misunderstandings, and the only totally useful methods are natural ones bound up with beautiful tone production and smooth, free movements of hand and arm.

I once heard an idea that sounds somewhat paradoxical but which is essentially very true: In order to make progress in the art of piano, 'one must play well as often as possible, and play badly as rarely as possible.' A pianist should indeed keep all his work under strict artistic control. The most mundane exercises should be performed with physical freedom and be made to sound beautiful. One should never learn fragments of a work using a deliberately hard, dry touch – this is bound to impair the eventual artistic results.

The pianist should train himself always to feel like an artist when seated at the instrument. His every contact with the keys should be designed to facilitate keen artistic attention. He must rid himself of all carelessness, and ward off any signs of flagging attention or indifference. The pianist should never permit himself to play any work worse than he is actually able. And all these qualities should become a habit with him that is taken for granted whenever he plays. The pianist must also love his instrument and its expressive capabilities, and indeed the very sound of the piano.

ON EXERCISES

In spite of its many false conclusions, Steinhausen's book, *The Foundations of Piano Playing*, makes one point that is unquestionably correct.[4] His basic idea is that there is a fundamental difference between gymnastics and exercises, and this idea can also be applied to the problems of piano technique.

The aim of gymnastics is to strengthen one's whole body, develop one's muscles, increase physical endurance, broaden the chest, and improve strength and stability. By contrast, the aim of an exercise is to inculcate a particular correct habit, to perfect a particular movement, whether simple or complex.

Let me give a very elementary example. Suppose that one of your friends wants to learn to ride a bicycle. Of course, any form of sport requires strong muscles, powerful legs, and a heart that is in good condition. Yet when someone has bought a bicycle but not yet learned to ride it, he is not first of all going to indulge in gymnastics to improve his musculature. Quite simply he will have to practise until he picks up the particular habits required to keep one's balance on a bicycle. I believe that the pianist, too, should overcome specific technical problems by performing particular exercises, and not through indulging in general manual gymnastics.

If we compare the physical features of a splendid piano virtuoso and someone unable to play the piano, it may well turn out that there is little difference in their musculature. The difference between them is simply that one of them can play the piano and the other cannot.

I am the last one to deny the importance of training for piano technique. But a pianist should focus his main attention not on gymnastics but on exercise, if only because there is an element of gymnastics present in every exercise and every practising session.

The main obstacle to achievement of total mastery usually lies not in a pianist's lack of physical fitness (although good health, strength and stamina undoubtedly have a part to play), but in his lack of sufficiently correct and efficient habits of movement and tone production. If a pianist does not have the highly developed specific dexterity, if he is awkward in performing movements that have to be executed with total perfection, then it is essential that he try and eliminate these shortcomings by means of exercises.

How, then, should one perform exercises? What are the requirements of an exercise? How best to construct genuinely useful exercises that lead to the highest level of technical mastery?

First of all, for clarity's sake, I am going to list ten basic requirements, and then I will try to discuss each point in more detail.

1 So far as possible, an exercise must relate directly to a pianist's current artistic work. It must be directed to the resolution of a particular aesthetic problem.

2 It is essential to learn to distinguish what is difficult from what is easy, what one can do from what is unmanageable. A pianist should not work on imaginary problems.

3 An exercise should be easier than the difficulty that you want to master.

4 An exercise should be based on simple, natural elements of piano technique.

5 An exercise should be short.

6 An exercise should be based on the principle of 'from the simple to the complex', and not vice versa.

7 An exercise must yield positive results in a short time.

8 An exercise should be based on the exchange of experience between the right and left hand.

9 An exercise should be executed with maximum technical perfection.

10 It is essential when doing exercises to concentrate on beauty of tone, and on efficiency and complete freedom of movement.

À propos of the first point above, I should point out that finger dexterity and a mastery of fairly rapid tempi are often achieved earlier than a true and complete piano technique. Technique in a broad sense is a way of describing genuine mastery of the piano. Everything should emerge 'firmly', as we say, and fairly fluently, and it should sound completely artistic and be beautifully polished. It is vital, of course, not only that all technical problems should be mastered, but that one's playing as a whole should be on a high artistic level. Yet one also senses that the exercises on which a young pianist spends so much time and energy and which enable him to achieve a basic level of technique, will not automatically lead to the highest level of mastery.

Here one should definitely distinguish various levels of training. Those methods of drill that were essential in a school of music may become unnecessary and burdensome if a more accomplished pianist continues them out of mere habit. Indeed it is likely that exercises that were helpful at an early technical stage may even delay a pupil's achievement of the ultimate heights. Also, even a talented student may not always be inclined to abandon a beginner's work habits and to move on from training exercises to more artistic ones. This may be a sign of the student's lack of confidence in his own artistic powers. Sometimes students even have a subconscious fear of higher artistic challenges and prefer to remain at the level of mere pupils. The experienced teacher should be able to notice this tendency in good time in order to counter it and develop platform confidence and artistic assertiveness in his students.

A secret fear of artistic responsibility may also take on various forms. Sometimes the student himself may not be aware of it. But usually this inner timidity, which must be overcome, is apparent in a novice's urge to replace artistic concerns with purely mechanical ones. He, as it were, clings to habits acquired in school and continues devoting many hours to general training exercises, and new pieces are only learned slowly by dint of dry and inartistic hammering out the notes, or else by reverting to a large number of mechanically contrived variants.

Lack of confidence in one's abilities may also express itself in a reverse tendency, when a student shows an unseemly haste to assert his own artistic individuality. Self-assurance and a proper confidence in one's abilities are quite different and even contradictory traits of character. Behind confidence lies strength, but self-assurance often merely camouflages an inner sense of weakness.

Striving after effect and originality are harmful precisely because they conceal an aversion for serious work caused by a student's fear of genuine artistic responsibility. In such cases the teacher's task is more than a mere formality. He has to arouse his pupil's aspiration toward genuine mastery and toward those artistic summits that can only be reached by a path that he at present conceals from himself behind a superficial snobbery. In fact, the teacher must stimulate in his student a sense of noble duty and a faith in his proper calling.

There comes a time in every pianist's development when the only way to further advancement has to be based on exercises directly related to the actual compositions he is studying. Of course, only a player with a keenly developed artistic ear both has the subtle control and makes the high demands of his performance that are essential to achieve a high level of artistry. But it becomes clear to an experienced pianist that every age, every composer, every composition – and furthermore every passage, figuration, and detail in texture – require their own artistic approach and specific technical resolution. Moreover, a really fine pianist demonstrates the high level of his artistry partly by an ability to find instantly the solution to every problem he encounters.

Exercises must become part of one's creative work. They must always be linked to the particular task in hand, to the work that a pianist is studying at that particular moment. An exercise is based on a form of creative initiative, an ability to find the most effective solution to any given problem.

The greater the pianist's level of mastery, the harder it becomes to say exactly what things are easy and what are difficult. On the one hand, a virtuoso with a big technique deals effortlessly and as a matter of course with many difficulties. On the other hand, a perfect performance of seemingly simple pieces or episodes also demands great artistry and attention.

The division of pieces into difficult and easy is thus to some extent arbitrary. This problem is often encountered by teachers looking to set their pupils something simple and well within their grasp. Sometimes teachers observe in pupils a measure of disdain for simpler works. But a pianist should be able to play everything, and it is precisely in simple compositions that pianistic shortcomings often come to light.

In the same way, there is no justification for turning up one's nose at slow pieces. To produce a good sound on the instrument is an integral part of the pianist's art. It is impossible to play well without fine tone control, and it is primarily in slower pieces that we learn how to produce a beautiful sound on the instrument.

So far as purely muscular or 'physical training' problems are concerned, one encounters them fairly rarely. In fact we hardly ever find works that require super-powerful muscles or extreme motoric ability. Certainly, there is a branch of musical literature that I would describe as 'athletic'. In this category I would place certain compositions by Franz Liszt. There are episodes in his work that require exceptional, almost superhuman stamina and dynamics. But I must admit that I do not regard those moments that require such overexertion as among the best features of Liszt's style.

I have sometimes heard his *Dante Sonata* referred to as an exercise in physical fitness. And it is true, one needs exceptional strength and endurance to overcome all the difficulties of this work without excessive exhaustion, playing with total freedom, without either slowing the tempo or needlessly forcing the pace. Maybe one really does need special training to perform such pieces. Yet the majority of Liszt's works, including the B minor Sonata, are perfectly accessible to players with 'normal musculature'.

All the difficulties in Chopin can be mastered by any pianist with a good technique, irrespective of his muscular strength or particular stamina. This, too, is true of the demanding passages in Beethoven's piano sonatas, as also of the difficulties in Bach, Mozart, Schumann, Brahms and Scriabin.

The pianist should be able to distinguish genuine difficulties from imaginary ones. Many things seem hard not only to young but also more seasoned players, because it is not always clear to them how to break up a complicated episode into its simpler elements. And the function of an exercise is to assist in finding the 'easier solution' and thus achieve a higher level of perfection.

Many seeming difficulties occur because of preconceived views about the role of exercises. Sufficient to recall how we used to play scales at the beginning of the century. The main difficulty we encountered was in tucking under the thumb. It is hard to pass the thumb under the fourth finger, and even harder under the fifth. But we were made to practise this for hours on end. The result was to create utterly unnecessary difficulties for pianists. When compiling his manual of exercises, Hanon worked along the following line of reasoning: if it is hard to tuck under the thumb, then student should be challenged with something even more difficult, and once he is used to negotiating this extra difficulty, he will find it much easier to deal with tucking his thumb under the fifth finger. Unfortunately, this approach leads only to habits of unnatural hand position and unnecessary tension, not to mention the defective playing that results from them. Nowadays most of our major pianists maintain that in normal technique the thumb should be tucked under no further than the third finger.

The above is one example of eliminating an imaginary problem, and we realize once and for all that this difficulty really does not exist. There is no need to practise overcoming it, it simply needs to be jettisoned. Just remember that the thumb is never passed under beyond the third finger, and in scale playing you have to find a natural fingering that never requires such artificial and difficult movements.

It often seems to pianists that they lack strength in their fourth finger, and they start searching for complex ways to develop this most unfortunate finger of the five. Lengthy exercises to increase its strength are usually followed by attempts to raise and stretch it artificially, but with no apparent technical improvement. It emerges that this too is a non-existent problem. It is all a matter of rationally distributing our hand weight. Then, if the finger stroke is correct and if the hand moves supportively, the fourth finger is capable of producing a quite beautiful tone.

Exercises should be easier than the difficulty we are trying to master. If, on the contrary, we make them harder than the problem they are meant to solve, we are not going to improve our technical mastery but actually impede its development. Difficult problems yield to our efforts only because we work our way forward gradually, from the simple to the more complex.

I once saw a truly frightening manual of exercises that was compiled as a *Selection of the Hardest and Most Awkward Passages from Beethoven*. If we work through this book with dogged persistence, we are actually going to unlearn how to play Beethoven. On the other hand, if we can learn to perform perfectly all the other not too difficult passages that are typical of Beethoven, then assuredly we should find some way of mastering the two or three other problem passages we meet along the way.

I am no sportsman. But it strikes me that an athlete who has problems with the two-meter high jump is hardly likely to say to himself: 'I think I'll raise the bar by another thirty centimeters and try, no matter what, to master that height. After that two meters will seem quite trivial.' Surely any experienced trainer would forbid such an experiment, because it would be not only pointless, but actually harmful or even dangerous. Similarly on the piano, if when you encounter a series of difficult skips, you force yourself to practise even bigger ones in the hope that this particular leap will then seem easy, you will be making a grave error. If you have an episode with a series of such leaps, you should first try and ensure that you can play the easier ones accurately and easily, after which the harder ones will also begin turning out right. In this way, the exercise should always be easier than the problem that you want to overcome.

In my youth I often had to work on complicated passages or difficult figuration with the help of so-called 'variants'. I persisted with these exercises without at the time feeling any direct benefit. Subsequently I convinced myself of the limited effectiveness of this method. Indeed, is it really necessary to learn twenty different variants of a passage in order to overcome one single difficulty? I think the majority of these variants create their own special difficulties not directly related to the basic one being studied.

First of all, most of the variants are more difficult than the problem arising in the work itself. Usually, too, they are built around a group of new problems surrounding the basic one, rather than on the extraction of simpler elements that are easily mastered. In addition they all involve replacing something vital with something dead, the natural with the artificial, and, most important, the artistic with the mechanical. And unfortunately, young talents fall most easily for this type of bait.

Surely, though, it would be more useful to learn twenty-four different études rather than twenty-four variants of one and the same étude?

However we break up a complex episode into parts for separate study, these individual elements should not be unnatural or inartistic. For as we practise, we should still be striving to achieve a fine perfection and a beautiful sound. There is no need to create long exercises. An exercise should be as short as possible and constructed for maximum efficiency. It should, as it were, condense and absorb precisely that difficulty that we have to contend with, and it is important we should so construct it that the particular difficulty appears in easier form and is more easily executed.

It takes considerable experience and creative initiative to devise such exercises. Many things seem difficult not just to the young but also to more experienced pianists precisely because they do not perceive the simpler elements from which a complicated passage is made up.

It is essential to school oneself in composing this sort of short exercise on the spur of the moment in the course of working on a piece. These exercises can help 'polish' difficult transitions, awkward turns in certain passages, and unusual sequences of fingering. Especially rapid results can be achieved with exercises so constructed that they can be repeated over and over several times as part of a continuous movement. This sort of *perpetuum mobile* based on a difficult passage can help overcome a particular problem sometimes in a matter of minutes.

I frequently resort to this method in my own work, and if it helps in working on some étude I refer to it as a 'study within a study'. I once showed one of these exercises to Alexeyev who included it in his article on my pianistic principles in the collection *Masters of the Soviet Piano School*.[5] I will quote this example again here, taken from the finale of Beethoven's *Appassionata*:

From this passage we can derive the following two exercises:

Ex 2

These are just two exercises for practice. Many similar examples could be devised, but in each case one must select that feature that most nearly corresponds to the particular difficulty encountered. The fingering of the exercise, of course, remains the same as that in the passage under study.

As can be seen, the exercise must be short and yield rapid results. And if while practising you do not immediately notice some progress in overcoming the problem, this means you have not correctly isolated its constituent elements, and you will need to discover some better version of them. Occasionally, too, an exercise may give a one-sided effect, and a second one may need to devised as a harmonic supplement. A pianist should study thoroughly and objectively the faults in his own technical apparatus and take them into account when devising exercises.

I have often heard teachers complaining that there are very few études written for the left hand. Yet for any passage one can construct a symmetrical exercise that is playable by the other hand. In this way, both hands can, as it were, 'exchange experience' and one hand can help train the other.

The right hand can execute certain passages better than the left. But there are some figurations specially adapted to the left hand. More often we encounter situations where the right hand can pass its technical experience on to the left. But the left hand, which is adapted to dealing with its own specific problems, also has plenty that it can teach the right.

In devising such exercises there is no need to require total, mirror-like symmetry, since this cannot always be achieved. But it is vital to observe the same fingering in both right and left hands. As an example one can take the opening bar of Chopin's Prelude No 3 from opus 28:

For this the following exercise can be devised:

Once you can master this exercise, it becomes clear that one hand is passing its technical experience on to the other.

If while studying a piece, you sense there is something holding up the execution of some passage or other, you should immediately try and devise a symmetrical exercise for both hands. Then, over and above any conscious efforts, you will sense that one hand is actually helping correct the movement of the other.

Under this heading one can also mention the method of coordinating the fingering of both hands. The simultaneous performance of passagework in both hands is made easier if the fingering is made to correspond. Then, when the keystrokes of the thumb or fifth finger coincide, this provides a support point or fulcrum that facilitates the execution. In parallel passages the important thing is to observe that groups of fingers coincide. Within each group of course the fingers play in reverse sequence, but the actual changes of finger groups occur at the same moment.

As an example of coordinated finger grouping in parallel motion, we can cite a passage from the opening movement of Tchaikovsky's First Piano Concerto, opus 23.

[Andante non troppo e molto maestoso]

Here the finger groups of both hands are distributed as follows:

RIGHT HAND	2-3-4; 1-2-3-4; 1-2-3-4; 1-2-3; 5
LEFT HAND	3-2-1; 4-3-2-1; 4-3-2-1; 4-3-2; 1

In playing any exercise we should strive for total perfection and accuracy. If this cannot at first be achieved at normal tempo, one should work out the exact coordination of finger strokes and hand movements at a slower pace. A direct switch from one tempo to another is especially easy in exercises of the 'study within a study' type where continuous motion is involved. Here, in a series of slow, then faster repetitions, you can immediately sense the problem simply melt away and disappear.

Once you can perform the exercise to perfection, you should continue repeating it for a few more minutes in order to make the movements automatic and free yourself completely of any unnecessary effort and unwanted tension. If you have practised properly, then later on when playing through the whole passage you should feel not the slightest difficulty when you reach the problem point.

However, it is essential to remember when practising that we should always keep check on the evenness and beauty of our tone, and on our freedom and efficiency of physical movement. The pianist should be able to sense that exercises free him of all superfluous movement and unnecessary tension, and that the precision, efficiency and plasticity of his technique are constantly growing.

When practising correctly, a pianist learns actually to hear his own playing. He can then evaluate it accurately as if from outside and maintain careful control over it. Later on, any recording of his performance will then cease to strike him as something alien and unexpected, and he will unmistakably recognize his own playing when recorded on tape.

ON STYLE IN PERFORMANCE

It seems to me essential to pause and discuss the question of style in piano performance. A good many works have been written on the subject, presenting a great variety of different views on the problem of style. Some of these works attempt to embrace the subject of style as a whole, offering general solutions and overall guiding principles. Others touch on individual phenomena, the interpretation of certain composers, or even one single composition. Some of these statements strike me as fair enough, although I find it impossible to agree with others. Let me begin, though, with some remarks on the role of tradition, in particular the importance of the Russian pianistic tradition.

Russian pianists can celebrate many accomplishments over the last century. Traditions in the field of style, interpretation method and approach to particular works, which have come down to us via such figures as Balakirev, Rakhmaninov and Scriabin and their artistic legacy, are not only precious to us but they make up that great school on which the progress of our modern pianism is founded.

More than once I have pointed out that the piano style of Rakhmaninov is rooted in the type of pianistic statement characteristic of Tchaikovsky. If we study the texture of piano works by Rakhmaninov and note some of the features of his own performance, we frequently observe that they derive from elements contained in the work of Tchaikovsky.

I also believe that we Soviet pianists should be specially aware of these invaluable traditions going back to Tchaikovsky, Balakirev, Rakhmaninov and Scriabin. We should study them and nurture and cultivate them in our pupils. I would also issue a reminder of the value of Liadov's unique and subtle pianism, and of the remarkable compositions and playing of Medtner.

We are aware of many pianists who perform older works in such a way that they come alive for us. If the performer is excited by the experience of a distant age embodied in the works of a great composer, he should be able to pass on this excitement to us. But sometimes we find an old composer is interpreted without any deep understanding, and his work remains as nothing more than a dead weight. One must know how to breathe life into these works of a past age. Frequently, though, a performer resurrects not so much the spirit and sound as the single dead letter of the past, not so much the creative idea behind a work as some point of empty dogma.

There exist several so-called 'traditions' of performing classical works. However, we frequently confuse tradition with mere habit, and there is a dangerous pitfall in this. The inertia of habit runs quite counter to living tradition. There is a vital creative impulse in tradition, whereas habit is founded only on lifeless inertia. Not every interpretive method to which our ears may get accustomed can rightfully be described as tradition. Year after year we teachers are used to hearing juvenile performances of the classics. And although many students do play well, nevertheless we are used to hearing performances that are frequently devoid of any real artistic initiative or genuine aesthetic tension. And without realizing it, we ourselves are guilty of turning mere habit into a tradition.

But a noble tradition should inspire in us a creative approach to every work. It should not limit but extend the stylistic frontiers. The traditions coming down to us from great pianists of the past demand individual realization and a genuine aesthetic effort on our part. But we are still not sufficiently skilled in detecting and developing the individuality of our pupils. Students are used to picking up and adopting many things from one another, and already at the level of our music schools supposed 'traditions' of performing Mozart, Bach, and Beethoven are developed. We know all too well exactly how each note of a classical composition should be played. Yet even the most over-played pieces can be made to sound in a completely new way. We can learn this from the art of such pianistic giants as Sergei Rakhmaninov. Every time we hear a popular work, we are involved in newly resurrecting its musical ideas and images. We have to listen with unbiased ears to music that has become much too familiar, we must check the freshness and sincerity of our perception, and force ourselves to be ready for yet further artistic exertion.

The strength of the Russian piano tradition lies in its breadth and in the range of individual approaches that it permits. Rakhmaninov's performance of classical works differed vastly from, say, Nikolai Medtner's interpretation of Beethoven, and the pianism of Prokofiev was often the diametrical opposite of Scriabin's. Traditions are valuable and bear fruit if they are bound up with the legacy of Rakhmaninov or the work of a whole series of other splendid interpreters. But if by tradition we understand some preconceived ideas about style, if we link tradition with some particular approach only because it has hardened into habit, we can easily fall into error.

Especially dangerous is a tendency to place too much credence in supposed eyewitness reports. We should not forget how hard it is to convey in words our impressions of some interpretation, or how difficult it is to curb a natural desire to exaggerate our impressions of some great artist's playing. These distortions and slips of memory occur unconsciously and arise from an understandable enthusiasm that a narrator tries to arouse in his listener. I once jokingly referred to such exalted accounts as 'fishermen's tall stories'. Very many music lovers tend to embellish their memories of the playing of great virtuosi with their own personal sympathies and attitudes. For instance, we are supposed to believe that Josef Hofmann played a piece in a certain way, while Busoni allegedly did just the opposite! Of course, the testimony of a great artist about the playing of another remarkable performer is extremely valuable, but the tales of less qualified authorities can sometimes lead to a total distortion of the musical image. Once again, however, we are bound to recall that we now have at our disposal a superb range of unimpeachable evidence thanks to modern recording methods on tape and gramophone.

ON AUTHENTICITY

The performer can derive most information from the text of a work itself, and musical notation is a live object for study, providing useful clues to the style of interpretation. But this alone is not sufficient. It is also essential to understand the circumstances in which a particular work was created. One needs to know something of the character of that epoch and also the complete range of the composer's other works. How, for instance, can one fathom the particulars of Tchaikovsky's piano style without a knowledge of his songs, symphonies and operas? Everything in the composer's oeuvre is interrelated, and one area of his work is affected by another.

There are some performers who are in a hurry at all costs to demonstrate their own original manner of playing, and they are afraid of losing their own identity and individuality. This is of course not always a sign of the originality of their talent. Such performers feel cramped within the confines of the musical text and are eager to 'enhance' it with at least some minor changes, hoping their playing will sound fresh and new if they leave a personal imprint on the actual text of the work. But in most cases they miscalculate. Pianists with the greatest original gifts are usually particularly scrupulous in following a composer's text, and, conversely, editors and performers who make additions and changes to what the composer wrote rarely turn out to be genuinely original interpreters.

This form of pseudo-inventiveness is often associated with a stubborn desire to impart to a performance features that are manifestly foreign to the style of the work itself. Or else, on the contrary, we find a desire to resurrect with museum-like precision the sound of old instruments that at one time appeared to be consigned to antiquity. Strange as it may seem, these two opposing tendencies co-exist quite happily. I believe that a museum approach to early classical works is mistaken, although I do not deny there may be a measure of charm in such stylized performance. But one can easily see that a work decked out in the antiquated adornments of clavichord performance and sound quality loses some of its impact. A performer playing on the harpsichord nowadays is not able to restore the complete musical image. The sound we hear is only a sort of arbitrary depiction, a moving doll from the ethnographic section of a museum of antiquities. Attempts at the arbitrary museum reconstruction of sounds of the past produce results that relate to the true impact of those magnificent examples of ancient music in the same way as shadow theatre relates to the theatre of live actors. The shadow theater can give pleasure and successfully evokes a certain mood, but it cannot claim to have the same power of impact to which the live theatre aspires.

In her performances of old music, Wanda Landowska sought to reproduce all the tonal features of early instruments, and in them one seemed to hear the echo of old castles and palaces. But the natural shortcomings of such instruments as the harpsichord and clavichord on which Landowska played were something she elevated to the status of an artistic dogma, believing that a work written for harpsichord should on no account be played on the piano-forte (although she herself was an excellent pianist). This sort of museum-style approach to performance is therefore something that I think is mistaken. Yet, despite her erroneous views on style, by her unique performing talents Landowska was able to produce performances that were nevertheless of some interest and significance.

It should not be forgotten that the modern grand piano is the result of an immense evolutionary process from earlier instruments like the clavichord. The construction of the violin has not changed since the times of Stradivarius. In its main characteristics, tonal range and sound quality, the modern organ also hardly differs from the instruments that Bach played upon. In its breadth of keyboard, mechanical perfection and in the beauty and power of its sound, however, only the piano has reflected the evolution that went on in European music from Bach to Scriabin.

More correct in my opinion are those pianists who perform old music but at the same time take into account the remarkable qualities of the modern piano. In their interpretation, ancient music comes to life with a power that would astonish the original composer if only he could hear his work performed on a modern instrument. The very sound of the piano, which is powerful, transparent, and flexible, and has a rich diversity of timbre and colour, would have delighted the ears of those used only to the feeble and monotonous tones of the harpsichord.

A work composed even in some distant epoch should thus come alive for us not like some musical ghost, not as a faint echo of bygone times, but as a powerful, full-blooded creative entity capable of making an impact on a modern audience. Nor should one think that the main stylistic elements are lost in modern piano performances of works by Bach and Mozart. On the contrary, with the perfect sonority of the piano old-style music is revealed with a precision, strength and freedom beyond the powers of any artificial stylized presentation. The legitimacy of transcriptions for the piano of old organ compositions is based on similar considerations.

Questions of style in music generally, and in piano performance especially, are so complex, broad and various, that I can here touch on only a few problems, and then only in passing.

Whatever our attitude toward authentic style and 'stylization', we can never go wrong if we regard a deep and direct musical impact on the audience as our main criterion of performance. By its very the nature the role of the performer is a *lyrical* one, and in a sincere performance it is virtually impossible not to reveal one's own individual relationship to the work in question. To substantiate this, let me quote from the Russian critic Vissarion Belinsky who in a discussion of the poetry of Lermontov talked about the relationship between the individual and common humanity: [6]

'In a great talent an excess of the inner subjective element is a sign of his humanity. Do not fear this feature, it will not deceive or lead you into error. In talking about his own self, his own "I", a great poet speaks also about what is common to all, about humanity at large, for the poet's nature contains everything by which all of humanity lives. And therefore in his sadness everyone recognizes their own sorrow, in his soul everybody recognizes their own and sees in him not just a poet, but a living person, a fellow who shares in their own humanity. And in acknowledging him as a creature incomparably higher than themselves, everyone is at the same time aware of their own kinship with him.'

Here Belinsky is talking about subjective lyrical experience, about the poet's feelings that are objectified in the perceptions of a broad circle of listeners and readers. But this idea is one that can be applied as a whole to the performing arts.

THE HARD AND SIMPLE, DIFFICULT AND COMPLEX

I would like to return again to the question of what is difficult and what is easy in the art of the pianist. Here there is a distinction to be drawn between what is difficult and what is merely complex. Very often some episode may strike us as difficult, whereas in fact it is only a complex one made up of a series of elements each of which, taken separately, would never be perceived as difficult. In bars that seem difficult a pianist must be able to discover those simpler elements that together comprise the difficulty. And in the majority of cases we can discern apparent difficulty as nothing more than complexity: a complex motion can be divided into a series of simpler movements.

Working from the music itself, a musical pianist will usually discover intuitively an efficient resolution to some difficult complexion of movements. But sometimes intuition is not sufficient and we have to resort to conscious analysis in order to discern the simple within the complex. It follows from this that it is vital that a pianist be able to give immaculate performances of simpler pieces and episodes. Yet it is a fault even with some great virtuosi that they cannot perform simpler works with adequate perfection. This may emerge in the pianist's lack of emotional expression, lyricism, poetic quality, or whatever, but often it is also a matter of technical perfection, of evenness and smoothness of execution, or of tonal control.

All too often, as well, technical mastery and rapidity of execution are confused. But they are different concepts. And it is due to this confusion that young pianists often acquire finger dexterity much sooner than they achieve genuine complete mastery of the instrument.

From time to time every teacher should therefore set his pupil some simple composition to study, because in his urge to master greater technical difficulties a young pianist is sometimes inclined to forget the need to be able give a faultless performance of some simple piece. Nor should the student take offence at this, since simple does not necessarily mean easy, just as complex does not necessarily mean difficult.

Inability to perform a simple episode often emerges when some virtuoso with a superficially impressive technique comes to some lyrical theme and is forced to resort to arbitrary devices such as excessive *rubato* or arpeggiating in order to conceal the flaws in his artistry.

So often, too, we pianists are unfair to orchestral musicians who only have to play one line of music, and we imagine it is easy for them to do this. One would like to suggest that the pianist step in for the orchestral player and perform, say, the clarinet solo in Tchaikovsky's *Francesca da Rimini*. Surely this is quite a simple melody? So let us suppose that the clarinettist is sick, and there is only a pianist to replace him... It will probably transpire that the pianist is unable to give a very good performance of the orchestral solo part – not just because the piano lacks the tonal qualities of the clarinet, but simply because the pianist cannot play the melody on the piano with sufficient precision and perfection. A good clarinettist is a great artist, and he knows many secrets about playing a melody which any pianist would do well to adopt. Many pianists display the same unfair and sceptical attitude when talking about the musicianship of singers. Yet assuredly, even an ordinary singer knows things about the art of lyricism and performance of a simple melody that are unfamiliar to a pianist who plays much more complex works.

FAST AND SLOW PRACTICE

Yet another question concerns the relative merits of practising slowly or at a fast tempo. I set great store on the value of slow practice in exercises. However, one should never linger too long over playing things through slowly. My suggested method of devising short exercises for overcoming difficulties simplifies the question of tempo. Automatically, after playing a short exercise slowly several times you will try and play it up to speed, and by varying the pace you can discover for yourself the correct movement and most efficient placing of the hand, elbow, and body position.

Slow playing enables one to check thoroughly every detail of finger and hand movement. If after playing a passage rapidly, however, a pianist is still unable to play it through slowly, this means the passage has not yet been learned sufficiently. I believe it is useful to play through a work slowly from time to time, checking on accuracy and beauty of sound, without artificially forcing the tone, and maintaining complete freedom and smoothness of movement. In doing so, one should never for a moment relinquish complete artistic control over what one plays, and one should never turn this slow play-through into a purely mechanical process.

I do not agree, however, with the view that one necessarily loses accurate visual control of hand movements when playing at rapid speed. Every tempo creates its own specific optical image, and like an experienced juggler the pianist gets used to controlling his precision of movement at a tempo dictated by artistic considerations.

We can more readily achieve a beautiful sound when playing slowly. Yet many advocates of persistent slow practice surprise me by their obvious refusal to concern themselves with artistic tone production during these hours of slow practising.

In Vitsinsky's article on 'Psychological Analysis of a Pianist's Work', among a variety of expert opinions I read a statement by one of our pianists (who shall remain nameless) to the effect that technical work on a piece consists mainly of honest and steady 'hammering out' of the notes.[7] This pianist, a great master and splendid virtuoso, was also asked whether in such practice the aesthetic aspect of the music was left to one side. To this he replied, 'Yes, deliberately and consciously.' The pianist in question thus believes that in studying a piece, one's playing should be slow and firm, and one should concentrate only on seeing that each finger falls on the 'centre of the key'. (It is unclear to me exactly what point on the key he is referring to, since the geometrical centre of the white keys is located somewhere between the black keys, which is a most awkward place for the keystroke to fall.)

Pronouncements of the sort quoted above lead me to reflect sadly on the despotic power of habit. The pianist in question gets accustomed to a particular method and practice routine, and by this he achieves significant results. Yet he is unable to realize that he achieves the heights of mastery not thanks to, but probably despite, his many hours of persistent 'hammering'.

And yet the negative results of such a method may show through in certain artistic shortcomings – in an uncertain memory, dryness of tone, and in incomplete freedom of physical movement. This form of 'technical slag' may be almost unnoticeable if overshadowed by a performer's great virtuoso talents. But for someone with lesser gifts it may prove disastrous.

It is extremely rare for a great artist to achieve perfect mastery by a direct and unswerving route, and without occasional and sometimes dangerous wanderings from the way. Studying the biography of some great virtuosi, we frequently observe that the heroic efforts they made in their youth are comparable only to the feats of Hercules, or even the labours of Sisyphus. There is certainly good reason for us to be impressed at the persistence of these future great artists. Nonetheless, it would be wrong to follow exactly in their tracks at every stage. Again, it is worthwhile noting that in the nineteenth century piano teaching methods were less well worked out than they are today. In those days there were many misconceived, and even quite harmful views in circulation. This explains why the average level of pianistic achievement was then much lower than it is now. Even highly gifted musicians had to find their way through a forest of perilous misconceptions, like the legendary hero forging his way past a row of monsters guarding the entrance to some forbidden land. And some of them, like Robert Schumann, ruined their technique and failed to slay one of those dragons, which in Schumann's case bore the dreaded name of 'hand extension'!

We should also not forget that only Hercules was capable of Herculean efforts. And even if one outstanding hero can steel himself and overcome great perils, it hardly makes good pedagogic sense to put everyone through such trials. The average talent may be overtaxed and defeated, wasting its strength on 'exercises' that a performer of genius might well survive without apparent harm. Modern teaching is absolutely correct in rejecting such methods.

Returning to the role of habit, I should issue a reminder that habitual methods of practice seem to us much easier. And habit helps a pianist devote himself to several hours of practice each day. This is the advantage and positive aspect of habit. On the other hand, each one of us should from time to time return and critically reassess all of our artistic habits. We should take a fresh and unbiased view of our entire practising routine in order to avoid it becoming infected by habits that could actually handicap our progress. This sort of self-analysis, however, is something a young pianist is rarely capable of.

Even experienced players quite often tend to divide their work on a piece into two parts: the basic work when they study and practise and forbid themselves any creative inspiration or artistic emotion, and then a second stage when they allow themselves to play artistically. In this sequence the first stage lasts far longer than the second. I would not wish to condemn this method of practising out of hand. Perhaps indeed it may bring some benefits. I myself, though, have never resorted to it for a long time since I find it highly unproductive.

Performers accustomed to devoting long hours to slow and persistent plodding through every piece should, I think, realize that essentially they are trying to learn a quite different piece from the one they expect to perform on the platform. An *allegro* movement constantly played slowly and without passion acquires new and alien characteristics, quite different from the piece that the pianist is hoping to learn. Played at slow tempo, the form of a rapid movement is perceived differently and in a more fragmentary way. The work cannot breathe freely and easily, and the longer lines of its form are not perceived. Moreover, when every single note is pounded out slowly and loudly, it is hard to ensure that the motions of hand and fingers reproduce exactly the efficient and economical movement required when playing at speed. Consequently, habits picked up while playing through slowly may become useless ballast when playing *a tempo*.

At the same time, I cannot quite understand why precisely those pianists that pay so much attention to repeated practising at slow tempo often avoid playing slow pieces. Could the explanation be because of the habit of learning pieces at a different tempo from the one at which they will be performed on stage? Furthermore, maybe a pianist too accustomed to harsh, dry practice methods is repelled at the need to persistently cultivate playing with a beautiful singing tone at slow tempo.

In this way habit may prevail over free artistic initiative. It is hard to overcome habit by logical argument. In fact, one habit can only be conquered by acquiring another new one. Having recognized one habitual practice method as incorrect, the pianist must gradually absorb a series of new procedures that have to be learned by dint of insistent, repeated effort. And he has to wait patiently until these become second nature.

ORGANIZING PRACTICE

I want briefly to touch on three further questions that are all interrelated: how to distribute one's practice time, how long to practise, and, finally, what to do in the run-up period before a concert.

There is no doubt that practice has to be systematic. It is important to play every day, and it is best to begin in a morning when the mind is fresh. One should train oneself once and for all to work at the piano in concentrated fashion, with all one's creative attention, but without unnecessary tension. Special attention should be paid to the latter point.

Sometimes it appears to a conscientious student that if practising comes easily and is a pleasure, such practice is less effective – a too fastidious conscience, supposedly, requires great effort and works best under stress. This is a mistake that should be countered. If a pianist practises with deep and complete concentration and senses no tension or fatigue, these hours of practice are the most useful ones.

The student should always remember that one hour of concentrated work is more fruitful than two hours of careless or mechanical practice. Particular hours should be set aside for practising. But even more important is to train oneself during these hours to work with concentration and active attention. Technical difficulties should be overcome not by playing an excessive amount of exercises but by creative use of exactly the right exercises.

It is essential to train oneself, also, to like one's work and enjoy one's hours of practice at the piano. It is hard to set an optimum number of hours for daily practice. But it is best to avoid over-exhaustion, either emotional or physical.

On the other hand, if for some reason you only have the chance to play two or three hours a day, do not forget that you can double the benefit of this by gathering all your creative resources and attention for this period.

Apart from consistent practice, it is also important to arrange and divide one's practice time. The time factor is important in mastering technical difficulties. Many players have noticed that one can persistently practise a difficult piece for a month without mastering it. Then, if one works on some other pieces and returns to the 'stumbling block' after a few weeks, one finds that all the difficulties can be ironed out without any special effort.

Many things in a performance become automatic of their own accord. One needs only to provide sufficient time for the intuitive assimilation of a piece. With two months to go before an examination, a student sometimes starts work only five days before the deadline. He may then practise for twelve hours a day, yet it would still have been better to spread these five days of work over the preceding two months.

Regular practice also affects the breadth of one's repertoire. Every pianist should strive hard to extend the repertoire that he plays. To do this, one constantly needs not only to learn new pieces but also to retain a memory of pieces already learnt. In revising these pieces, one should never play them through hastily and 'any old how' simply in order to restore one's memory of them. If you play carelessly through a work that you have not played for some time, you may easily have a disappointing sense of regression. You might believe that now, at the second attempt, everything should fall into place of its own accord. You therefore skim over those passages that go wrong so as to get a complete grasp of what is already a familiar work. You play the piece through in this way several times by heart, but alas, the end result is often a 'gabbled' performance, with wrong notes and stumbling over difficult passages. And after a few days of this sort of practice you might even persuade yourself that the piece now sounds worse than it did a year ago!

In returning to old repertoire, it is essential to force oneself to go, however briefly, through those stages by which the piece was first learned and assimilated. The best way is to play it through carefully several times with the music and then move on to polish the difficult passages, using the same short exercises that you used before. After this, the work will probably return to the forefront of your memory. You will also feel you can now play it easily, that the time spent on organized practice has worked to your advantage, and that your interpretation of it is deeper and more perfect than before.

It is important to train yourself to use the above method and to return from time to time to works learned earlier. Every pianist should feel that he has several variegated programmes within his grasp. The question of how to refresh a memory of earlier pieces is thus bound up with that of learning each new piece.

Having a broad repertoire has more than purely practical importance. In working on many different pieces, the performer grows as a musician. In extending his programmes, the pianist broadens his artistic horizons. But in all this the most important thing is the growth and development of one's mastery.

In piano playing everything is interconnected and interdependent. Each new composer sets a series of particular tasks for the performer and forces him to overcome particular difficulties. Technical mastery grows along with the variety of methods, exercise devices and musical styles that one takes on board. A line extends from Beethoven to Schumann, and via Tchaikovsky, to Rakhmaninov; similarly from Haydn to Prokofiev; and a mastery of the world of Bach's polyphony can assist in the interpretation of contemporary works.

The broader the pianist's repertoire, the more easily he can learn new pieces. The memory of an artist is not to be compared with some vessel of limited capacity which, once filled to the brim, cannot easily accommodate new items. On the contrary, the more works a performer can retain in his memory, the more easily he will memorize new ones. And in answer to the question as to how to memorize a new work as rapidly and firmly as possible, one general principle is the following: among various possible methods, one of the most fundamental is to maintain a constant concern for the breadth of one's repertoire.

BEFORE THE CONCERT

I have not managed to touch even briefly on many aspects of the art of the piano. I have hardly spoken at all about fingering, and have said nothing about use of the pedal. By way of conclusion, however, I would like to say something about how to comport oneself before a concert. This is a question of vital importance. I have noticed that many students, including my own, make a great mistake in starting to prepare in earnest for a concert only a few days beforehand.

Karl Avgustovich Kipp, a splendid teacher who at one time worked at the Moscow Conservatoire, maintained that it was necessary to ease up slightly on practising just before a concert. At such moments the entire complex of acquired technique and the results of one's struggle to surmount difficulties should be allowed to settle and become firmly assimilated. And one should never be learning difficult passages just two days before a concert appearance.

It is true, in some cases it is necessary to be able to learn and master a new work in the shortest possible time, and I would be the first to welcome an ability to quickly find your way around a new piece and learn it inside a few days. But why, when a student knows he has an important performance coming up, can he not begin preparing at least a month or two in advance? Why does he have to wait until the very last week? This concerns not only conservatoire students, but also many other young pianists. They evidently fail to realize the importance of having time to completely learn and master a programme. I think that Karl Kipp was absolutely right: the basic material should be fully prepared in advance, and then just before the performance one needs only to reinforce what has been learned already. This is the only way to guarantee complete confidence on the platform.

So, in answer to the question how to conduct oneself before a concert, my considered answer would be: One should conduct oneself well! That means not getting wound up, overtired, or distracted, and not over-practising.

In the artists' room before a concert should one play through various passages and episodes from the programme? Certainly, most pianists indulge in this, although I am convinced by experience that one should refrain from the habit. I once had the following experience. At the end of Prokofiev's Third Concerto there is a tricky passage where one has to play at speed between the black keys. I had been having problems with this passage and had devised some minor changes that made it slightly easier. Somewhere I have even noted down my version of this passage. But once, when I was due to play the Concerto in Kharkov, just before the performance the pianist Alexander Kamensky called in at my dressing room and asked me how I played that particular passage. 'Well, I don't play it exactly as written,' I admitted. 'Oh, how do you play it then?' he asked. I went to the piano in the dressing room to show him the version I had thought up, and found I simply could not remember it. I tried, and I racked my memory, but to no avail. Then, at that moment, I was told that it was time for me to go on stage.

Of course, I walked out onto the platform feeling irritated and unconfident. But I was saved when I got to the end of the third movement, because I suddenly remembered the version I had thought up and I played it successfully.

If a performer has cold hands or if he is used to warming up just before a concert, then it is best to play through pieces other than those in the programme, or limit oneself to encore pieces. When warming up in the artist's room before a concert you should try to play as well and as carefully as possible, so as to muster your complete technical apparatus and have it functioning and ready.

As a rule, the pianos standing in dressing rooms are third-rate instruments. Precisely because of this, it is important to avoid playing through any difficult passages from your programme before going out on stage. On a piano with imperfect mechanism they may not work out, and the slightest setback just before a performance may rob the artist of his confidence and inspiration. Hasty practice just before a concert is of no help to the pianist. He must rely on his artistic intellect and the knowledge that he has thoroughly learned the programme, and he should go out and play with fresh energy, clear imagination, and a confident memory.

Pianistic artistry over the past 250 years has undergone a colossal evolution. This growth has gone hand in hand with a general expansion, perfection and emotional enrichment of the whole of music, both in composition and performance. An excellent illustration of this has been the change in function of the piano étude as a genre. In the early classical era, the étude was important chiefly as material for technical training of students. Since Chopin, however, it has acquired independent validity as an artistic genre and stands alongside other accepted musical forms. And since Chopin's time this line of development has continued in the remarkable études of Debussy and Scriabin, and in the *Études-Tableaux* by Rakhmaninov. I believe that every pianist who organically develops his gifts passes through a similar pattern of evolution. As he develops, the material that served in school during the first stages of his training is gradually replaced by exercise and study in which his emotional strength and artistic attention never falter. It is in this light that we should view the development of every pianist as he follows the path to pianistic perfection.

NOTES

1 Alexander Sergeyevich Pushkin (1799-1837), one of Russia's greatest poets and foremost representative of the Golden Age of Russian literature. Mozart

and *Salieri* is one of four 'Little Tragedies' composed in 1830. Pushkin's po-
etry has been set to music by several composers; operatic settings such as
Tchaikovsky's *Eugene Onegin* and *The Queen of Spades*, and Mussorgsky's *Boris
Godunov*, are based on works by Pushkin.

2 See the recollections of Vera Skalon in *Vospominaniya o Rakhmaninove*, Moscow 1988, vol.II, 435-7. Pavel Yulyevich Shletzer (Schloezer) (1840?-98), Russian pianist, pupil of Kullak and Liszt, professor at Moscow Conservatoire
1891-98; some of his piano studies still enjoy some popularity.

3 Charles Louis Hanon (1819-1900), French pianist, organist and composer,
author of various instructional manuals that enjoyed wide currency in the
nineteenth and earlier twentieth century.

4 Friedrich Adolf Steinhausen (1859-1910), German pianist and doctor, author of various works (now superseded) on instrumental technique based on
an anatomical, or physiological, approach.

5 A. Alekseyev, ed., *Mastera sovetskoi pianisticheskoi shkoly* |(Moscow, 1967).

6 Vissarion Grigoryevich Belinsky (1811-48), prominent Russian literary
critic; Mikhail Yuryevich Lermontov (1814-41), a leading Russian Romantic
poet.

7 A.V. Vitsinsky, 'Psikhologicheskii analiz protsessa raboty pianista-ispoln-
itelya nad muzykal´nym proizvedeniem' in *Izvestiya Akademii pedagogicheskikh
nauk*, 1950, No 25.

ALEXANDER GOLDENWEISER

Advice from a Pianist and Teacher

Although one of the greatest teachers of his age, unlike his colleagues at the Moscow Conservatoire such as Heinrich Neuhaus and Samuil Feinberg, Alexander Goldenweiser published no major monograph of method that summarized his views on teaching and performance. His philosophy was set out very completely, however, in many lectures, archive notes, lessons and masterclasses. Many of the latter were recorded in memoirs and shorthand notes by pupils and other listeners, including his wife Anna Goldenweiser. The following 'Advice' is a systematic compilation of his ideas drawn from various sources, written and spoken, edited by musicologist Dmitrii Blagoi.

'A work can be played many times, but each time is a different time.'

GOLDENWEISER

ARTISTIC APPROACHES TO MUSICAL STYLE

In Russian fairytales one sometimes encounters the figure of a knight of old setting out to perform various heroic feats. On his way, he meets his old enemy, engages him in battle, but falls defeated and is hacked into little pieces. Then, along comes his protector, a kindly magician who first of all sends off a raven to bring him the 'water of death'. The magician sprinkles this on the hero, and all his pieces are suddenly joined together again. Then the magician sends the raven off again, this time to bring the so-called 'water of life'. He then sprinkles this on the knight who is miraculously restored to life. In the field of music, unfortunately, one finds many performers who rest contented after only the first stage of this operation... But any truly artistic performance first and foremost requires an interesting and engaging content. Naturally, this does not at all mean one has to think up some interesting 'programme' for the pieces one performs – such inventiveness is often in fact quite harmful, and it may even distract the performer from the music itself, which has its own content and speaks directly in its own language.

One of the most important and complex problems in teaching the art of performance is to educate a sense of style in one's pupils. It is very hard to define exactly what we understand by artistic style, but this does not at all mean that the actual concept of style is superfluous, or that it involves some purely fictitious quality. It is also wrong to think that musical style is contained not so much in the work itself as in its actual performance – anyone who plays music by a good composer with his own original style must realize this.[1] At the same time it is essential that the performer, too, should have his or her own style. Again, this is often difficult to define in words, but the main criterion of judgment lies in the degree of correspondence (or, conversely, the contradiction) between the performance and the style of the actual composition.

I should add that 'stylish' performance should not at all be confused with 'fossilized' performance. A good performer should not need to live another ten years, or become an old man in order to play a composition differently. Even after the elapse of ten years one might play very similarly to how one played before – or else very differently just ten minutes later! There, on the actual concert platform, a genuine artist might well discover an artistic intuition that completely overturns his original concept of a work. The main thing here is to play in such a way as to appear convincing – one might even play in a paradoxical way, yet one should still perform convincingly.

APPROACHING THE COMPOSER'S TEXT

People often speak and write about the supposedly approximate nature of musical notation. But even if printed notes are only a rough and ready indication of the composer's intentions, they should certainly not be altered except in case of extreme necessity.[2] There are of course certain compositions that are written 'sketchily' and require further working out (e.g. figured basses, some of Bach's unrealized textures, Handel's violin sonatas, some episodes in Mozart's piano concertos, cadenzas, et cetera). However, this does not at all entitle one to change other works that have been fully written out.

It is also a mistake to refer to performance as a form of 'improvisation' (as Busoni did, for instance). Even if musical notation is only an approximation to the composer's ideas, any improvisation by the performer, whatever its freshness, is obviously the most imperfect of such approximations.

In modern science people often speak of infinitesimally small quantities, which, despite bring infinitely small, have a decisive effect on entire worlds. In art too we can observe something similar: all sorts of minutiae can acquire immense significance, and it is extremely important to perceive these in any musical text and to realize them in performance. True, an ability to read what is there in the text does not come immediately. One sometimes finds things that are not clearly spelt out in a musical text, and one has to weigh up how to perform such episodes. But if you look carefully, you can often find else-where something that clarifies the confusion. And in general it is extremely important to comprehend and make sense of one's approach to everything on the printed page. Suppose there is an arpeggiated chord in the left hand, while there is no such arpeggio in the right – here, evidently, the right hand should play its chord simultaneously with the top note of the left-hand ar-peggio. Conversely, if an arpeggiated chord appears only in the right hand, then it will be most natural to play its first note together with the left-hand part, since there must be a rising sequence of notes in the whole chord.

There is also the question of melismatics, or ornamentation. Even if the origin and abundance of such embellishments arose from a lack of sustain-ing power in old keyboard instruments, obviously this latter circumstance gave rise to a specific artistic idea 'from within' that is bound up organically with the spirit of the composition. Nobody nowadays would compose for our modern instrument in this way, but it is possible, and a matter of duty, to play older composers without distorting them.[3] Here, again, it is wrong to believe there is nothing decisive or precise in old ornamentation. And it is even more mistaken to think that one can play whatever one decides, and even alter or omit the ornamentation.

One also comes across other instances of inaccuracy in performance. For instance, a common feature in many pianists, from music school students to mature performing artists, is that they play the written notes with great pre-cision but are appallingly inaccurate in releasing the notes. They often also fail to heed the composer's dynamic markings. In fact, however, you should know the text in such a way that even if my own copy of the music had all the dynamic nuances removed, I should be able to restore them again by merely listening to your performance.

TONE

At one time there was much discussion and debate about whether a pianist can in any way influence the quality of piano tone that he produces. Things eventually reached such a state that at one musical conference placards were hung on the doors stating: 'It is forbidden to raise any question about the variability of pianoforte tone!'

Despite all this, those involved with the construction and tone qualities of the piano have concluded that it is in fact possible to alter the tone of the instrument – even in depressing a single note, not to mention whole chords in which it is possible to emphasize one note or another. And facts are obstinate things: we all realize perfectly well that one pianist has the power to make an instrument sound well, while another is unable to do so. The manner in which we produce piano tone is of decisive importance, and the seemingly 'dead' instrument in fact reacts to every slight movement of our hands, arms and bodies. For this reason the coordination between bodily movement and sensation and the sound that we strive to project is of such importance. This affects both the visual impression made on the listener and the physical sensations of the performer, as well as the actual sound produced by the instrument.

There are several great truths about the sound of music in performance that we ought to tape-record and constantly play over and over again to our piano students. Here are some of them:

When the right hand is playing a melody, the extreme top notes are highly important, and when the left hand plays an accompaniment, no less vital are the lower bass notes. In general, our manner of hearing and listening is such that we usually perceive the upper notes as most important. However, these notes are invariably played by the fifth or little finger, i.e. the weakest finger of all. One should thus particularly concern oneself with this finger in order properly to 'reveal' it in the playing of treble notes.

It is highly important that the endings of melodic phrases and passages should sound clearly, just as the start of all such phrases should be clearly audible.

It is essential to remember once and for all that all notes – even those of lesser importance – should be clearly heard. At the same time one must notice and be aware of all notes that have a particular significance. It also often happens that while hearing the actual notes played by the pianist's right or left hand, one does not hear the projected voice of these notes. (This is closely bound up with the idea of 'singing' on the piano, which is so characteristic of the Russian pianoforte school.) In playing a melody on the piano, the pianist must create the illusion of power and control over each single note, but this power consists not merely in producing the sound as violinists or singers do, but in properly hearing and sustaining it.

One often encounters a mistaken idea adopted by piano players – namely that louder playing involves more tension. In fact, however, the reverse is true. Muscular tension is more permissible in *pianissimo* playing, whereas in playing at *forte* level one should try to be free and relaxed.

It is also essential for teachers to remember the great difference between working on tone production with adults and with children. A child should first of all be taught to hear the sound, and one should talk with children in the most concrete terms possible. Thus, for instance, one can suggest to a mature adult student that he play the upper voice with 'different tone' in relation to the lower one (e.g. when two voices are combined in the right-hand part). But what can such an expression mean to a child? Children will understand if one says 'louder' or 'clearer', but will hardly grasp such expressions as 'brighter', 'deeper', or 'more buoyant' tone, and so on and so forth.

RHYTHM

Rhythm is also a form of basic foundation that plays an immense role in the art of music. Unfortunately, there are cases where even those with a good ear have no sense of rhythm, and it is especially hard to counteract this defect. Moreover, those who lack rhythm in playing the piano usually also lack it in the rest of their lives. Concerning the rhythmic distribution of sounds in time, there are a number of basic truths that constantly have to be reiterated in classes. They are as follows:

Hasty playing and rapid playing are two entirely different things. It is possible to play *presto* yet still play unhurriedly, and it is possible to rush even in *adagio* passages. [Goldenweiser warned especially often against rushing the climactic moments of a composition, and considered this a major artistic failing – ed.]

Rhythm is easier to hold and maintain in that hand which plays a lesser number of notes.

One should never rush the figuration in one hand if the other hand is at the same time sustaining a single note. I recall one instance when I played with a violinist who was a highly skilled and interesting artist, but who when holding a long sustained note always asked me to 'play a little faster' and took offence when I refused. [This is not to be confused with playing with a sense of movement and rhythmic impetus, which is presumably what the violinist really wanted - ed.]

One should always remember a wise piece of advice from Egon Petri – namely that one should play the end of a passage in such a way as if one intends to make a *ritenuto*, and then the passage will turn out exactly as intended.

One must first of all feel the flow and rhythmic movement of the music within oneself, and only when one senses this should one begin playing. Otherwise one is bound first of all to produce a sequence of disorderly sounds rather than a vital, rhythmic musical flow. And if, say, you have to 'jump aboard' after actually starting, you will always have to run alongside for a certain distance before you can pick up impetus and leap on board.

When there is a combination of, say, three triplets spread over four beats, there is absolutely no need to count up to twelve; rather one should simply count 'one-two-three' four times. This method always helps quickly and without fail. This point should be learned once and for all, and not in music where this has been encountered, but in the most simple elementary exercises.

While it is painful to listen to unrhythmic playing, it is also quite intolerable when someone plays entirely by the metronome. However, the musical text must first of all be set precisely on its 'rhythmic rails', and only then can one move on to play with a free and lively sense of rhythm. Otherwise disorder and anarchy are inevitable. It is necessary first of all to be aware of a scheme before departing from it. Where pianist beginners are concerned, one should avoid any talk of so-called 'free' rhythm; one must treat matters in such a way that the pupil himself unconsciously feels this and yields to the sensation of his own accord.

If there is a broadly arpeggiated chord, then a certain rhythmic inexactitude or delay is permissible and even necessary. At the same time, though, however free the execution, a triplet rhythm should never turn into a dotted rhythm. [Goldenweiser's warning on this account was usually aroused by the false pathos occasionally noted when some pupil played a theme of emotionally exalted character – ed.]

I recall how even Rakhmaninov, who had a rock firm sense of rhythm, admitted that when he was playing a concerto and there was a pause on a long held note, he always counted out this note to himself. True, there is the question of exactly how to count. There have been orchestral players, for instance, who counted out five beats like so: 'One, two, three, four and five...'

PHRASING

Declamatory mistakes in a musical performance affect me in the same way as wrong stress or pronunciation in speech – I feel as if I have been cuffed in the back of the neck. When performing myself, I have occasionally allowed some note or other to stick out unnaturally, and when this happens on the concert platform I feel ashamed in front of myself, as well as all those listening. One should not permit oneself such things even when practising at home.

Any melody has certain strong points towards which it aims and which provide its shape and character. One should imagine a smoothly flexing line in which there is a certain high point – or maybe a curve, or possibly a zigzag (although as a rule no performance should move in a zigzag line: otherwise some notes either jump out or get lost, or else the whole phrase will seem monotonous but with sudden unnecessary accents). Thus, for example, when two notes are followed by a pause and when the second note is the resolution of a dissonance, pianists very often play in such a way that the second note sticks out. However, if one lets one's hand sink into the first note and gently lift off the second note, the resolution will automatically emerge as more gentle than the dissonance.

Often a short note of some motif or phrase may lead into the phrase itself, or else form part of the preceding phrase. Harmonic considerations should solve any doubt: if a particular note resolves a dissonance or is harmonically related to the previous phrase, then it must form part of its conclusion; but if harmonically connected to the next motif, it is more natural to play this note as a lead-in to what follows.

It must also be remembered that the balance of phrases is not cancelled out by any dynamic nuances. No matter how a phrase is played - *forte*, *piano*, with or without accent – it must always make sense as a declamatory phrase group. If when playing *marcato* every single note is stressed, no line of phrasing can result. But a phrase should always remain a phrase. With accented notes one must always perceive their sense within the phrase. An accent may sometimes fall on the main note, sometimes on an auxiliary note, sometimes on an upbeat, and so forth. Often, too, a theme may consist of repetitions of a single rhythmic figure. In such cases one must particularly avoid mere mechanical repetition and ensure that all notes form a single line. [Goldenweiser made this observation particularly à propos of pupils performing Beethoven, e.g. the second movement of the Sonata opus 101, or in Schumann, e.g. the central movement of the C major *Fantasia*, opus 17 – ed.]

PEDALLING

Sometimes one gets a stain on one's fingers and cleans it off, only to find that it reappears again. The same can happen with pedalling: one changes the pedal and everything seems nice and clean, but suddenly a smudge appears, lingering from the previous chord. In such situations one should never remain 'sitting in the dirt': one should clean up the sound with very slight further movements of the pedal.

Experienced performers always lift the pedal slightly before a pause, since if one raises it when the actual pause begins, the previous note or notes may continue sounding faintly. Some players, on the contrary, have another nasty habit: when a phrase or motif comes to an end, they depress the pedal on the final note and instead of a breath, or slight caesura, a cloudy or even downright muddy sound is left lingering. The ends of phrases also must always be clean, except of course in cases when the phrase ends on a long note or chord that has to sound on at full strength.

In using so-called 'delayed pedalling', some players are often late in depressing the pedal and manage to pick up only the second or third notes of the bar. Here again a muddy sound will result. As a rule, a new and full pedal should be used on the appearance of a new bass note (i.e. with new harmony) and this usually coincides with a strong beat.

When working with beginners, it is best to begin by teaching them to use 'short pedal', i.e. depressing the pedal at the same instant when the note is played. Only later should one move on to use 'delayed pedal'. The essential point, however, is that from the very outset pedalling should be regulated by hearing and should not merely follow some metrical scheme or other.

PHYSICAL MOVEMENT WHILE PLAYING

I do not think anyone would ever suggest that the process of physical movement should actually impede a pianist's artistic intentions or the sound images he tries to project. But there is no doubt that bodily movements play a primary role in the realization of our artistic aims. Sometimes of course a pianist indulges in such manual 'fuss and bother' that almost nothing remains of the actual music. In fact, however, what I observe when I watch someone play should actually assist my aural appreciation and not interfere with it. If in the process of this hand and arm movements are reflected in the psychological state of the performer, then the converse is even more vital and essential.

One of the important principles in piano playing is that of economy of means and movement, although unfortunately we do not always find this even in some great artists. Teachers and theoreticians will often recommend literally hundreds of physical devices and tricks, but the wisdom and self-limitation imposed by public performance usually prevent these from cluttering our mind. In practice the same thing is true of so-called 'placing' of the hand. The very idea of hand 'positioning' is psychologically inhibiting and creates the false idea that there is some opposition between a 'piano hand' and a free and vital one. In fact the hand should demonstrate or 'depict' what it is about to play and what it has just played. In my view, despite his great artistry, Egon Petri was no poet of the pianoforte, and his idea of the 'prepared hand' even seems to indicate some sort of psychological constraint. Generally speaking, the motto of the performing pianist should be: 'Don't try and teach movements to the body, but learn them from the body.'

Here are some further observations and advice connected with the physical action of piano playing and with pianists' use of particular movements:

The custom of 'over-sustaining' notes in *legato* playing is a great mistake. There is a vast difference between holding notes down for their proper duration and over-sustaining them.

There are times when one should lift the hand off the keyboard in the same way as one jumps off a moving streetcar – in the direction of travel.

In octave playing the middle fingers should not be held out straight. This considerably coarsens the tone produced. Apart from which, a low wrist and hand position generally tends to produce hard and heavy tone.

The technique of bending the fingers under when playing *staccato* was regarded as essential and applied with consummate virtuosity by Nikolai Medtner. Hardly any pianists could compete with Medtner in the precise articulation of fast passage work.

To reject completely the idea of passing the thumb under in playing arpeggios is just as extreme a resort as refusing to allow 'sliding' of the thumb. In passing the thumb under, there should be a corresponding slight tilt of the hand in the direction of the thumb.

The alternation of fourth and fifth fingers in playing octaves involving the black keys assists economy of movement. It does not at all require a very large hand, and only exceptionally small hands find it uncomfortable.

Chromatic scales are one of the hardest forms of passage playing, and to achieve rapid execution the use of a maximum number of fingers is quite reasonable.

In practising *tremolando* passages, especially at *forte* level, one can often recommend first of all playing the complete chord(s) or interval(s) on which the *tremolando* occurs.

Feeling the keys first before depressing them is a practice more harmful than beneficial.

It is useful to practise double notes by breaking them, playing and sustaining first of all the upper note followed by the lower, and then also vice versa.

THE PURSUIT OF PERFECTION

I have observed that students often play harder passages better than easier ones. The reason is that once pupils notice some difficulty, they try hard to master it and frequently succeed, while deciding that simple passages need no special study, and they therefore play them quite badly. This is a frequent story. Also, if one hand part is especially important or difficult, they forget that the other hand also requires to be studied. In the Schubert-Liszt *Serenade*, for instance, it often appears as if the man serenading beneath the window of his beloved has not troubled to learn to play the guitar that he has brought along as accompaniment!

There are many examples of what at first sight seems to be quite simple musical statement, even in the mature and profound compositions of Chopin. But it is often precisely this sort of passage that presents immense difficulty. To achieve a musical background accompaniment that has its own vital independent line and yet at the same time fully reflects and supports the main melodic theme often seems to present an extremely complex and almost insoluble problem.

Another grave problem occurs with pupils underestimating the importance of detailed study when they come to revise pieces that they have already played. Yet it is vital to remember that work done on a new piece one is just starting to play and on something one has played for a long time should be basically the same. The difference lies only in the amount of time involved, but the type of work should in each case be completely identical. When you play through something you have performed earlier, everything at first may seem to fall into place. But once you begin probing, it turns out that some things are no longer clean, others are inaccurate, and yet others have been forgotten.

Often, too, performers playing a rapid piece believe that in order for it to turn out properly at the right tempo they must immediately strive to achieve this aim. But it rarely occurs to them that to play something very slowly is also extremely difficult, and this too requires a great deal of work.

When working on a piece it is dangerous to try and achieve everything at once. It is important to concentrate attention on various problems in turn. First of all one must have a sense of the basic shape of the work, construing the piano texture in simplified form. Thus if there is a melody with some figuration as accompaniment, it is worth playing it through first in a simpler harmonic version. Then, once one has a clear idea of the basic lines of the passage, one can usefully start work on secondary difficulties. Only then is it possible to try and realize the complete musical picture.

When learning a new work, one should first of all insert various 'punctuation marks'. Furthermore, if some phrase does not turn out when working on the piece, it is useful to isolate it, pause, and linger over it. Obviously, one must later ensure that this pause does not remain in place in actual performance.

Further, in any rapid episode or passage there are always certain significant strong points. And when practising in a calm, relaxed manner it is essential to pay attention and take care over these to ensure that they do not go awry when playing rapidly.

One is often asked how to study and learn passages with skips and leaps. The solution is to practise the passages with pauses and halts, but always with quick movements [i.e. isolate the rapid movement between notes from the actual act of depressing them – ed.]. In doing so one must develop a movement that is unrushed and rhythmic and involves a minimal sweep of the hand and arm. There must be nothing feverish or jerky.

I am no advocate of abstract exercises when working at the piano. However, long ago when working on chord passages, I wanted to develop an ability to stress one note requiring particular emphasis, and I invented the following exercise: Place the five fingers of each hand on five different keys, then raise one finger, followed by the next, and so on, and when only one finger is left, I have to feel the increased weight of hand and arm on this one finger. (This exercise can also be tried on the closed lid of the piano.)

When working, there is nothing more beneficial than abandoning the well-worn path of playing passages in a hasty manner. Indeed, when I hear pupils play rapid pieces in an uncontrolled and 'gabbled' manner, I feel like ordering a large placard to hang on the classroom wall, reading as follows: 'Rapid playing can develop from good playing. But good playing can never emerge from rapid playing!'

THE PROCESS OF PERFORMANCE

Pupils frequently complain of tiredness after a performance. Here it should be said that the exhausting effect of playing is bound up not just with the character of the actual work, but also with the performer's ability or otherwise to discover certain points of rest within a piece. The art of discovering such points of relaxation comes largely with platform experience. To some extent this is also connected with the sense of strength conveyed by a pianist's playing, and this depends more on an ability to distribute one's energies rather than on any absolute strength.

Incidentally, sometimes performers suffer not from an insufficiency, but from an excess of strength. (This always reminds me of the fairytale knight who took someone by the hand and the hand came away, and who when he placed his own hand on someone's shoulder, drove the man waist deep into the ground.) Pianists possessed of great virtuosity and physical strength would do well to think of how to curb and limit themselves. I remember once when visiting a blacksmith's forge I was shown a huge steam hammer that could flatten anything and everything; yet it could also crack a tiny nut with a thin shell in such a way that the kernel stayed whole. That is how one should learn to handle one's own strength.

It is also no less important to be able to control one's own temperament, since an excess of the latter can often adversely affect the technical side of a performance. Thus, for example, I believe that occasional wrong notes from such a great pianist as Artur Rubinstein are caused not through faults in his technical equipment, which is really first-class, but because of excessive impetuosity and what in my view is an insufficient sense of moderation in relation to his own movements. It is the presence of this sense of measure that is the main guarantee of clean playing.

Much worse than this, of course, is a show of indifference and absence of involvement in the music. It frequently happens that pupils play as if they are not fully 'there'... But when a pianist sits down at the instrument and starts to play, nobody should be left in any doubt that the performance has begun – otherwise it is not always clear whether he has really begun playing or merely struck a note inadvertently! Similar impressions may occur at the end of a performance. I remember Taneyev once said of some composition that it merely 'came to a halt' rather than 'reaching a conclusion'. Performances also can end in this way.

The hardest thing in the world is to play simply and naturally. Only if a performer displays clear artistic intentions, and if the music sounds within him, can he use all his technical resources and, so far as possible, overcome the instrument's own imperfections. And the main thing is to carry one's audience with one without resorting to tricks and mannerisms.

SOME MISTAKES IN THEORIZING

Sometimes excessive claims are made about the number of people who have allegedly been 'crippled' as pianists owing to irrational teaching or methods of practice. The main trouble is that too many people have striven not merely to play the piano (something accessible to almost anyone) but actually to become pianists (something to which very few are called). Because of this there have been many disappointments and ruined lives. But true catastrophes befalling genuinely gifted pianists are not so very frequent (one recalls the cases of Schumann or Scriabin). But the large numbers of ordinary, uninspired folk who play the piano are not at all the victims of unscientific teaching or practice methods, but simply normal cases resulting from the irrational use of energy.

Mountains of books have been written on how to play the piano, and in many of them the authors have merely thought up one particular device and tried to present this as the basis of some all-embracing method. For instance, Steinhausen bases himself on the claim that mere rotation of the forearm will cause everything to fall into place, while our fingers, the most sensitive and vital parts of our body, he regards as nothing more than the spokes of a wheel! Similar such books usually tell us not so much how as how *not* to play the piano!

Some knowledge of neurological processes or the physiology of movement is of course useful to any educated person. But what does the pianist as such gain by it? I believe that to know the practical reason that causes students to bolt or gabble passages of music is far more important than any anatomical or physiological descriptions. It is precisely because of unreasonable theorizing that an inexperienced performer often un-learns how to play the piano after reading such specialized textbooks.

To state that piano playing is carried out via a series of motive processes without which it is inconceivable is the same as saying that, because thought is accompanied by a series of processes going on in the brain, Immanuel Kant first needed to study the structure of the brain in order to write his *Critique of Pure Reason*.

In any case, why imagine that all we need do is talk about muscles, nerves and other technicalities of piano playing, when all this is secondary and can be applied if only we have the will to engage in the most important endeavour? Apart from which, in my view to talk about the separate elements of physical movement is a great heresy. Any vital motion is totally different from the sum of its supposed components – this is no better than trying to gauge the flow of time by the ticking of one's watch. Any precise laboratory study of the living process of movement is hardly possible, especially where art is concerned. Even a cine-film cannot provide an unbroken record of continuous motion and cannot help us. And in general, any record of the hundreds of minute shifts taking place each second is useless, since we are dealing not with the mere quantity of such movements (remember Achilles and the tortoise!).

But if the opportunities for precise observation and analysis of another person's movements while playing are limited, to be aware of and observe one's own movements is obviously not only possible, but should be actually encouraged. But it is worst of all when a student unconsciously follows a teacher's instructions without thinking for himself. Such 'imitation' is preached only by people whom one should never on any account imitate... The pupil should definitely think things through for himself, yet the main question is where the centre of gravity lies in these various reflections!

Finally, as for regretting that the process of artistic performance on the piano still remains unsolved to the end, I totally fail to understand such regrets. Otherwise that would spell the very death of art.

NOTES

1 These remarks by Goldenweiser are part of a polemic with musicologist Grigorii Prokofiev, who claimed in his book *Igra na fortepiano* [Playing the Piano] (Moscow, 1928) that 'Style is a myth. Style ... comes alive in performance by an artist, and only there.'

2 Here again Goldenweiser is arguing with Grigorii Prokofiev who in *Igra na fortepiano* also maintained that one should accept the idea that musical notation is only a 'highly approximate' expression of the composer's intentions.

3 Goldenweiser is here disputing an opinion that the profusion of ornaments in old music is not altogether a function of the 'aesthetic taste' of former ages, but that the ornamentation appeared in keyboard compositions because of the brevity of the sound produced by old instruments.

LEV OBORIN

Some Principles of Pianoforte Technique

The principles of piano technique in general are a most important concern of mine. Here, though, I want to concentrate first and foremost on one fairly narrow aspect, but perhaps the most vital one, that of finger technique.

It is slightly arbitrary, of course, to talk about finger technique on its own. After all, the fingers cannot be isolated from the rest of the hand, wrist, arm and shoulder. That is to say, they form part of the overall human physique, all of which should be actively and usefully involved in the pursuit of our artistic aims.

Questions of technique have attracted the attention of performing musicians of every age and calibre, and there are many different schools of thought and various published 'methods', all designed to expound and solve the problems of instrumental technique. I personally am not an adherent of any one of these systems. It strikes me that musical performance involves such multifarious problems and possibilities that there is no way of forcing it into the straightjacket of some 'school', which inevitably hems the player about with limitations and prohibitions. I thus make no claim here to be expounding some elegant and complete system. I want simply to share some of my performer's experience and some observations that may be of use in working on finger technique on the piano.

I believe every player would do well to have about a score of rules to follow concerning 'good behaviour' at the keyboard. These rules would concern both the thought and the technical problems behind interpretation, tone production, pedalling, et cetera, and they should offer direction in the hard task of building up a piano technique. Nowadays it is regularly accepted that music and technique are inextricably bound together, and that technique divorced from artistry is as senseless as form without content. Moreover, technique is not just a matter of playing rapidly and accurately, but a compound of very diverse elements, some of which are amenable to conscious control, while others are intuitive or subconscious. Put briefly, however, technique amounts to an ability to present and realize one's artistic intentions in practice.

Unfortunately, there is nowadays a widespread opinion, especially among the young and inexperienced, that everything depends on technique. One hears phrases like: 'If only I can work up my technique, then everything will be all right musically.' Clearly this is a mistaken view. Any artistic idea or 'image' requires no less devoted effort than technique itself. Feeling and understanding can, and should, be educated as well – they have no right to be neglected or regarded as a mere piece of additional baggage. Furthermore, as long as we make a sharp distinction between technique and actual music, there will forever be a yawning gulf between our ambitions and their fulfilment. This disparity between artistic intention and execution is familiar to all performers, and all of us have a lifelong task to try and reduce or eliminate it.

I well remember the bitter experience of youth. When I was a conservatoire student, I pursued studies in three different faculties simultaneously – pianoforte, composition, and conducting. I was already a fairly accomplished musician and knew quite a lot for my age. But my piano technique lagged badly behind my other accomplishments. I was physically cramped and often had difficulty coping with the problems of virtuoso technique. I became convinced that I was doomed forever to play only lyrical miniatures and that the big virtuoso pieces would always be beyond me. Nor did my professor at the time, Konstantin Igumnov, try and shake this conviction of mine – partly because he tended at that time to pay attention more to the musicality of his students' performance than to technique.

But since I could envisage no profession for myself other than music, and especially the piano, I began to make my own way along the road of technical progress. I devised exercises for myself containing as many aspects of piano technique as possible, and every day I worked at them for between one and a half and two hours. These exercises involved scales and arpeggios, double notes, chords and octaves, as well as some exercises by Hanon, Tausig, Brahms, and Joseffy. Each day I played through all this at the start of my practice before working on any pieces. After two months of this training, I could move my fingers incredibly fast, although at the same time they still seemed to move in a very disorderly fashion. I had no idea how to correct this, especially since all my hard work had hardly any effect on the technical polish of the pieces I was studying. I then cut down the time spent on technical drills to half an hour, and used them mainly as warming up exercises. And as I worked, I tried to adopt the more 'direct' method of performing actual pieces while striving at the same time to achieve a condition of maximum psychological and physical freedom and comfort. The aim was to get the physical aspect of playing to function as a reliable support for my artistic endeavours, to assist rather than impede their development. After fairly hard work on this for about a year, I found that playing the instrument had become both comfortable and pleasurable, and I also felt much greater freedom. Studying sonatas by Chopin and Liszt and other large-scale works from the repertoire finally convinced me that there are, as it were, two principles at work in piano technique – the creative, or artistic, and the physiological. Put more precisely, there was the artistic presentation of a composition on the one hand, and the actual physical act of playing it on the other.

During the history of piano playing, views on the physical aspect of playing have altered radically. At one time, exclusive importance was attached to the placing of the hands and to mechanical exercises that were often at variance with the pianist's own true physical nature. Subsequently, various 'natural' theories evolved, but they to failed to produce any significant results in terms of actual piano playing. In more recent years people have adopted an extremely negative view of mere mechanical exercise, and rightly so, but this has led to regarding any insistence on hand positioning and any form of exercises as unnecessary and almost harmful.

I would therefore like to say a few words in defense of the 'physiological principle' of piano playing, which I would like to see rehabilitated. Certainly, those who regard technical systems as a universal panacea are badly mistaken. Even the most perfect schooling cannot teach someone to play well when this is based only on physiological laws. On the other hand, any professional must be sufficiently aware of himself and his physical abilities to realize that they can be a serious handicap if wrongly applied, no matter how brightly the fires of inspiration burn. Playing the piano is, after all, an act of touch, a tactile operation, and dependent therefore on efficiency of movement. This being the case, a pianist must try and instil some sort of order into his movements.

What then are the requirements for successful development of technique? The first essential is psychological and physical freedom, and associated with this a sense of maximum comfort and confidence in one's movements at the keyboard. Unfortunately, what sounds clear and simple is not at all so easy

in practice. The idea of comfort and freedom should not be interpreted absolutely literally of course. There is not – nor can there be – total freedom while
playing the piano: any movement is bound to involve tension in some muscle
or other. Complete freedom is only possible in the absence of all movement,
when everything is at rest. The sense of freedom I am talking about means
that only the essential muscles are involved in any work, and the whole of
piano playing is in fact based on the rapid successive tensing and relaxing
of muscles. Exactly which muscles and ligaments are involved is still not
entirely established despite various interesting scientific experiments. But I
think that this can only be of general interest rather than practical use to the
performer, since hardly anyone is capable of thinking about all his muscles
and controlling each one of them while playing. In the art of the piano, intuition plays an enormous role as well. Very often when playing, and especially
on the concert platform, a performer discovers the best technical approach
and the best sound only by intuitive means.

Does a pianist need to observe a particular hand and arm position? To what
extent would there be a definite set manner of placing one's hand on the
keyboard? I have often heard objections like: 'Isn't it all the same how I hold
my hand, so long as I get the effect I want?' And the answer is: No. I am
convinced that positioning is by no means a matter of completely random
choice.

Consider the string instruments – the violin, say – as another example. For
a violinist, correct hand and arm positioning are absolutely essential. Only a
particular (and initially highly unnatural) placing of the hand will in the long
run produce correct positioning on the fingerboard and accurate intonation.
And the piano, too, has its own specific requirements. It is of course easy to
play 'in tune', and the hand and arm positions required may not be quite so
rigorously standardized as on the violin. Nevertheless, only some sense of a
'standard' position, even though it may at first seem awkward, will produce
positive results, consistent and even tone, as well as an individuality of style.
Also, whereas the violinist carries out different tasks with his left and right
hands, both hands of the pianist have to perform every role, including articulation, in which it is vital to have some standardized hand position, as I shall
now try and demonstrate.

So what sort of hand position should a pianist have? And what type of hand
is reasonably a 'good' one for learning the piano? First of all, good piano
hands differ greatly in size, breadth, length of finger, and relative propor-

tions. Provided it is not cramped, every normally shaped hand has its own advantages, and it is often difficult to say what sort of hand is best for playing. Undoubtedly, the breadth of the hand is of importance. A broad hand serves as a sort of 'dome' to support the fingers and gives the player a general sense of broad control. Narrow hands of slender 'aristocratic' form are, as a rule, less suited to successful playing.

Before talking about the position of the hand on the keys, first a few words about arm movements and posture at the piano. One should sit calmly and comfortably. One should somehow sense the feeling of one's own frame, and feel the spine as a foundation that should be straight yet flexible. It is in fact preferable to sit absolutely straight, although a slight forward inclination is permissible. The shoulders should be loose and low. Both feet should rest on the pedals in an absolutely natural position.

Arm movements I would envisage as follows: Since both arms are attached at one point to the shoulders, their extremities when moved will describe part of a circle. Similarly the fingers are attached to the hand and therefore also move along a circular arc. It follows from this that any natural motion of arms and fingers will usually be a movement away from the piano and towards the player, rather than a forward 'thrusting' that one occasionally observes in some players. Hammering the notes forwards, 'into' the piano, might occasionally be used for obtaining certain tone colours, but it should never be a basic normal movement when playing. Employed in this way, the hand moves towards the keys and strikes against them as against some sort of obstacle; and the fingers naturally behave accordingly.

The most natural finger position in the right hand is generally the position required for playing this chord

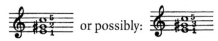

The choice of position will depend on the structure of the individual hand. Those with a large span between the thumb and index finger will find the first variant more comfortable.

The hand will feel most natural when the thumb and fifth finger are on white keys, while the second, third and fourth rest on the black keys:

This position, which Chopin used to recommend, is the most practical one for developing a natural hand position. Once it is mastered, one can move on to practise less comfortable positions, with fingers 1 and 5 on black keys, and 2, 3 and 4 on white, or else all five fingers on white keys, et cetera.

The hand's position on the keys can vary according to its individual features, but in principle it should be as follows. The fingers should be slightly bent and lie with their cushions (not the nails) on the keys and be supported on all three joints. The hand should remain on a level with the forearm, and should in turn be supported flexibly on the joint of the wrist. The forearm and upper arm should function as compliant intermediaries, and in order to give maximum assistance to finger and hand movements, they need as much freedom as possible. The elbows should not be pressed in against one's sides but should be held in a low 'suspended' position, and the weight on the fingers should, as it were, 'flow down' from the shoulder to the finger-tips without getting stuck en route at the elbow.

I believe it is essential to use the whole arm, hand and finger when playing. The unusual exertion or difficulty this may initially entail will be justified in the long run by the results. An ability to play with the whole finger enables one to achieve maximum strength, evenness and precision of touch, while the involvement of the whole arm helps one to play passages with a heavier and more complex texture. The movement can thus be likened to a lever mechanism, and the lever in this case is the pianist's arm. The only difference is that one's muscles are divided into extensors and flexors, which have on the one hand to be free while remaining coordinated with one another. But freedom and coordination must be sharply distinguished from slackness and disorganization. Sound is obtained from the piano in various ways, by various movements, depending on the character of the music, but basically it should be created by using the entire arm, properly coordinated. (To strike the key with the finger on its own is bad; striking from the wrist is even worse; from the forearm is better; but the firmest finger position is one where the action and weight of the whole arm support it.)

Apart from accuracy and firmness, this method also has the advantage of evenly distributing the weight onto all the fingers. Our fingers, as we know, differ not only in size but also in strength, and each finger has its own character. On the one hand we should try to preserve this character, striving for maximum independence of the fingers and working to develop equal strength in each of them. Yet to obtain equal strength in all the fingers on their own is virtually impossible, and it is here that the weight of the whole arm comes to our aid, 'flowing down', as it were, from the shoulder to the fingers and creating an equal load on each of them.

How should the fingers move when playing? Should they be raised, and if so, to what extent? Any public performer knows that when on the platform there is no time to think about actual finger movement. A pianist absorbed in his playing hardly controls (nor should he try to control) his movements, and he carries them out largely intuitively. From my own experience of playing in public I would sum things up as follows: there is no harm in raising the arm and fingers as high as you like while playing, so long as this serves a purpose and is artistically justified. While practising, however, the pianist must have a clear view of the coordination and movement of his fingers. I am not an advocate of either lifting the fingers too high or playing with fingers that constantly lie upon the keys and are never raised. In the first instance, the fingers tend to make too broad a sweep as they play, and raising them too high thus creates extra tension. In the second instance, freedom of movement, phrasing (i.e. clear 'diction'), and tonal quality are all bound to suffer. I personally prefer the golden mean: the fingers must have some free play or 'breathing space' in which to move, but they should never be raised above the general level of the hand. Finger action should amount to depressing the finger and then letting it rise to its starting position, rather than deliberately lowering then raising it (in this case there is again excessive swing and unnecessary movement of the finger).

The hand should thus be lowered freely and flexibly onto the keyboard, and the finger, slightly curved, moves down and rests with its cushion on the key. In doing so the finger should, so far as possible, be opposite the key it is playing and be parallel with it. The other fingers at this moment should be in an attitude of rest and should lie as close as possible to one another. They should not project sideways. Keeping the hand compact both assists relaxation and helps concentrate energy in the finger that is playing.

As the next finger descends onto the key, the supporting weight is transferred to it from the previous finger, and the latter is actively removed from its key when once the next finger has produced its sound. In effect a double process is going on here: one finger is depressing a key at the same moment as another is returning to its original position. And the fingers should not be passive elements, but active and rapid in their movements. If the fingers 'dawdle', the player can never move quickly from one key to the next and he will never learn to play rapid passages well.

Once when I was a conservatoire student, I had to play in front of Egon Petri. He was not only a brilliant virtuoso, but also a musician with enormous professional expertise. He had an exceptionally clear idea of what each finger should be doing as it played. After I had played to him, Petri's observation was: 'You sometimes depress and release the keys very slowly. When you play *forte*, your finger movements are all quite normal, but when playing *piano* you are delaying the movement and smearing the sound as a result. When playing softly surely your fingers should be just as active as in *forte*?'

There was probably some truth in Petri's words. Later on I was able to convince myself that only rapid depression and raising of the fingers leads to clear and precise playing. But in achieving speed and accuracy perhaps the most important thing is an ability to think, see, and hear clearly at high speed. All of us at various times have looked out of the window of a moving train as it gathers speed. While travelling slowly you can still see each individual rail-tie, or sleeper, and every pebble on the rail track, but once you start moving faster all these things merge together in a blur. Yet I think if one trained oneself and got used to one's speed of motion, one could maybe still make out the sleepers, stones and pebbles even at high speed. In the same way, when playing exercises and other passages one should be able to register individual notes with precision and clarity even when they are played rapidly. I have more than once ascertained that pianists who are technically fluent are able to register and control every note they play with great accuracy. To them any passage they play is not like the way things appear to the inexperienced eye when travelling on a speeding train. They see and hear everything with unerring accuracy and clarity.

There are many different ways of tone production on the pianoforte. They depend partly on the character of the individual performer and on his approach to the style of this or that composer. It is impossible here to list and describe all the various means of tone production. Briefly, though, I see tone production as something carried on between two governing limits, those of *staccato* and *legato*, and of *leggiero* and *tenuto*. And these opposites constantly vary and alternate, passing at varying speed from one into another. By *tenuto* I understand an actively supported tone production, by *leggiero* – the gentle free fall of the finger.

Differentiation of sound is the basis of piano tone colouration. Recall, for example, the start of Chopin's D flat Nocturne, opus 27, No 2. The right-hand melody is played *tenuto*, while the left-hand accompaniment is *leggiero*. The use and blending of *legato* and *staccato* requires no special explanation. It should be noted, however, that the main condition for *legato* is a smooth, unhurried depression of the finger and a similar slightly 'lazy' release of the previous finger. If the previous finger delays very long in leaving the key, then the *legato* becomes *legatissimo*. Conversely, the quicker a finger presses down the key, the less *legato* will be the tone, and it would then be described as '*non troppo legato*' or '*non legato*'. The speed with which the finger strikes the key is highly important. I believe it is essential for a pianist to cultivate speed of finger movement. It is this that develops activity and purposiveness and assists all the motoric aspects of technique. Obviously, when playing legato it is essential that the hand be flexible and mobile, and at the same time properly coordinated.

Probably many pianists have been taught as children to let their hand 'fall' or 'sink' into the first note of a phrase and to raise it on the last note. How exactly is this done? I am no great advocate of 'sticking' on the first note of a phrase, or of releasing the final note with special deliberation. I prefer phrasing that combines both smoothness and gentleness with a certain masculinity. It thus seems to me best of all to let the wrist sink on the first note of the phrase, and on the last note to straighten it and return to the starting position while trying not to 'flap' the hand unnecessarily meanwhile. Turning the hand and forearm toward the particular note or notes being played is of course perfectly permissible and legitimate. Raising and lowering of the hand is also allowable, but only when necessary. The whole approach described here is of great importance in structuring phrases and in correct articulation. And although articulation marks are not usually so crucial for a pianist as for a violinist, they should nevertheless be mastered fully in order to achieve proper expression and reproduce accurately the composer's intentions. A passage might, for example be played as follows:

or like this:

or in this way:

Now a few words on playing scales and passing the thumb under the hand: It seems to me that on no account should the thumb be held too low. A 'supine' thumb is clumsy and awkward in its movement, and more tense, than one held high. It is vital for the thumb to move freely and easily. A high thumb is therefore probably more comfortable to play with and is easier to tuck under. There are various opinions about passing the thumb under, depending probably on individual preferences and feelings. But smoothness of execution is what I would emphasize as the prime requisite. Take the fairly simple scale of E major. It can be divided into two convenient segments (1-2-3 and 1-2-3-4):

The transition from one position to another is made smoothly, without raising or lowering the hand and without any jerk or awkward twisting. I rest on the third finger and then, as it were, slide onto the thumb, which is held lightly and high. In a descending scale, conversely, you support on the thumb (still held high) and spring off onto a lightly held third finger. When playing scales any superfluous movement should in my view be avoided altogether.

The above are a few ideas and observations on pianoforte technique that I would offer to young players. I repeat, I have not set out a complete and coherent technical system or offered any universal remedy for every pianistic ill. In art nothing is worse than fossilized dogma. Life itself changes, and so does music – and together with it technique and aesthetic norms and criteria also change. I will be happy simply if the ideas that I have set out and which are the result of long experience are of real use to young pianists in their daily toil.

KONSTANTIN IGUMNOV

Some Technical Observations

The following remarks were made by Igumnov towards the end of his life in one of a series of conversations with Professor Grigorii Prokofiev, the Soviet musicologist and pianist, who graduated from Igumnov's class at the Moscow Conservatoire in 1909.

PROKOFIEV You said that in recent years you have acquired some settled ideas on the subject of piano playing. Do you feel and consider that this result is something basic and essential?

IGUMNOV I can't formulate anything absolutely precisely here. But muscular sensations when playing the piano are something that has to be felt. In playing, one must strive to fuse together with the piano, so that nothing, not even a slip of tissue paper, can come between the bedrock of the piano keys and your fingers. One should somehow become at one with the keyboard and adhere to it.

PROKOFIEV So I am going to lay my hand on your armchair, and you have to imagine that my hand is on the keyboard: I shall be able to feel the sensation, but this is not something one can see.

IGUMNOV Of course, and it's not just a question of one's fingers. You have to cease feeling your elbow as something separate. It's as if all the separate links of your arm and hand flow over and become part of one another.

I don't like it when pianists' fingers spring up off the keyboard in playing *staccato*. On the other hand, this does become necessary in order to play some single sonorous chord. The difference is in the fact that there are people who constantly play the piano like that: they lift the finger then lower it, lift and lower, lift and lower. But I believe you need a calm finger position and with just downward movement, not up and down. Why should I separately raise one finger and then lower it? All one needs is one downward sweep of the finger...

Freedom of the arm and hand is essential. But why then should the hand need to stop and hang in the air? To produce a sound it is better to slightly raise and then immediately lower the hand. The hand remains calm, without any movement; it touches the key but without any sudden sharp jolt. You should lift the hand immediately before the sound, and not in advance. The weight and fall of the hand play an important part. But you shouldn't throw the hand weight around. You need just to raise and lower, but without any throwing. And I strongly dislike any rapid downward movements, just as I don't like upward flourishes.

One needs to control the positioning of the fingers and to be able to change it. If you place the fingers in a sharply curved attitude once and for all, this is going to interfere with the variety of tone you can produce. Apart from which, it will impede *legato* playing, and that is something I regard as very important. Fingers that are drawn in often produce a duller tone. In the olden days, for instance, they use to say of Arensky 'How can he manage to play with fingers extended?' But it isn't really a matter of the shape of the fingers. The important thing is the relationship between separate parts of the arm and shoulder, their proportion and coordination. Perhaps this is the reason...

PROKOFIEV But in octaves, too, the fingers are active, and then really the whole technique is exclusively in fingers that work and feel the keyboard. Yet it's obvious that tone production depends not just on the fingers...

IGUMNOV True. The source of our tone is also somewhere here in our back.

PROKOFIEV In recent years I think you formed an opinion that in placing the hand a certain inclination toward the fifth finger was more comfortable than the traditional one toward the thumb...

IGUMNOV No, I don't like any inclination toward the thumb. Generally, there should be some inclination toward the fifth, but sometimes the structure of a particular passage may require the opposite. At one time I used to like sitting low, and I also held my wrist very low. But a higher sitting position helps one to move, and it brings you nearer to the keys. But it's not so good when you sit low. But there are various views on this. One old lady who studied with Nikolai Rubinstein used to say that he considered you had to have straight fingers and a high wrist. I don't know about Nikolai, but Anton's fingers were not at all long. He had a very broad hand but short fingers. So Anton would have found it awkward to maintain a high wrist. But Liszt used to hold his wrist high, and he had very long fingers.

PROKOFIEV Have a look at the plaster cast of Rubinstein's hand in the Conservatoire museum. Actually, Ippolitov-Ivanov[1] once told me that this isn't in fact Anton Rubinstein's hand, but that of the third brother – Iosif, who was not a professional musician. But the two Rubinstein brothers Anton and Nikolai had the hand position they learned from Villoing[2] with the joint between the tip and middle phalanx of the finger pressed in.

IGUMNOV They played with their fingertip cushions.

PROKOFIEV But that's a sensation one can feel even with a usual and normal finger position. But if one places one's fingers as Villoing taught, then the wrist will be much lower...

IGUMNOV The first finger, or thumb, is very important. A well-cultivated thumb is essential. It was only later that I thought about Safonov's words and his remarks about how terribly important the thumb is. The thumb is a lever on which the rest of the hand moves and shifts. It is necessary for it to be alive, able to 'move around' and 'twist round'. It has to be strengthened and supported all the time. It has to be a sort of support point that helps the hand to move around. Otherwise no arpeggios will turn out *legato*. And it's essential that its neighbours are all able-bodied, because the thumb lies on its side on the keys. There was a story from Busoni about everything being built on horizontal movement of the hand and arm, and about there being no rotary movements. That's not good, though. You have to make a transfer on the thumb by moving in a slight arc. A player has to be in control of his muscles and be able to isolate the one from the other, and not by means of pressing, but by allowing everything to lie passive and activating only those muscles needed for playing. One shouldn't permit any pressures that hold up one's movement, whether deliberate or unconscious.

Fingering is also of absolute importance... At one time I was fond of passing fingers over one another, over the third, fourth or fifth. But then I started playing the old way again – tucking the thumb under. Then I came to the conclusion that in playing it is the third finger that is the basic one. I also have a terribly long fourth finger....

Yet I don't think much of any mystical ideas about the specific role of individual fingers (there's an echo of Chopin's ideas here). I often argued with those who ascribed some mystic meaning to individual fingers and their individual role. I always maintained that this was pure mysticism, and the *fingers have to be of equal strength and value...*

PROKOFIEV I was very interested by your phrase that 'there has to be a sensation that the fingers step over one another', and I can well imagine the possibility of this. But why in view of all the rotary movements that we make should it be the fingers that 'step over', and not the hand that shifts? And why do the fingers 'sink' into the keyboard?

IGUMNOV I do realize that the hand does move laterally. It shifts its position, while the fingers actually depress the keys. In cantilena playing there will be a movement of the hand from finger to finger. If I want to learn, say, the first study in Clementi's *Gradus ad Parnassum*, I'm not going to make any arm movement, and my fingers can move around quite easily. It's true, though, that together with the fingers the actual hand is consequently going to shift up and down too... But maybe this is a piece of mystification, and at rapid tempo something else is going on?

Perhaps what I said isn't going to happen quite like that in rapid tempo. But as I work I'd like all parts of my hand to feel they are shifting their position, and that the weight is shifting from the first finger onto the second, then onto the third, and so on. But it's necessary to slightly support the hand however, so the motion can continue freely by inertia. If I have to keep making jolts of the arm and hand all the time, that's no good at all. But if I slightly support it, that's very good for developing the right sensation in the fingers. Therefore one must have this feeling in the fingers. The fingers are capable of sustaining a certain load, and they need strengthening in order to do this.

And when I play exercises by Tausig, let's say, weight and lateral movement of the fingers are important all the time.

PROKOFIEV But perhaps there is no weight as such, but there's simply effort being applied in the fingertips? And it is this that concentrates the complex muscular effort. In a large *forte* the initial fundamental energy even comes from the torso – all the remaining links of arm and hand are merely transmitters of energy. Here all the links of the hand, upper arm, shoulder, and torso are called into play.

IGUMNOV Yes, sometimes the whole of the upper body plays a part.

PROKOFIEV In cantilena playing, of course, it's a different question. There comes a moment of contradiction between slow and rapid movements – a phenomenon that every pianist encounters sooner or later.

IGUMNOV Quite correct... But as regards sonority, and economy of movement, a sense of weight plays an enormous role... At the moment in the Conservatoire we have lots and lots of low stools and chairs, which is quite unpleasant. Recently Alexander Goldenweiser told me that at one time he used to try and sit at the instrument as low as possible, but now he does quite the opposite. We agreed on this, and I am beginning to think that it is far more convenient to sit higher. This is a very important matter. Anton Rubinstein used to sit terribly far away from the piano and with his legs stretched out, while Liszt sat high up and with straight back. It's not impossible that his way of sitting was bound up with the fact that he produced a very sustained and ringing tone, although it lacked the density of timbre that Anton Rubinstein had.

PROKOFIEV Rubinstein increased the power of his tone by coordinating every part of his arm and hand in a movement 'towards himself', whereas Liszt used movements that 'pushed away' from him. You were saying that in cantilena playing the fingers have to step across laterally. But what is going to happen in arpeggios? Can one here really do without a certain horizontal shifting of the hand?

IGUMNOV In arpeggios the sensation of fingers stepping from one to the other is essential in slow tempo in order to make them even. And then at fast tempo there is tucking under of the thumb, but no further than a fifth... I am a supporter of the idea that there should be exercises on the piano. Gymnastics are always essential – in moderation of course. For this it is useful to practise movements involving turns of the hand, as in the following exercise:

Here I like to have the fingers stretched out... You know, 'stretching' is constantly ignored with us, totally, and this is absolutely wrong. Chords you will of course play with 'prepared' fingers, and they have to be absolutely freed up. In order to play chords well, one has to let the fingers move apart uninhibitedly, without their interfering with one another. Incidentally, a single sonorous chord can be played pushing the hand away from one and bringing the fingers slightly closer...

NOTES

1) Mikhail Mikhailovich Ippolitov-Ivanov (1859-1935), composer, conductor and teacher; between 1893 and 1922 he was successively professor, director and Rector of the Moscow Conservatoire.

2) Alexander Ivanovich Villoing (1804-78), Moscow based pianist and teacher, of French descent, famed principally as teacher of brothers Anton and Nikolai Rubinstein.

GRIGORII GINZBURG

Notes on Mastery of the Piano

1 TEMPO

Discovering the right tempo can take a performer a long way toward mastering the whole conception of the work. As the stage producer Stanislavsky
once observed, 'The rhythm and pace of the action can intuitively and directly
suggest not only the corresponding feeling and arouse experiences, but can
also assist in the creation of images'. More specifically: 'If the rhythm and
tempo have been correctly picked up, then correct feelings and experience
are created naturally, of their own accord. On the other hand, if rhythm and
tempo are wrong, then in just the same way wrong feelings can arise, and this
can only be corrected by reverting to the correct rhythm and tempo.' [1]

The tempo of a piece is decided by the performer, based on the composer's markings of *allegro*, *andante*, *presto*, et cetera. However these are all fairly flexible notions, and to make them more precise composers sometimes
add metronome markings. But even the latter should be taken as a very approximate guide, and not as an absolute requirement. The history of our art
knows many instances where great composers put in metronome markings
and then proceeded to disregard them themselves, only to be surprised and
irritated when their own markings were later pointed out to them. This hap-
pened, for instance, with Rakhmaninov in his Second Concerto for piano
and orchestra.

Alexander Goldenweiser recalled that when preparing to perform this
concerto publicly, he asked the composer to listen to him, and they met at
Goldenweiser's apartment, since Rakhmaninov did not have two grand pianos at home. Goldenweiser had heard the composer's own first performance of the concerto, and he kept to the tempi played by Rakhmaninov as he
recalled them. Before Rakhmaninov's arrival, however, he decided to check

his performance against the metronome markings in the score, and consequently found that at various points he had to change the relative tempi. In doing so, Goldenweiser discovered several things that were not altogether convincing. However, such were the composer's instructions.

At last Rakhmaninov turned up and together with Goldenweiser played through the concerto. But although he approved the performance in general, he asked Goldenweiser to alter the tempi of some episodes in a way that confirmed precisely Goldenweiser's own earlier intuitions. However, when the latter pointed out to Rakhmaninov the disparity between his remarks and his own metronome markings, the composer was unpleasantly surprised. After this incident, he hardly ever placed metronome indications in his compositions.

It is significant, too, that Anton Rubinstein never placed metronome indications in his compositions, but at the start of a piece he very often indicated 'the basic metrical unit defining the relative speed of movement'.[2] Without inhibiting the performer by prescribing a precise speed for the music, this indication provided an important central guideline for his thoughts.

The tempo of a performance is in fact a highly individual matter. The tempo cannot be 'ordered' in advance – the performer has to discover it. If we listen carefully to the performance of one and the same piece by several major artists, we can often see that while expressing the idea of the work with exceptional clarity, profundity and perfection of thought, they play at tempi widely differing from one another. Nevertheless, the individual choice of tempo has certain bounds and limits that are defined by the character, concept, and content of the work in question. Vladimir Stasov observed that 'it is known that in a musical performance the meaning and appearance of a work are altered by a change in movement, to such an extent that the most familiar piece can sound like something strange and unfamiliar.'[3] The performer should never for a moment forget that his art is like that of the actor, orator, or narrator, and therefore his musical 'speech' should proceed at a pace that makes the composer's ideas intelligible and accessible to listeners, conveying them with maximum clarity and expressiveness.

This point should be especially remembered when performing so-called 'rapid' compositions or passages. Almost always, especially at the start, the pianist tends to play them extremely quickly, or as fast as possible. The dynamics and passionate impulse of the music, and the composer's markings – let us say, *presto*, or *presto possibile* – push the player in this direction. And without having a sufficiently clear picture of the work, the pianist surrenders totally to his own motor instincts and follows their lead. But does the composer's artistic idea really demand 'supernaturally' rapid tempi that can only be achieved by 'supernatural' finger drill? Any musical thought develops in time, and in order to be correctly perceived and understood, it ought not to be conveyed with excessive speed. One might even say that the more significant, thoughtful, and expressive the artist wants to make his performance, the more restrained should be the tempo that he selects.[4] The situation is similar when we try to convey other ideas in as convincing, weighty and impressive manner as possible, and we therefore express these by reducing our rate of speech and space it out into phrases.

Borodin has left us a description of Liszt's playing: 'Contrary to everything I had so often heard about it, I was struck by the simplicity, sobriety and severity of the performance. There was a total absence of mannerism, affectation or aiming for superficial effect.' In Borodin's words, Liszt 'chooses moderate tempi, he does not force the pace, and he does not get worked up. Nonetheless, despite his age, one is aware of a mass of force, energy, passion, élan and fire.'[5]

Of course, one should bear in mind that when Borodin penned these lines, Liszt was aged seventy-two. Yet probably that sage and restrained performance was far more profound and meaningful than the playing of the young Liszt, at a time when he was once caricatured as sitting there amidst a heap of pianos pulverized and shattered by his playing!

At the same time it would be wrong to conclude from what I have said that a performer aiming at the most expressive possible rendering can slow down the tempo to an unlimited degree. Imagine, for example, that the composer expounds his musical idea at an *allegro* pace. Without going beyond the bounds of this marking, as we said already, the performer can be relatively free in his choice of tempo for conveying this *allegro*. But the limit of any slowed performance will always come at the moment when alteration of the tempo produces an actual qualitative leap, when gradual change breaks down and a new sensation is created – of *andante*, let us say, instead of *allegro*. And this will inevitably happen if the performer forgets the composer's basic marking, that is, if he lacks moderation in his own choice of tempo. The same is true of any undue acceleration. Consequently, the performer is limited in his freedom of choice of tempo by the quality of movement indicated by the composer. He enjoys freedom only within the bounds of this. For instance, whatever its individual variation in performance, an *andante* should not lose those features inherent in *andante* ('in walking rhythm', 'as though walking', or 'in gehender Bewegung', as Beethoven described it). And, finally, even the slowest *lento* should still be supported by sufficient inner movement for the musical fabric not to fall apart into individual notes....

Conservatoire teachers occasionally encounter another widespread student mistake. Having listened to the piece he is studying in a performance by some major artist, the student usually begins by firmly seizing on the tempo adopted by this artist and tries to copy it as exactly as possible.[6] Yet after spending much effort to achieve this aim, he is surprised to discover that something is not quite as it should be, and that in his own performance this tempo creates a quite different effect from the one produced by his favourite artist. This is because tempo is closely bound up with the artistic conception as a whole and is inseparable from its other constituent components. A change in any one of these components requires a corresponding adjustment of all the others. Otherwise the whole conception is thrown off balance and the standard of performance suffers. There is no sense at all in removing and isolating one element from the sum total.

Our conclusion is that in deciding on a tempo, the master performer does not proceed from any exact notion of playing speed imposed from without, but from his own individual ability to convey the composer's thoughts with maximum clarity and accessibility. The tempo of a work is defined by the performer bearing in mind the composer's indications, the content of the particular work, the character of dynamic shading, the degree of expressiveness, brilliance, impetus and other elements in the concept of the performance, as well as the technical abilities of the performer himself, and the physical strength required to give an artistic rendering of the work in question. All these factors come together, often contradicting and colliding with one another, and out of the struggle of these contradictions the performing tempo emerges. A successfully discovered relationship between all these elements and a true sense of measure lead to a realization of the 'correct tempo', that is, the tempo that best assists this individual performer to present this particular work with maximum artistic conviction and roundedness. Yet at the same time this tempo will not be in any way absolute. It will however be relatively correct: since performers differ in the nature of their talent, and in the development of their performing abilities, they will always play the same series of works at different speeds while retaining an ability to offer varying presentations that are nevertheless alike in their richness, profundity, and realism.

2 ON USE OF THE PEDAL

The ideas set out here are based on a careful study of the pedal indications provided by Shostakovich in his *Twenty-four Preludes*, opus 34.

Any survey of the hundreds of editions of classics, Romantics and other so-called teaching literature will show that countless editors have spared neither time nor energy on writing in the pedal markings in each bar, and almost on every note. One wonders what was the guiding principle of these editors? Careful analysis reveals that there is only one principle in force – namely the holding of a single harmony on the pedal. One might indeed think that teachers and students studying one of these works are so illiterate and deaf that they are unable without the editor's help to understand or hear where one harmony ends and another begins. Of course, one cannot deny that when playing the piano such a principle for applying the pedal is often absolutely essential. But is it worth bothering to write in such pedalling? And yet in other cases when the performer is faced with realizing the composer's intentions that do not fit this pedalling scheme, very often the editor avoids providing any pedal indications! In other words, while not trusting the ability of teachers and pupils to sort out a quite elementary piece of pedalling, editors at the same time trust them totally in places where the problem of pedalling is far more complex!

Everyone knows and agrees with Anton Rubinstein's pronouncement about the pedal being 'the soul of the pianoforte'. But in very many cases this 'soul' is on display in strikingly primitive form. Indeed, when Beethoven or Liszt indicate pedalling in their works that does not fit in with a primitive notion of 'harmonic pedalling', one often hears discussions to the effect that, first of all, 'pianos in those days were different'; secondly, that this is a 'misprint overlooked by the author'; and thirdly (probably the most widespread explanation), that the composer was haphazard and careless about marking in the pedal since he was too lazy to bother about such trivia.

If argumentation such as this might seem more or less convincing in the case of the classics (although without sufficient foundation), it is certainly totally inapplicable to the music of Shostakovich. Quite apart from the state of the modern piano, the care with which the pedalling is marked, and the amazing precision with which it has been thought out, remove any apprehensions regarding the composer's carelessness or misprints that he failed to notice. Furthermore, if we examine and reflect on Shostakovich's pedalling and the subtle mastery of its execution, we realize that it is an integral element in the performance of his works. I would say that any performer who does not observe Shostakovich's pedal in fact undermines the composer's intentions no less than if he played different notes or different phrasing.

But serious doubts arise also with respect to the classics: did great composers of the past hear their work in the way that it appears to us? Is this how they imagined the sound or the performance of their works? We should recall, for instance, that Mozart played on instruments that had no dampers. Consequently any compositions performed on them had a hollow resonance and lacked any sharp clarity of harmony. The first thing to strike one on examining Beethoven's pedal markings is their amazing boldness of treatment. If we take, for instance, the last few bars before the coda of the first movement of the *Appassionata*, we see that the composer obviously wanted the tonal mixture of D flat and C in the bass register. But this is incompatible with the otherwise clean and 'sterile' pedalling of the whole movement up to this point that is recommended by the majority of editors and teachers. And when truly great performers such as Medtner or Schnabel turned their hand to Beethoven, their pedalling sounded strange and unacceptable to our 'academic' ear. Chopin was very pedantic in the placement of pedal marks, and in his work we also often find extremely bold pedalling. And when we turn to certain editions by Liszt (e.g. of Weber's *Perpetuum mobile*), we can convince ourselves that Liszt too very often put pedal markings where no teacher could ever bring himself to place them.

Probably teachers and editors are most terrified lest two contiguous notes of a melody fall on the same pedal. And yet they never seem to consider that on a good modern grand piano there are powerful 'tolling' bass notes capable of completely masking false overtones in the upper register. This, for example, enables one to play each bar of the *Funeral march* trio in Chopin's B flat minor sonata on a single pedal, and the pianist who changes it on each melody note thereby displays not a keen ear but an ignorance of the nature of the modern instrument.

In the same way there are several cases where a fear of mixing two harmonies on the same pedal is quite unjustified. It is no mistake when Shostakovich in his E flat minor Prelude, opus 34 number 14, prescribes the following pedal:

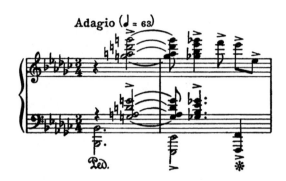

This pedalling is not only permissible but is the only one that achieves the desired effect in this particular passage.

Frequent 'cranking' of the pedal is unreasonable not only acoustically but also in a purely technical respect. Modern instruments have extremely heavy dampers, and they become more so especially toward the lower register. Anyone can easily convince himself of this by playing some rapid passage in the bass register both with pedal and without it. Playing without pedal requires far more effort from the fingers, since one not only has to strike the keys, but also raise the dampers. When playing with pedal, however, the dampers will already be raised. Thus by too frequent changes of pedal the player puts himself at a disadvantage: playing one note with raised damper and then another with damper lowered creates a 'rough' or uneven keyboard...

3 THE PERFORMER'S WILLPOWER

Whether he is a modest pupil or a first-class performing artist, every player is familiar with those tormenting moments when in his enthusiasm he exceeds the limits of his abilities and his performance falls a long way short of perfection. The urge to insure oneself against failures of this sort rouses the player to even more persistent work on so-called 'technical aspects'. Yet the trouble here is often bound up not so much with lack of technique as with a lack of urge and willpower.

The same is true in a series of other instances. Many things fail to come off with pupils only because of the insignificant effort of the will expended by them on fulfilling the task in hand. Hearing pupils come out with phrases like 'I cannot' or 'I'm not in a condition' to do something, I am often reminded of a splendid phrase I recall from the Italian poet Petrarch's essay *On contempt for this world*: 'I would like you to admit that where you said "I cannot", you in fact did not wish to.'

What exactly is meant by a piano performer's willpower? By this we mean his ability to consciously perform on the instrument the brilliant artistic idea created in his imagination, a task whose execution requires the mobilization of all the performer's psychic and physical resources. And the performer's willpower is a most important, often decisive, factor in achieving artistic success. Its presence or absence invariably affect the results of a concert performance.

There are many people who have a good feeling for music. There is also no shortage of people able to create an interesting and vital conception of how to perform a particular work. But it is one thing to create such a plan, but quite another to realize it in terms of physical sound. It is one matter, let us say, to define the tempo limits and relationships in a work, but quite another to stay within these limits and to execute and realize these relationships once identified. The number of artists capable of realizing their performing plan in terms of actual sound (if not totally, then at least in a sufficient approximation) is relatively small. And yet, what earthly good is the most brilliant plan if the artist lacks sufficient willpower and urgency to realize it?

Constant efforts to educate this quality should begin at the very earliest stage of the music teaching process. And this acquires particular importance as the artist reaches maturity. Yet to this day not enough attention is paid to this problem.

At every step the performer encounters the need to overcome all manner of obstacles. Inertia and a tendency towards motoric rapidity tend to push him towards irrepressible speed at a time when any concern to convey the musical content demands relatively restrained tempi. An explosion of impulsiveness and emotional absorption with the music of one particular episode may lead the pianist to spend all his physical and emotional strength on one passage. But in the process the interests of the whole, the artistic value of the entire performance, will suffer if the culminating point of the composition appears to occur in an entirely different episode.

On the other hand, the worry and fear that grip many musicians as they approach a 'dangerous' passage often give rise to rushing and to 'mangling' not only this difficult passage but also quite simple episodes directly preceding it. Repeated playing of this sort leads to the habitual 'gabbling' of whole passages.

What can one do to counter such bad habits? What power can overcome the temptations and fears described above and free the performance of unnecessary and harmful fussiness, keeping it within its planned limits? Only a well educated, trained, and rigorously organized willpower.

In the training of one's will a crucial role is played by work done away from the instrument. In itself this method is not at all new. Many pianists think over the pieces they are working on without using the instrument, and many even learn the musical text without touching the piano. However, I would emphasize that the most important thing in the method I am suggesting is the vital presence of an element of willpower when mentally playing through pieces away from the instrument. This should be not just a hasty read-through of the work, but a steady and committed self-critical analysis reminiscent of the chess-player's examination of a game he has just lost. As we know, the reason for defeat is almost always some wrong move made long before the end of the game. In just the same way, if something does not work out at the piano, the reason by no means always lies in the 'last move' that you made. Much more often the reason has much deeper roots that lie hidden. To discover these and find ways of eliminating them is the task of the mental work done away from the piano.

A hike or walk offers the best conditions for achieving this aim. Not surprisingly, walking is a constant ingredient in the creative process of many artists. Thus, for instance, Tchaikovsky wrote in one of his letters in 1879: '... From time to time I need that sort of lifestyle, that is, I need to discover myself in a *tête à tête* with mother nature... I spend the whole day walking, dreaming, reading, playing, and saying nothing...' [7] Beethoven too used to roam the streets and fields alone with his thoughts, and the sound of a galloping horse gave rise to the metrical figure in one motif from the finale of the Sonata, opus 31, No 2.

As he walks around and reflects, the performer should mentally play through a composition, think over and reinforce its framework, strength of tone, fix its exact tempi, their interrelationship, the finest rhythmic divergences, et cetera. One should strive to ensure that not a single choice of tempo arises on stage arbitrarily, and that all the elements making up the complex process of platform performance are harmoniously combined and unified by the single artistic will of the performer.

Mental work is particularly beneficial where rapid passages are concerned. Many teachers of the past and the present advise mentally 'singing though' such passages. This advice is particularly helpful in giving a clearer understanding of the melodic nature of the passage. However, when mentally singing though a passage we must do it at a tempo that is often much slower than that at which the passage has to be performed, since the speed achievable on the piano far exceeds the resources of the human voice. Thus, singing through the passage is not in itself sufficient to master the passage and ensure its reliable performance on the instrument. Only by thinking through the passage, directing his will towards playing it through mentally as part of the whole piece, can a performer learn to keep the passage in the tempo and tonal framework required in the overall scheme of performance. In particular, even those so-called 'gabbled' passages are best of all corrected by strenuous mental work, repeated mental playing through of the troublesome passage in a frame of mind where one's will is concentrated and directed towards a deliberate, highly articulated, and slightly slower 'delivery' of the passage in question, with deliberate slowing toward the end and at those points where the performer is tempted to accelerate. If the pianist works in this way at overcoming his own motoric impetus, he can guarantee to eliminate any hint of 'gabbling' from his playing.

Obviously, what we have said above is addressed not to each and every performer, but to those that are fairly mature and experienced. In order that the work done away from the instrument on one's musical imagination and performing willpower bears proper fruit, at least two conditions are necessary. First of all, this presupposes adequate musical maturity in the player, and a developed ability to imagine things with one's inner ear (something that should be trained from the very outset of any musical study). Secondly, it demands a stage of mastery of the work such that it already lies in the memory and in the fingers of the player.

Of course, work away from the piano does not totally replace or remove the need for work at the instrument, it merely complements and completes it. And one should constantly return to the keyboard in order to check experimentally what has been achieved by mental effort. When we discover at the piano further faults, we should examine and mentally revise the whole piece, trying to find out our mistakes and understand and correct them. After this we should reexamine them again at the keyboard and establish what has turned out correctly in practice and what requires further revision. To repeat, we are not concerned with doing away with actual work at the keyboard, but with significantly shortening and rationalizing it, and with rejecting excessively long and at the same time insufficiently artistic and unproductive drilling at the piano. This, despite the fact that many stick to an old-fashioned view that this is the principal and even the sole means to overcome any technical faults in execution. In reality work at the instrument is only part of the performer's daily routine – an important part, but only part, moreover not the greater, but the lesser part.

Essentially, the player's creative work, the agonizing search for correct solutions, the construction of a complete performance and the polishing of details with the help of a performing willpower fill the whole conscious life of the artist. He goes to sleep with these thoughts in his head and wakes up with them next morning. Even when eating, drinking tea, talking with friends, somewhere deep down inside him the performer continues with his professional work. The person who can walk away from the piano and forget all about his work is not a real performing artist, and will never become one. Art, just like science, 'demands the whole of a person's life. And even if you had two lives, that would still not be enough. Science demands from a person great passion and great exertion. Be passionate in your work and in your searchings.' Our young artists should mark, learn and inwardly digest these remarkable words by the scientist Ivan Pavlov.

NOTES

1) K.S. Stanislavsky, *Rabota aktera nad soboi* (Moscow-Leningrad, 1948), pt 2, p 220.

2) K.Igumnov, fn.3 in A.Rubinshtein, *Izbrannye sochineniya* (Moscow, 1945), vol I, p 3.

3) V.Stasov, 'Muchenitsa nashego vremeni', in his *Izbrannye stat'i o muzyke* (Moscow-Leningrad, 1949), p 151.

4) It appears to us that when a composer writes a passage, he has in mind a declamatory delivery that will be slightly slowed precisely at those points which strike the performer as most difficult.

5) A.Borodin, *Pis'ma* (Moscow, 1950), vol 4, p 19.

6) In this category belong also the frequently encountered cases of students who have heard recordings of Rakhmaninov and then try to reproduce the inimitable rhythmic peculiarity of this great Russian pianist's performances.

7) P.I. Chaikovsky, *Perepiska s P.I.Yurgensonom* (Moscow, 1938), p 94.

PART TWO

Lessons and Masterclasses

SAMUIL FEINBERG

Beethoven's Appassionata: A Performer's Commentary

The following notes were made by Samuil Feinberg, presumably at some point in the 1950s as a summary of his remarks on Beethoven's Appassionata in classes with students. The Sonata was one that Feinberg performed especially often, holding it in particular regard as a work whose dramatic and lyrical power probably surpassed even that of the late Beethoven sonatas. The following notes, edited by Feinberg's brother Leonid, have been supplemented by various extracts from Feinberg's monograph Pianism as an Art. The fingerings are Feinberg's own, preserved in his personal copy of the Beethoven sonatas.

FIRST MOVEMENT: ALLEGRO ASSAI

The opening of the Sonata offers the listener little assistance in obtaining a true and precise idea of the basic tempo of this whole movement. The groups of repeating eighth notes that first appear in bar 10, and later – at reduced tempo – in bars 12 and 13, and also the passage in sixteenth notes in the following bar, are still not enough to convey a sense of the basic rhythmic pulse. This only becomes more apparent when the main theme is repeated at bar 16. But final confirmation of the movement's tempo comes only at bar 24, with the start of a chain of eighth notes in the bridge passage.

This initial metronomic uncertainty requires the performer to observe particular rhythmic precision in playing the main theme. This especially concerns the performance of trills in the four alternate measures beginning with bar 3. Here it is essential to be rhythmically precise in performing the passage in sixteenth notes while also preserving exactly the 12/8 meter and the basic tempo of the movement. Also, despite the marking of *poco ritardando*, the insistent motif of eighth notes in the bass should also help prepare listeners for the repeating eighth notes in the subsequent accompaniment to the theme.

The new episode that opens the bridge passage at bar 24 is also very important in establishing the basic tempo of the movement as a whole. It would thus be quite wrong to reduce the long series of eighth notes to a secondary role forming a simple light accompaniment. Here for the first time we find concentrated the entire energy of this basic rhythmic pulse, and its emergence should be made clear and emphasized by a slight *rinforzando*. The expressive power of these eighth notes can be conveyed by a simple fingering based on the alternation of thumb and second finger. Despite the *piano* marking, the pronounced *sforzando* in the right hand at bar 26 should be matched by the stressed thirds in the left hand that make up an augmented version of the triple-time theme:

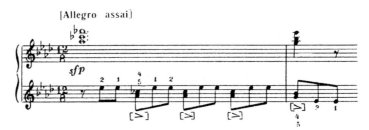

This episode is followed in the fourth quarter of bar 24 by a light, scherzo-like statement in which the same theme of repeating thirds is broken up and distributed on weak beats in various octaves. This is actually the point where a *piano* marking should be placed. After the return of the *sforzando* in bar 30, the left hand part descends chromatically, forming a natural diminuendo that leads into the second subject.

The second subject, built on elements of the now transformed main theme, sometimes causes special difficulty for the performer, since it is not easy to combine the broad and song-like melody with a metrically exact execution of the short sixteenth notes that divide in half the eighth notes making up the accompaniment figuration. These sixteenth notes should sound as a faint echo of the rebellious excitement of the first subject. The trills in bars 44-46 introduce a brief moment of calm, and it may well be useful to perform these in quintuplets rather than groups of six, which would be too busily energetic for this transition passage.

In the closing section of the exposition one should not only point up the top notes of the melody, but also make a *rinforzando* on the first quarter note, underscoring its relative weightiness (in bars 51, 52, and later in bars 55 and 56).

The left-hand octaves at bar 53 may be joined by a slur, with the second octave played *sforzando*, after which the ensuing upward flight of eighth notes begins *piano* and rises to a new *sf*:

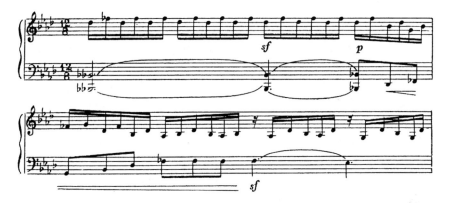

In bars 58 and 59 each *sforzando* in the left hand should be matched by a corresponding *rinforzando* in the right. In the first half of bar 60 an intense *fortissimo* also develops into an immense *rinforzando*. At the end of bar 64, the C flat in the left hand that together with the following A flat forms a falling third is best left held on the pedal: this is perfectly in keeping with the style and sonority of Beethoven's chordal writing.

The modulation at the opening of the development in bar 65 can be emphasized by means of a sudden *pp*:

It is essential to vary the colouration in the following phrases with their trills. These trills are first of all energetic (in bar 71) and then more gentle (in bar 73). It is worth issuing a reminder that the transition to groups of five notes should not lead to an overall increase in tempo. The episode in repeated eighth notes starting at bar 93 is subject to the same principles mentioned already à propos of the exposition.

At bar 105 the quarter notes in the left hand should be distinctly felt as an additional thematic layer:

In bars 123 and 124 there are gradually increasing halts in the left hand. These interruptions continue over the next five measures.

In the recapitulation the faint and alarmed pulsation of eighth notes can be demonstrated more noticeably on the diminished fifth by means of a clear rise and fall in dynamics (at bar 143).

As in the exposition, the *piano subito* at bar 151 should produce the impression of a sudden revelation of the background accompaniment. It is as if this barely audible drumming was earlier concealed by the energetic passage in the foreground and only now emerges.

In bars 203-9 the right-hand figuration has been altered and redistributed in several editions without any justification.

Starting in bar 218 and over the next eight measures, it is essential that the performer have a correct sense of the metrical scheme of these sixteenth notes, which move in twos and not in threes.

Beethoven's marking of *sempre Pedale* in bars 234 and 235 is there as a somewhat sketchy general suggestion, and the player must correct, define and differentiate this in performance.

In the final statement of the second theme, in bars 243-4, and 246-7, Beethoven places a *sforzando* on the strong beat, unlike the earlier statement in bars 214-17 where the *sforzando* appeared on the weaker second beat. The resulting shift of emphasis to the strong beat here reinforces a sense of impending conclusion to this movement.

(In Feinberg's personal copy of the Urtext, the timing for the first movement was marked in by him as 8 minutes, 5 seconds, a note probably dating from the mid 1930s when he was preparing his first public performance of the complete cycle of 32 sonatas. Regarding Beethoven's own markings, Feinberg writes further in his monograph, Pianism as an Art:

'In the first movement of the *Appassionata*, when the triple-time theme first turns into a continuous movement in eighth notes, there is a general marking of *piano* for ten whole measures. By carefully following the musical image sequence that leads into the second subject, however, one can see a much greater differentiation in the changes and contrasts than would be compatible with one single uniform dynamic level.

'It is natural to underline the start of the continuous rhythmic motion with a slight *rinforzando*. After Beethoven's *sforzando* on the right-hand six-three chord, the theme occurs in augmentation in the left-hand thirds. These three repeating beats cannot conceivably be played *piano*. There can hardly be any doubt that a series of accent marks, stylistically so typical of Beethoven, have been omitted here.

'Subsequently the theme is split up into light, syncopated thirds for which a marking of *pianissimo* would be most appropriate. After another *sforzando* the three beats of the theme in augmentation return again, and a gradual diminuendo ensues, suitably marked to lead into the second subject. Quite apart from Beethoven's *sforzando*, it is surely impossible to play this entire episode within the limits of the *piano* that is marked. Otherwise the three pounding beats of the augmented theme would be upstaged and turn into an ineffectually imposed harmonic accompaniment; the scherzo-like lightness of the syncopations would be lost; the whole episode would sound monotonous and inexpressive; and the spirit of the music would be sacrificed for the sake of a too literal interpretation of the printed expression marks. This can often be heard in performances by pianists who stick with pedantic rigour to the composer's markings... Of course, it is vital to follow the composer's instructions and expression marks. But they have to pass through the prism of each performer's consciousness, and every shade of expression should become an integral part of an organic and unified interpretation. As I mentioned earlier, the composer's markings should not be reduced to the status of some alien presence that merely jogs the pianist's elbow each time a *sforzando* is called for.')

SECOND MOVEMENT: ANDANTE CON MOTO

The second movement combines and varies two basic elements: the choral sonorities of the main theme (with various transformations by diminution in a series of variations) and the measured character of a march-like *con moto*.

Both these motifs are varied in an apparently free and independent manner. Thus, for instance, the march-like bass voice in the first variation takes on the character of a series of fluctuating syncopations, while the sustained choral chords in the right hand sound more faintly, and are interrupted as if by purely acoustic pauses beyond which one suspects there may be other sounds that recede and fade and somehow never quite reach the ear.

The impression of sounds receding is also underlined by various 'interruptions', when a logical series of alternating octaves is replaced by a series of 'intentionally random' alternations:

[Andante con moto]

Here is an instance of Beethoven's particular love of the quasi-accidental – new and unexpected sound combinations created by the obstinate continuing development of earlier thematic material.

In the second variation it would be wrong to highlight particular voices among the general harmonic chorus. However, it is necessary to 'tie' separate notes like, for instance, the upper voice in the figuration of sixteenth notes:

In this variation the bass line does not need to be accented since its function within the harmony already gives it a certain prominence. Thus the role of the left hand can be represented in chords, which Beethoven does in certain bars.

In the third variation, which now moves in rapid thirty-second notes, performers usually fail to observe strictly Beethoven's markings of *sf* and *f*. One also hardly ever hears anyone play the *fortissimo* in the falling passage at the end of the variation. This divergence from the composer's markings may be explained by performers' desire to give this whole variation a more tender, emphatically lyrical character. It may well be that the music itself prompts such an interpretation.

In the next episode, which rounds off the movement, the theme is stated in different registers in turn, and the performer has to reveal the meaning of these shifting transpositions. In the soprano register the melody sounds more lyrical and poignant. It is, as it were, a personal response to the fading and receding voices of the chorus. Thus the final *crescendo* may well be replaced by a *smorzando*, if it proves possible to play it thus with sufficient conviction.

(In his monograph Feinberg writes in more detail about Beethoven's occasional striving after the quasi-accidental, the unexpected and even contradictory:

'One finds a remarkable example of such "artistic disorder" in the coda to the first movement of the Fifth Piano Concerto, in the piano accompaniment to the horns, where the blend of harmonic functions gives the passage a particular coloration. In the first variation of the slow movement of the *Appassionata* one also observes seemingly accidental, but in fact justifiable collisions in the figuration. One could cite many similar examples, including the well-known horn entry on the second of a dominant seventh in the reprise of the first movement of Symphony No 3.

'These elements of an integrated harmonic system that Beethoven literally "breaks up" point to his striving to go beyond the limits of established style and overturn its constraining canons.'

In his book Feinberg also discusses the two main elements developed in the Appassionata second movement, and links this with a method of pedalling that he calls 'acoustic pedal':

'A characteristic of organ sound is its ability to create an impression of lofty vaulted buildings and intricate Gothic ceilings. Every instrument not only sounds in particular conditions that are more or less favorable acoustically, but also evokes ideas of the aesthetic source of the musical image, such as a landscape or building.

'The second movement of the *Appassionata* might unfold before us as a prayerful chorus of knights. The theme combines the harmonic unity of choral singing with the restrained march movement of the dotted rhythms. The chorus then recedes into more distant halls as their measured tread echoes down corridors. The sound of singing reaches the ear only intermittently, and the voices are barely audible and keep disappearing... The melodious chorale soars ever higher and more gently, and is lost in the vaulted ceilings of the enfilade of castle rooms.

'For the performer it is immensely important not only *what* is sounding, but also the setting *where* the sound is produced. Thus part of the problem of pedalling is not only in adapting to particular acoustic conditions, but also knowing how to create in the listener's mind a setting in which poetic images can be completed. The pedal is thus subordinate to acoustic conditions, but at the same time it creates its own sphere of sonority, and in this sense it must be *acoustically active*.')

THIRD MOVEMENT: ALLEGRO MA NON TROPPO

Beethoven's tempo indications are not always totally precise, and occasionally some measure of correction is needed to evaluate their meaning. In some cases the change from *Allegro* to *Presto* is a sort of figurative suggestion based on an artistic impulse. At other times, however, it clearly indicates an acceleration of tempo, even a *doppio movimento*.

At the end of the final movement in the *Appassionata* the distinction between the final *Presto* and the basic tempo of the movement as a whole (i.e. *Allegro ma non troppo*) cannot be so great – if only because of the previous sixteenth notes that in the coda return us to the original theme, and it is hard to imagine Beethoven would have omitted to mark 'Tempo 1' at this point.

The stormy and agitated character of the main theme of the finale certainly requires a fairly rapid tempo from the very outset. Otherwise one risks falling victim to the dogmatic approach of those players who set more store by the word than by the actual work. In this particular case it is most natural to regard the difference between *Allegro ma non troppo* and *Presto* as merely the composer's intention that the performer should step up the basic tempo somewhat in the coda. It is useful to compare this tempo acceleration with a similar example in the finale of the D major Sonata, opus 28, which is marked *Allegro ma non troppo*, but with an adjustment in the coda to *Piu allegro quasi presto*, instead of *Presto*.

The opening theme, played *pianissimo*, suggests the first and still restrained surging of an elemental restlessness. Here the dynamic ebb and flow should follow the rise and fall of the melodic line.

[Allegro ma non troppo]

In bars 21-2, the left hand here reinforces the movement of sixteenth notes. To achieve a complete unified sound here, one should not emphasize too much the final sixteenth note in the bar, thus avoiding an excessive *sforzando* in the octave doubling. Here the pause in the right hand should be covered by a short touch of pedal that will slightly prolong the previous note (F). Both octave notes in the bass can be felt as two sixteenth notes, in which case the resulting line of thematic figuration will be even smoother. It is worth comparing this with a similar feature of the bass part in the fourth bar of the finale of the Waldstein Sonata.

In bars 28-9, the *sforzando* in the left hand coincides with the falling melody in the right, which makes this left-hand emphasis particularly expressive.

In bars 34-5 it will always sound better if accents in the right-hand part are made to synchronize with the short syncopated eighth notes in the left. While theoretically one could justify setting the syncopated bass notes against an accented strong beat in the right hand, in practice this leads to excessive fussiness as well as sounding unsatisfactory.

At bars 38-9, the resolution of the left-hand chord coincides with an emphatic suspension in the right-hand melody. The same figure occurs in bars 43-4. However, here the suspension occurs in thirds in the middle voice of the right hand, and it is essential to bring this out in performance.

In bars 52-3 the powerful *sforzando* in the right hand is matched by an expressive *rinforzando* in the sixteenth notes of the left hand.

Alexander Goldenweiser is quite correct in pointing out the need to bring out the melodic element in the sixteenth notes in bars 76-85, especially since in bar 86 this voice appears in the left-hand chord sequence. The *sforzando* here can be extended also to the last eighth note of the measure, with the following bar played *piano*. This treatment is also applicable to bars 88 and 90.

The *sforzando* in bar 98 is applicable to both hands. In the left hand this is closer to a general *rinforzando*.

In bar 102 there should be a *rinforzando* in the left hand on the last three sixteenth notes of this measure.

In bar 226, almost all editions incorrectly have a *ritardando* marked instead of *rinforzando*.

As in all similar cases with Beethoven, his marking of '*sempre Ped.*' is too generalized and should therefore be clarified and made more specific in each case.

The final two *sforzandi* before the coda (i.e. seven and five bars before the *Presto*), which have been shifted onto the strong beat, are possibly printing errors that were never corrected. It is also possible that, as before the conclusion of the first movement, Beethoven intended to give this passage a more direct and affirmative character.

At the end of the movement (in bars 36-51 of the coda), the left-hand figure that is repeated sixteen times and used to underline the appearance of the main theme, emphasizes a *rinforzando* in the second half of the bar, which should also be reflected in the right-hand part.

(The notes in Feinberg's 'Performer's Commentary' are more thorough and detailed for the first and second movements, and less so for the finale. In his monograph, however, he amplifies on some matters of pedalling in the Appassionata that are only briefly touched on in the 'Performer's Commentary':

'One of our greatest pianists once spoke of the pedal as the "soul of the pianoforte". Certainly, thanks to the sustaining pedal, the piano displays its most characteristic and sonorous aspects. And quite naturally, those sounds that are picked up and sustained on the pedal are the most 'pianistic'...

'The pedal markings made be Beethoven in the first edition often strike us as somewhat sketchy. One can hardly approve some pianists' efforts to follow exactly Beethoven's pedal indications in such episodes as, for example, the recitatives in the first movement of Sonata 17 in D minor, opus 31, No 2, or in the coda of the first movement of the *Appassionata*.

'Evidently, in these passages either Beethoven did not sufficiently appreciate the structural or tone-enhancing qualities of the pedal, or else his indications are to be understood as being of a general nature, suggesting the desirability of pedal, but without providing any details of its use, which are left up to the performer. Unfortunately, even in those cases where Beethoven indicates the use of "architectural" pedalling, as in the finale of the Waldstein and other late sonatas, the pedal markings contained in the first editions give no clear indication either of the exact intended duration of notes sustained on the pedal, or of when the pedal should be changed.')

SVIATOSLAV RICHTER

Three Answers to Questions about Beethoven's Sonata Opus 57 (Appassionata)

'In the music a performer should attempt to sense the pulse of the age in which the composer lived, and to convey its most characteristic features.'

SVIATOSLAV RICHTER

In your opinion what place does the Appassionata Sonata occupy in Beethoven's oeuvre, and what is your own view of this work?

The *Appassionata* in my view occupies a quite special, unique place among Beethoven's other works. One can speak in general about the composer's early sonatas that are marked by an unusual freshness, youthfulness, and directness, although of course each of them is also unrepeatable and individual. I might add that that some of these sonatas – for instance, those in C major, opus 2, No 3, in D major, opus 10, No 3, in B flat major, opus 22, and the *Pathétique* – are especially close and dear to me (subjectively, maybe even closer than the late sonatas). One could also talk about a series of common qualities shared by Beethoven's late sonatas which like his other late works I would regard, objectively, as the composer's most perfect creations (the Sonata, opus 111, in particular is truly unique). But the *Appassionata*, I repeat, stands in a place quite apart, and one has no desire or need to compare it with any other work. As a performer, though, I would say it is a real 'monster' to handle; with it one feels stuck between the perils of Scylla and Charybdis...

How do you perceive the imagery of the Appassionata? Do you feel any programmatic elements in the music, especially in light of Beethoven's words about Shakespeare's The Tempest?

Just now, after a ten-year break in playing the *Appassionata* (I played it a lot at one time, perhaps even too much, which probably caused me to abandon it for such a long period), I can only say a few words about the imagery of this work. It seems to me that everything here takes place at night. I remember the words of Heinrich Neuhaus who once compared the second movement of the *Appassionata* to a mountain lake. That is a very accurate and finely observed simile: one genuinely senses in it the mysterious winking of stars reflected in some mountain lake...

It is obvious that the central movement contrasts sharply with the total cataclysm of the work's two outer movements. In these, incidentally, it seems to me that here humanity does not figure as a direct participant in events, but rather as an observer, which is something fairly rare in Beethoven. Could one talk of the cosmic breathe of the finale? Voices communicating and echoing in space? Maybe. In general, though, there are immense forces at work here, and the whole sonata is filled with their titanic power.

As for Beethoven's words that one should 'read Shakespeare's *The Tempest*', I think they are very important, since they are the composer's own words. On the other hand, for me at any rate, in my own work on the sonata, this association never played any part, and I think it is probably important, rather, for the audience who listen to the *Appassionata*.

What seems to you the most essential thing in interpreting this sonata? What relation is there between the performer's own creative initiative and the need to follow the composer's indications?

It is essential to be absolutely strict and scrupulous in one's treatment of the text of the *Appassionata*, as with all of Beethoven's compositions. In my view, here one cannot tolerate any pianistic simplifications or adding anything to the texture. It is true, of course, this applies to the entire classical repertoire (one can quote only a few exceptions – for example, the two-handed trill passage in Dvorak's piano concerto). So far as dynamic shading is concerned, in the works of Chopin and Rakhmaninov (and maybe to a lesser extent Schumann and Scriabin) if it is possible sometimes to vary it depending on one's mood (not to mention the works of Bach, who hardly ever placed any expression marks), in Beethoven's works any dynamic indications not originating from the author are out of the question.

I very much dislike the way in which many performers of the *Appassionata* change the tempi within one single movement. First of all, this concerns accelerations of pace at the start of the repeating triplets in the first movement.

The music loses a great deal because of such changes. It is also particularly nasty when people begin rushing over the alternating chords in both hands at the start of the bridge passage, whereas these chords should in fact sound very clear and distinct. Often, too, pianists are inclined to play the easier passages faster. I immediately lose interest in any performance that has these *accelerandi*, and, strange as it may seem, I get a sense of limpness as a result, despite the faster tempo. One has the impression of a wishy-washy lack of pianistic discipline. And although one can maintain that Beethoven was the first Romantic, his romanticism should not of course be displayed by resorting to these superficial methods, such as taking liberties with the tempo, which are alien to the spirit of his music.

I absolutely refuse to condone any abbreviation of the repeat of the development section and the reprise in the finale of the *Appassionata*. I think that if you do not observe the repeats here, then it is better not to play this work at all. Only by playing the whole text in its entirety does the sonata produce the impression of a really major work. Otherwise it just turns into a game of hide-and-seek – a bit of music followed by a coda that lacks sufficient justification.

In general if I hear a performer fail to repeat what the actual composer wanted repeating (this is true of the Chopin sonatas, the symphonies of Mahler, and the whole of classical music), I begin to have fears that he does not really love the music that he plays. Apart from which, after all, playing repeats makes public performance considerably easier: the second time round it is always easier to 'get into the part', and to discover and bring out the main essence of the music. And why on earth should one be scared of repeats? Out of fear of boring the audience? But, surely, if we are going to talk about fears and apprehensions, then the only person to fear is not the audience but the actual composer we are playing.

(*Based on a conversation with Dmitrii Blagoi in early 1960*)

HEINRICH NEUHAUS

Work on Beethoven's Sonata in A Major Opus 101

'*Only by demanding the impossible from the piano can one achieve everything possible.*'

I

Neuhaus: Today we'll turn our attention to late Beethoven, and we'll hear the Sonata No 28 in A major, opus 101.

(*A student from the Music Teachers' Institute of Advanced Studies plays the work.*)

What can I say? Your performance has plenty of positive features. You're a conservatoire graduate, which means you're a literate and cultivated musician with an appropriate level of knowledge. For a proper understanding of Beethoven it's essential to know and play all the sonatas, and the symphonies and quartets. Unfortunately, very few people here play the quartets, but I strongly recommend that anyone that wants to know their Beethoven well should study the whole of his work.

If we approach your performance critically, then I have several objections in regard to your understanding of the more subtle, poetic and artistic meaning of this music. There are several points I'd like to amplify. So where shall I start? Well, to begin with, in your performance the whole sonata sounds somewhat fragmented. There are some rhythms that sound haphazard, and even contorted, and this doesn't give the work chance to sound as it should in terms of timing. All the movements are very rhythmic in construction, after all. The first movement is a smooth, flowing piece in 6/8 time; the second is a rapid, cheerful march in 4/4, and also very rhythmic. Most of all I liked your third movement. Here there were some fine nuances in your performance. And finally there's the last movement, which is not too fast, but played with

110

great decisiveness. Here, too, the rhythmic side is very important.

The main shortcoming in your playing is that of timing. (I am starting first of all with the two most important musical categories – those of time and of tone.) You have to weigh everything up very accurately, and carefully check on the relationship of tempo and rhythm with the musical effect of the whole fabric. And it's precisely in these two main aspects of performance that you have a fair number of defects.

First and foremost, in the opening movement of this sonata the sound has to 'blossom'. I imagine this movement as it would sound if played by a string orchestra. Everything blossoms and sings and moves very smoothly. This wasn't apparent in your playing, though. On the contrary, I felt that everything was too broken up and even slightly tormented. You also lacked that freshness that's so evident here. This is the music of spring and blossom time. And after the *fermata* at bar 6, the music specially begins to blossom.

Your second movement also had a somewhat jerky rhythmic pulse. I least liked the trio from the march. Here I feel the basic idea is wrongly interpreted, and you're simply not following the composer's markings. On several occasions Beethoven writes '*piano*' and '*dolce*'. This is a canon for two voices, a sort of conversation between two people in very intimate tone. But with you the music had a rather energetic, challenging character. I can't agree with such an interpretation.

The last movement you could have been played slightly slower while making the rhythmic structure clear. I also didn't very much like the second theme from the finale. In this theme those sixteenth notes that played an important part in the first theme gradually turn into an accompaniment, the melody moves smoothly in quarter notes, and it sounds singing and sustained. But it wasn't quite like that in your performance (see bars 37 and following).

I also have a few more general comments, about purely pianistic matters, for instance. After all, the physical movements that we make are very closely bound up not just with our tone, but also with the rhythmic aspect. Sometimes, even though you played expressively, I found your *espressivo* was rather arbitrary. There was no point in emphasizing some things that could well have been slightly concealed. And on other occasions some things were made to 'stick out', to use student parlance. One has to convey the general 'countenance' of the work, beginning with its mood and character, and not simply play with pedantic accuracy, making things 'stick out'. Incidentally, this sort of thing often happens when people play Bach without feeling the music, and there the 'sticking out' turns into deliberate emphasizing of the theme, which also sounds highly unpleasant.

I'd like to say a little about your piano playing too. I feel your playing still contains a lot of what you simply learned at school. But maybe it would be better to think about the essential quality of this sonata, about its poetic substance, and not just about playing it in a grammatically correct way. Some of the rather angular rhythm and hard tone you produce, I think, has something to do with your convulsive way of moving. I would advise you to approach your piano playing in a more natural way: at the moment you have a somewhat 'tortured' relationship to the instrument. You need to have better control over the gifts that nature endowed you with. You have to feel and move more simply and naturally at the piano. And it's typical of your playing that the soft and muted colours come out more successfully. In the first movement there was plenty of intimate colour in your playing, although it's true it was often rather doleful and not always appropriate. But it was well suited to the character of the *Adagio*. So there are some movements, colours, and musical experiences that are more germane to you and which you control better than others. They turn out quite well and fairly convincingly. But you don't have complete control of other possible approaches, and these turn out less well.

Now play the first movement again from the beginning.

(The student plays the opening of the first movement.)

Now you've managed to add a flowing quality to your sound. But I'd like your tone to be even better. If you play a *ritenuto* at the end of the second bar, the music sounds very lugubrious. This is one of Beethoven's sonatas where he gives tempo and expression indications in German. He writes: 'Somewhat lively, and with innermost feeling'. And then there's a marking in Italian: 'Allegretto, ma non troppo'.

I don't sense any brightness of sound in your touch. And it needs a lot a work to maintain a brightness of tone and also achieve plenty of warmth. In the first few bars it's the upper voice that sings, and below it there's a second, and a third voice, and then finally the bass. These four voices are four elements. In your version, though, the middle voices are too prominent, and this shouldn't be the case.

The third bar should begin more brightly. And then all those chords in bar 12 should sound fuller. After that, in bar 14, there's a slight crescendo, and a diminuendo in bar 15. I didn't hear these in your performance, but they should all be gently conveyed. These are very expressive moments. It's interesting that Beethoven places two slurs, one above another, in bar 14: first of all, two notes are tied with a slur, and then all three notes are joined up by another slur. This is also something that needs bringing out.

I can sense one of your rhythmic defects in the sequence of quarter and eighth notes in the cadence at bar 15. There doesn't need to be any deep thought here, no brooding or philosophy. It has to be simple. You're reflecting too much here. The main thing is to feel the smooth rhythmic flow of the music, and you'll lose this if there are too many rhythmic fluctuations.

Here, at bar 16, you need to use less pedal:

In this passage I have the sense of a question and answer, as it were. Your bar 19 doesn't sound quite right. There's a certain dryness of tone, possibly because of your too careful use of the pedal. Without any pedal you make it sound as if you're playing 'on an empty stomach'.

I would play bar 24 slightly more freely, like a violin solo:

You're playing the whole of this episode with a very assertive tone. You should play it more gently. And why so many unnecessary movements? Here there should be a sense of calm and organized freedom. Any unnecessary movements seriously interfere with this idea. I recommend that you think seriously about this. Strive for a sense of calm and simplicity. Use the simplest possible movement to make the piano sound. But with all the movements you make, there can't be any simplicity of phrasing. You ought to train your body and technical apparatus more in the spirit of the piano. And your use of vibrato touch on the keys, as though you were playing the violin or cello, won't do any good either – and it doesn't do anything even for a great artist like Artur Schnabel, when he plays chords with vibrato touch at the end of the exposition in Beethoven's D minor sonata, No 17. [1] But with him it's an actor's way of persuading his audience into 'hearing' a vibrato. But to my mind, the piano should be played using pianistic devices, and without resorting to false gestures like an actor on stage. Among these false gestures I would include any fussy movements of whatever sort. I urge you to impress this not only on your own mind, but also on your pupils too, because students often tend not to copy the most valuable habits of their teachers. It so often happens that you play something really well for your student without his appreciating it; and then, when you play something badly, he immediately goes and copies it!

I think that on this particular instrument you should try and play *piano* and very gently. We pianists often find ourselves in very difficult situations: we have to deal with the 'resistance' of the material we work with, that is, play on a poor instrument. And we have to develop a skill that other instrumentalists never have to think about: we have to learn to overcome a bad piano and adapt to it. I frequently emphasize and drive home to my students that they need to be able to adapt to any instrument, and they have to make the audience listen to them even when playing on the very worst piano.

Let's continue. Starting with bar 25, I would try and bring out that line in the left hand, as if cellos and basses in an orchestra are playing. The basses have a slightly dull sound, whereas the cellos sound brighter. You need to apply every effort to bring out the bloom and depth and warmth and singing quality while still maintaining a gentle tone.

(The student plays, starting at bar 16.)

Bring out the tenderness in this question and answer.

(The student repeats the same passage.)

This phrase starting at bar 19 should be played crescendo throughout, without any diminuendo on the last note. You may be surprised that I'm making you repeat the phrase so many times. I was once told that when Valentina Shatskaya[2] played this sonata in Safonov's piano class, he made her repeat one phrase fifteen times. And there was an even 'worse' example, when Maria Nemenova-Luntz was studying with Scriabin and he made her repeat one bar fifty times![3] So play it once again.

(The student plays the passage again.)

Here, in bar 28, the upper voice has to be heard, like the violin section of an orchestra:

One of the most terrible things for the rhythm and whole life of a work is when metrical accents break up the phrase. In your playing I can hear accents on the strong beats, and the phrasing is getting lost because of this. Play the whole phrase at bar 35. First of all, in bar 34, you should play very quietly (pp), because the following crescendo develops very slowly and gradually:

At bar 41 Beethoven writes very few actual notes, so how do we deal with this situation so that it still sounds well? What I do at this point is to indulge in some 'incorrect' pedalling. I take advantage of the fact that we're building a crescendo, and I take everything on one pedal, and by that means I can achieve greater sonority. For the sake of the sound one has to resort to all sorts of trickery! Here in one bar you have to move from a *piano* to a full orchestral *forte*. But in your performance you have none of that. Your playing is too inhibited, and therefore some things don't come off. There's no flexibility:

Then here, in bar 41, there's a *crescendo*, and then a *forte* in bar 42, then *piano* again, then again *forte* and *piano*, and after that a long *crescendo* over four full measures. But if I might say so, in your performance this passage just sounds degenerate and rather feeble. That's not how Beethoven conceives it. He wrote very precisely: *crescendo*, then *forte* and a *fermata*.

Bars 50 and 51 present a problem for the performer: with *legato* in the right hand, and *staccato* in the left. Here you need to play a finger legato as best you can. Then suddenly after *forte* comes a *piano*.

At bar 58 the reprise begins. We should always pay some attention to the musical structure of a composition. In this first movement, Beethoven builds a complete sonata form from very homogeneous materials. There are no contrasts in it, and one could even describe it as a poem. Usually the themes used in sonata form are contrasting ones, but in this sonata there is comparatively little difference between them, and the development section here is very short.

(Neuhaus asks the student to begin playing from the reprise.)

One would like this episode, starting at bar 61, to blossom more, and you should bring out the small crescendo at bar 66.

(The student plays from the reprise.)

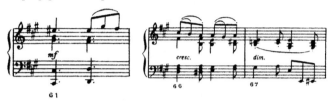

(Neuhaus stops the student at bar 67.)

In order to achieve a *crescendo*, you keep moving in jerks. But you should be depressing the keys without any jerk or tension. This is extremely important for the tone. I'm convinced that Artur Rubinstein, whose tone was unusually full and beautiful, played without any tension. On the contrary, he played with total freedom. Pianists who play in a fixed manner might play more cleanly than pianists who play more freely; but on the other hand they lose that ravishing tone quality that makes up for any wrong notes.

In this first movement there is a great deal that is joyful and spring-like, and this is typical of Beethoven when writing in the key of A major. All of these pieces have something in common in their mood. I always like talking about a composer's sense of key – it's a favourite subject of mine. Just think about all the occasions when Beethoven uses the key of C minor – and, incidentally, Chopin's Étude in C minor definitely has its origins in Beethoven. All of Beethoven's A major compositions are always very chaste works. This quality of the key of A major is common to Beethoven, Brahms, and Medtner. Tonality is a special type of language, as it were, a particular quality of the air, landscape and climate, just like the weather varies. A musician has to be sensitive to this tonal colouration. And if this sensitivity is lacking, that means there's something wrong with him. He evidently suffers from some form of aural colour blindness. In our day atonalism is a historically well-established category, but it has done considerable damage to those who got too carried away by it: it has led to the loss of a sense of key.

Moving on: you ought to make sure that these syncopations in bars 96 and 97 are noticeable. You need to articulate them quite clearly. At this point, in bar 95, there is a *diminuendo*:

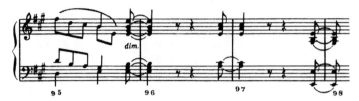

You should show this. Just as you should also show the *crescendo* that Beethoven indicates in bar 100:

To conclude this lesson, I want to make a general comment: I recommend that you pay more attention to your technical apparatus, your hand and arm movements, and manner of playing. What I'm talking about is enough work to keep you busy for a whole year. It won't come immediately. You need to think constantly, you need to educate yourself, and train your powers of self-control in order to improve yourself further.

II

Neuhaus: First of all, I'd like to recommend that everyone here take a careful look at all the Beethoven sonatas in the edition by von Bülow. And now we'll continue working on the Beethoven Sonata in A major, opus 101. Since 'X' played the whole work through last time, today we'll hear just the second movement.

(*The student plays the second movement of the Sonata.*)

I like it today more than I did last time, but I nevertheless have a whole series of comments. Speaking overall and disregarding several details, I believe you've successfully caught the general character of the movement, although your performance still lacks plasticity. All that we can see there in the music, in particular the slurs and pauses, has to be conveyed much more clearly. They should all be audible, whereas you only sketch them in. Furthermore, your tone would be much richer if you played more freely. Everything still sounds rather dry and constricted, and this is evidently because of your playing style and general tension.

From the very first bars, all the slurs and pauses have to be played with greatest precision. The entire splendour of this movement lies in this. The upbeat to the second measure and what follows are not quite accurate rhythmically. You're cutting short the left-hand notes - F, F and E; E, E and E flat: E flat, E flat and D. They have to be played accurately, absolutely accurately:

 etc

What is the unusual feature about this remarkable march? The answer is that it is a march, yet at the same time not a march: there's something joyful, light, and airborne about it, with temperamental exchanges in places. For all this you have to find the necessary elasticity of tone and rhythm.

It's essential to show the *crescendo* marked here in bar 2. Listen for the lovely harmony in the first quarter of bar 3. Any syncopations should be highlighted and accented more than passages in plain rhythm. Here, in the second quarter of bar 4, the note B flat is, first of all, syncopated, and secondly it forms a splendid harmony of C, G, D flat and B flat.

(The student repeats the opening of the second movement, and Neuhaus interrupts at bar 40.)

Bring out these wonderful pauses in bars 5 and 7. Then, in bar 12, the A octaves should sound like a full orchestra, followed by a sudden *piano*.

In this episode in bars 19-20 there is a splendid hint of lyricism. What exactly is going on here? The sustained F in the right hand should sound a little louder. Your F sounds too lightly. Seek out the right sonority and play into the notes a little more deeply:

At bar 21 in the left hand you should not make an accent on the third – the G and B flat – but listen out for how wonderfully it settles onto F and A. The entire splendour of this lies in the dissonances, 'false notes' that then resolve.

You may not agree with me, but the harmony in the unexpected D flat following the *crescendo* (in the last eighth note of bar 25) is amazingly bold. The unexpected chord on D flat gets slightly lost in your performance. I would play into it much more deeply. Then, after that, there are no pauses in this bar, and there is an immense difference between pauses and the dotted notes that we have here. But in your version we are getting pauses instead of dotted notes. You must hold on to those dotted notes:

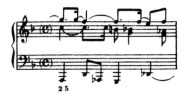

(*Neuhaus himself demonstrates both the correct and incorrect ways of performing this.*)

In this episode, in bars 30 and 33, all the editions have a pedal marked in. And it sounds splendid like that! When I analyze my musical feelings while performing such passages, I enjoy an aesthetic pleasure in the 'dangers' of such sound combinations and in preventing them from sounding wrong. That is, one hovers between pleasure and displeasure, fear that it might sound out of key, and pleasure at the result when it resolves on a concord. There is a particular splendour in all of this!

In order for bar 30 to sound well, you need to play the D flat in the bass more loudly, and all the rest quieter.

You should bring out the fourths in the left hand at bar 28 a bit more clearly. Play this passage once again. The D flat appears so unexpectedly that I would separate it slightly from what went before. Apart from which, it also helps the pedal. Bar 30, starting with the organ point, should be slightly separated from the previous one.

At bars 38-39 there is a slight divergence from the constant march-like rhythm, and here I allow myself to slow down and broaden out very slightly:

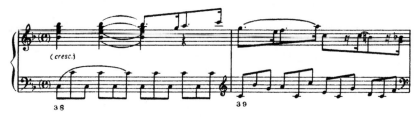

Do you sense the splendid feeling of 'emptiness' in these bars (Nos 34-35)?

At bar 40 a new series of exchanges begins, with brilliant imitation. There should be a big build-up here, more than you are giving it (bars 40-41):

This spot, at bars 45-46, is especially hard. Beethoven often has passages like this, where there are not many notes but a great deal of meaning – like an orator who expresses a lot of deep thoughts in very few words, without any decorative rhetoric. And Beethoven is like that – full of meaning, but without any external trappings, simple, economical, and significant. Pushkin, Shakespeare, and some other great artists had this trait in common. Starting in bar 45 there is a moment very typical of Beethoven: these modest thirds and sixths have to stand out in relief, and the octaves in the left hand must not drown them out. This is difficult to play. There's no doubt that Beethoven is much more difficult for a performer than any other composer:

Here, at bars 49-50, one wants to hear a good big sound. Beethoven writes *fortissimo* and even *sforzando*. And after that build-up we need a brilliant *ff*:

In the concluding phrase, bar 54, there are very few notes, so one therefore needs to very slightly exaggerate them to give them more sonority:

Moving on, in bars 55-56, try immediately to play *piano* and *dolce*, and to find a new colouration for this passage:

Here, despite the speed of the two sixteenth notes in the theme of the trio, they still have to have a melodic character. Here everything converses and sings. This is a canon for two voices. This sort of dialogue in canon form is quite often met in Beethoven. You should play this passage and admire it as you do so.

I'd like you to appreciate the richness and beauty of this melody. This is a real melody and a real dialogue, and if you work on the expressive sound of the actual melody, the habit will remain with you for life and will be applicable to other similar passages. Incidentally, this passage is close to Bach in conception. If you really work at it, it should develop beautifully.

In bar 60 there is a small *crescendo*, but you shouldn't lapse into even the slightest sentimentality. Also, the tone you produce is slightly monotonous. Last time I mentioned already that you can't play any melodic passage on the piano without some nuance of light and shade, as one can on other instruments, for instance. For us pianists it's absolutely vital to have richer nuances in our playing, so as to avoid the appearance of those 'telegraph poles' that I fear more than anything else. If instead of a melody we hear only separate notes, then the melody perishes and disappears. So give us more variety, and more light and shade. This is the most difficult passage, and it comes off worst of all in your playing, because it really is hard to play.

In bar 70 and after, thirty-second notes appear in both the left and right hand. But they shouldn't sound so aggressive as you make them. This is just a small and very expressive rhythmic nuance. The two thirty-second notes shouldn't be played too loudly, otherwise they take on a quite different character. In art every such minor detail always has some meaning and expresses a certain idea. It's like using words, and therefore you have to choose exactly the right words, and not just use any old expression:

In bar 70 a long *crescendo* also begins, but there is no *forte*. You're adding this on your own, but a *crescendo* that never reaches *forte* level is quite characteristic of Beethoven.

When the trill begins in bar 76, Beethoven immediately writes *diminuendo*, and there is no *forte*. This too is very typical, and it indicates that the dynamic gradation has to be gentle, and the volume increase never leads to any loud exclamation. Apart from which, there's no way of building a *forte* here since this is quite incommensurate with the tonal possibilities of two single voices. Considerations such as this must always be taken into account in order to play Beethoven well.

Starting with bar 84, one begins to sense a certain pensiveness. To start with there was a light and airy march, then a 'conversational' section, and now, finally, comes a moment of indecision and reflection.

At last there appear those long half notes that have not appeared before in this movement. It is a good idea to slow down slightly here, and listen to the bass part to prevent it becoming too dry. On the note C in the bass one should have a sense of double basses playing. There should be no clenching of the left hand. On the contrary, there should be nothing but calm, and no frisky playfulness. And in the right we want to hear the tune a little more – it's a wonderful melody.

One can well imagine the final bars in terms of orchestral sound, with flutes and timpani. This passage, again, is very hard to play because there are so few notes. But there's plenty there in terms of feeling, thought, and idea. This poses a special difficulty in playing Beethoven.

Now let's go on to the next movement.

(*The student plays the Adagio.*)

Here your *piano* sound – forgive the comparison – produces a somewhat 'consumptive' impression. In my view, all of this should be played rather more deeply, and then you can create more nuances; your sound is slightly restricted and superficial.

The first bar should be played completely freely. Listen how splendid it is. What a marvel that major is in bar 5, and the last sixteenth note of bar 6. I recommend that you look at von Bülow's edition. In his book *Lessons with von Bülow*, José Vianna da Motta talks precisely about this passage and also about the final chord, of which he says: 'It should sound as if it is something dear and familiar, and at the same time unexpected.'[4] The move from E minor transforms into the intonation of C major. It's difficult to substantiate, although I can well understand such pronouncements – although it's true, if one were to put together a whole piano method based on such statements, the result might well turn out as nonsense.

Try and play it once again. I want you to feel that miraculous change from minor to major.

One ought to learn how to play on such pieces as this. It should be played almost in an attitude of prayer. But you have too hard a hand. That style of playing might well be good for performing some pieces by Liszt, but it's not right here. Every move that one makes should be generated by some idea, by an attempt to create some particular expression, or a particular sonority. And you have to find the most appropriate habit of movement, like an actor discovering the most suitable gesture for a given situation.

The tone here should be songful and profound despite its muted level. And here it's all a question of one's way of playing. Your own playing is slightly anaemic, if you'll pardon my saying so. Last time when you played, your left hand was too loud and drowned out the melody. Evidently your manner of playing was not quite the right one. But you should search for the right one yourself – one has to learn how to search for these things.

There are certain things that one is allowed to enjoy and relish. But in the first bar all three notes of the first chord sound alike in your performance. You should make the upper voice sound slightly brighter.

The gentle, transparent chords in bar 5 should be delivered with modesty and care. Feel in these chords as if you would like to broaden them very slightly but are not allowing yourself to do so. The chords will then imperceptibly broaden out (in time) of their own accord.

(The student begins playing again, but Neuhaus once more interrupts.)

The thirty-second notes in the first bar should be made even more song-like, even more expressive. In bar 3 you had the upper voice emerge as a series of separate notes, but in fact there's a single slur marked here.

The aim of these classes is to help make your performance as accurate as possible, and to convey more clearly and profoundly all that the music expresses. It's worthwhile working at all this. Indeed this is the main thing, and perhaps the only thing, that needs doing. Everything else is relatively unimportant. When a person plays well, that's only the beginning. The real work only begins at the point where there's an understanding of the true difficulties. In addition, during this work one accumulates immense artistic experience, and a mastery on the basis of which you can later on improvise and create other performances.

Begin once again, please.

(The student begins playing again, but Neuhaus stops him after a few bars.)

The note G in your left hand (at the beginning of bar 9) sounds too forthright. It should sound as if played on the cello:

(*The student plays again but Neuhaus immediately stops him.*)

That's already better. But you'll have to do some more experimenting so that it's really expressive while retaining the same softness.

Moving on, I'd like the second eighth notes in bars 17 and 18 to be felt more. After all, these are syncopations and suspensions. And the chord in bar 19 should be played a little more deeply. And after that the *crescendo* continues, especially in the right hand; and I would play this figuration with the short notes more lively:

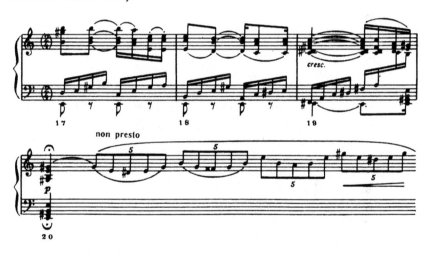

Incidentally, I'd like to tell you something that may not be of general importance, but it's a good example of an idea that to me is very important. This sonata was once played by one of our splendid women pianists. I had a good number of criticisms to make, but my main general objection was from a purely conductor's point of view, with an ability, as it were, to see things from a 'bird's eye view'. It was this vital quality as a performer that this lady singularly lacked. For instance, the entire third movement sounded very profound and expressive, after which the return of the theme of the first movement, which should sound free and lively, had a light and gracious character. This showed a failure to understand the artistic sense of the work as a whole. And in just the same way every day I hear my students play some detail very well, even many such details, but if one listens to the whole performance there is no sense of a complete whole. There is no plan. And this 'unplanned' work emerges in a lack of 'time flow', precisely the thing that creates a complete whole. Thinking about this compositional plan and the bird's eye view, I am always struck by the incredible intellectual stature of composers. This is often something difficult to grasp. You may easily understand and sense some detail, but it's far from easy to comprehend the work as a whole. This often requires a great deal of hard thinking.

To return to our work, I wasn't satisfied with this episode. Can't you hear what meaning there is in this indecisive phrase in bars 19-20? You need to create here an impression of marvellous indecisiveness. But I'm afraid that today we don't have any more time to work on this...

(Transcript of a master class)

NOTES

1 Artur Schnabel (1882-1951), the Austrian pianist, had made concert tours to Russia and the Soviet Union in 1911, 1924-25, and 1927-28.

2 Valentina Nikolayevna Shatskaya (1882-1978), Russian pianist, teacher, and promoter of music in schools. She succeeded Heinrich Neuhaus as Rector of the Moscow Conservatoire 1937-9.

3 Maria Solomonovna Nemenova-Luntz (1879-1954), Russian pianist, graduated 1902 under Scriabin at Moscow Conservatoire, where she was later professor 1922-54; author of memoirs on Scriabin as teacher and pianist (*Muzykal'nyi sovremennik*, 1916, No 4).

4 José Vianna da Motta (1868-1948), Portuguese pianist, conductor, composer and teacher, trained with von Bülow, Scharwenka and Franz Liszt; director of Lisbon Conservatoire 1919-38.

MARIA ESHCHENKO

Chopin's Études
[Based on classes with Samuil Feinberg]

The étude occupies an important place in Chopin's oeuvre. His works in this genre are distinguished by their profundity of idea and emotion, and their use of instrumental expressive resources was totally new at that time. Although they contain some piano writing of utmost difficulty, Chopin's études offer much more than mere exercises designed to develop pianistic virtuosity. Their technical complexities are always bound up with a great originality of ideas and poetic fantasy. So great is Chopin's mastery of form and content that even where he apparently starts out with some technical problem in mind, this ceases to be an end in itself and becomes the vehicle for some musical idea.

In his discussions of works by Chopin, Feinberg noted the peculiar étude-like character of several of his compositions. The finale of the Sonata in B flat minor, for instance, has a uniform texture, and the same rhythmic and melodic character throughout. Also of interest is the fact that this finale is in itself a creative reworking of the shorter Prelude in E flat minor. Maybe Chopin's initial pretext for writing his études was a desire to systematize and record his own achievement as a virtuoso pianist. Yet the result so far exceeded the initial aim that an entirely new field of creativity was opened up, Chopin in effect created a new genre in pianoforte literature.

Feinberg saw Chopin's compositions as irrefutable proof of his mastery as a performer. Only an executant of genius could discover the technical devices to express adequately such bursts of fantasy and inspiration. Chopin's instrumental resources were his own creation, and they were part and parcel of his compositional ideas. Even the most convolute forms of étude figuration doubtless arose in the course of his improvisations. Yet hardly any of his ideas occur in variant form, except for minor alternative readings in different editions. All the attempts made by numerous subsequent pianists and editors to 'correct' Chopin's texts have both lacked taste and betrayed an inferior level of artistry.

Many of Chopin's most difficult passages do not even permit alternative fingerings. Attempts by some pianists, such as Alfred Cortot, to supply the études with various alternative fingerings may well be of some interest, but they usually strike one as artificial or arbitrary in character. Seemingly the music itself was the prime stimulus for particular new movements of arm, wrist and fingers, and the result is a sheer perfection and total harmony of idea and expression.

In order properly to interpret Chopin's work, one must have some idea of his special qualities as a performer, and any approach to the harder and more complex études is only part of the broader problem posed by Chopin's pianism. How does Chopin strike us as an executant? Certainly, he was a great and in many ways unrivalled pianist. Various surviving contemporary accounts and Chopin's own remarks on the style and performance of his works suggest that his art was a rare example of the organic blend of form and content, and of the dependence of every technical aspect (tone production, touch, dynamic nuance, et cetera) on the composer's artistic intentions. If Chopin's playing lacked any qualities of rigidity, learning by rote, or pedantry, it was also devoid of anything that smacked of randomness: performance was subject to the logical development of musical ideas.

The soul of the instrument seemed revealed in Chopin's playing, and all his writing for the instrument was totally pianistic and barely conceivable in terms of any other sonority. One could say that Chopin's own playing was a sculptured and tangible manifestation of his lyrical ideas. In the dynamic, tempo, and other markings that Chopin placed in his compositions – sometimes in minute detail, sometimes scantily – he strove to record the vital, unrepeatable process of performance. These markings tell one plenty both about Chopin's own playing and also about correct interpretation of his works.

Chopin uses established musical terminology. Sometimes he uses a term such as '*Doppio movimento*' to give an exact tempo indication. At other times he provides only a general indication of sound quality such as '*Andante spianato*'. Very often he requires a reduction of tone to sotto voce, or *mezzo voce*. But the musical text is not overloaded with such markings, and excessive pedantic details are never there to hamper one's freedom of performance.

Samuil Feinberg emphasized the absolute distinction between some of

Chopin's performance markings and those of Beethoven. In Beethoven such marks do not just flow out of the style and texture, but are an actual guide for creating the characteristics of this style. Thus, for instance, an identical phrase or chord may in one instance be marked *forte*, in another – *piano*. In Chopin, though, texture and style are so closely connected with the manner of performance that they almost always predetermine the composer's written instructions. Without exaggeration it could be imagined that any adequately sensitive performer, even if unfamiliar with Chopin's own markings, would reproduce them in his own playing. Quite apart from what is spelt out by way of dynamics, tempo, *accelerando* or *ritardando*, Chopin's musical text itself always provides enough information on how to perform any piece. Therefore, if playing Chopin from an edition where one is uncertain about the authenticity of some marking or other, it is preferable to place one's trust in the stylistic features of the actual text.

In his lessons, Feinberg repeatedly emphasized the need to allow the character of the music to dictate one's entire approach as a performer, and he pointed out the mistake of some players in trying to vary and 'enrich' their performance with arbitrary dynamic or rhythmic touches that did not derive from the musical text itself. An example of an entirely congenial blend of Chopin's music and its interpretation is provided by Rakhmaninov's performance of the finale from the Sonata in B flat minor.

A lot can be left to the intuition of the talented player. However, one should point out a number of frequent misconceptions that lead to a distortion of Chopin's style. What in Chopin's playing was imagined to be a disturbance of the rhythm, or an absence of appropriately academic observance of meter, was in fact the free and natural breath of a genuine rhythm that did not always fit into an artificial metrical mould. The performer should thus carefully ensure that any rhythmic divergences are not merely arbitrary but are bound up with the style of the music. By carefully following gradual shifts in texture, and by observing the slightest movements in melodic line that may alternate broad and flowing phrases with short ones, the player can naturally discover that free and flexible rhythm that gives relief and brilliance to the composer's thought.

The basic tempo of a work is also decided by the same method. Feinberg described this as a certain 'average quantity that uniformly favours the general flow of the piece'. Feinberg also warned against any abrupt or unjustified changes of tempo or rhythmic outline. He forbade any *tempo rubato* that erased the distinction between note values – between eighth and sixteenth notes, say, or between sixteenth and eighth note triplets, et cetera. The more subtle and complex the rhythm of a work, the more painstakingly one should try to convey it. In other cases a metric sequence of equal notes (a melody moving in quarter or eighth notes) should sound fluent and flexible, with rhythmically fluctuating breath. But performance of the Études requires an especially precise rhythm, since when the same figuration keeps repeating, the slightest disturbance of tempo can be felt and destroys a sense of uniformity. In those instances when an étude's regularity of movement lies in the melodic line – e.g. in the A flat major and F minor of opus 10, the A flat major and E minor of opus 25, or the A flat study without opus number – the performer is expected to show some ability to breathe life into these sequences of notes.

The fact that changes of texture affect tempo can be observed in Chopin's variation forms. Often slight tempo changes are necessary when moving from one variation to the next. However, the composer does not always indicate a tempo change in such instances. Even with Beethoven, who does write tempo changes in his variations, one has to make small changes of tempo that are not indicated by the composer. This should convince us that a change of form in piano notation usually has some effect on the tempo. In Chopin's works, where the piano texture often plays a decisive artistic role, the character and style of musical statement are bound to cause some change or fluctuation in tempo. In the G minor Ballade, two different statements of a similar passage follow in succession, the second of these is almost always played slightly faster, and any sensitive pianist would here speed up to *agitato* even without any such indication from the composer:

Chopin's unusual polyphony demands understanding and careful attention from the pianist. Often a striking melody or theme starts in one voice and then, seemingly without completing its statement, turns into an accompanimental figure. Examples of this in Chopin are many, and some of them will be examined below in discussion of the A minor Étude from opus 25.

Chopin's first book of Études, published in 1833, contained several items written at an earlier date, and it represented a form of pianoforte compendium proclaiming new principles of performance and revealing unprecedented, rich new possibilities in technique and figuration. Liszt said of Chopin's Études that they would always remain 'models of perfection in this genre that he himself created, and like all his works they bear the hallmarks of genius'.

Both as composer and performer, Chopin aroused general astonishment at his new stylistic and technical revelations. Here there are inevitable comparisons with two great musicians from Russia, Rakhmaninov and Scriabin. However, whereas the full potential of Chopin's fantasy was unleashed in his own special area of piano composition, a large part of Rakhmaninov and Scriabin's creative powers crystallized in symphonic form, and also in vocal and chamber music in the case of Rakhmaninov.

In Chopin's rare combination of performing technique and creativity, not only does he conjure up new technical devices, but the actual technique of piano playing, the pianist's contact with the keys and his sense of certain fingering sequences often serve as pretext for the appearance and development of new artistic ideas. This is a special phenomenon in which technical performing skill is inspired by a unique combination in one person of both a great composer and a great executant. The loftiest achievement of this amalgam was probably manifest in improvisation at the piano – an art that Chopin had mastered to perfection, according to contemporary accounts.

A special feature of the piano is its capacity to offer the pianist-improviser opportunity to use every component of musical speech – melody, harmony and counterpoint. For Chopin this feature – the constant creation of a complete musical fabric – is his most inspired form of direct statement, never prescribed in advance and throwing up constant new discoveries. His melodic richness in itself is organically bound up with the variety of his pianism. In classifying his musical expression, we never revert to any stereotype musical cliché. His pianistic discoveries do not fit any pre-established categories of technical device. Indeed, one finds a tendency toward changeability rather than similarity, toward variety rather than repetition. Of course, one can trace certain trends in Chopin's invention of musical texture as well as a tendency to follow certain features of classical pianism: he writes études for broken chords and arpeggios, for developing 'independence of the fingers' or a light wrist, for chromatic scales, studies in thirds, sixths, octaves, and so forth – yet how far removed is their subtle and complex pianism from any routine understanding of such drills!

Naturally, every now and then one comes across cases of near 'duplication', exploiting one and the same formal discovery. Some of these are less striking, while others are full of new vitality, like the C sharp minor Étude, opus 25, and the central episode of Polonaise No 1 in the same key, the Prelude in E flat minor and the finale of the B flat minor Sonata, the Prelude in D minor and the F minor study from opus 10. Several further works, such as the G major Prelude and the C minor *Revolutionary* Étude, opus 10, or the larger A minor Étude of opus 25 and certain passagework in the C sharp minor Scherzo – works of diametrically contrasting mood – also emerge as related in the figuration that they use. On the other hand, every original composer has certain of his own typical turns of musical phraseology, or characteristic melodic or harmonic progressions. And in Chopin too we find favourite melodic figures or harmonic sequences that in varying degrees typify him and distinguish his musical language from that of all other composers. Yet here again one is astonished at the richness and variety of expression, and the composer's seemingly inexhaustible fund of imagination.

The virtuoso difficulties of Chopin's style can be seen as consequences of his own melodic animation. Here the actual melody generates complex, sometimes fantastically eccentric accompanimental figures that are indivisible from the melody itself, just as vocal timbre is often inseparable from the sung phrase. Almost always we find a fabric of subtle and bewitching sonority blending with the melody, completing it and revealing itself fully in the timbre of the piano. Once we have understood the quality and character of the musical fabric (what Feinberg termed as its 'textural cross-section'), we can better fathom the meaning and emotional saturation of the melody. The melody itself is not sung through to the end, and the listener's attention follows only the first appearance of the lyrical phrase, but at the same time the expressiveness and vividness of the accompaniment make so strong an impact that in one's imagination they already complete the composer's idea. The character of Chopin's exposition preempts the subsequent development of musical ideas, revealing the composer's concept already in the striking originality of his pianistic devices. At this point it would be useful to cite some of Feinberg's pronouncements concerning performance of some of the Études.

ÉTUDE IN A MINOR, OPUS 10, NO.2

This étude introduces the pianist to the difficulties of playing a melody based on chromatic sequences in which the upper voice is allocated to the third, fourth, and fifth fingers. It is extremely useful to practise playing it with four hands or on two pianos, using both hands to play the right hand part. It is also useful to learn to play freely the sixteenth note line, using the same fingering but without the accompanying chords. It is evident that a chromatic scale played with only the third, fourth and fifth fingers cannot be completely *legato*, since this would require the fifth finger to bend under sharply when playing rising sequences of 5-2 or 5-3, or conversely when descending with 4-5 or 3-5. However, this consideration should not be allowed to alter the basic character of this Étude, which should be fairly smooth and flowing. Moreover, ease and transparency do not preclude a *leggiero* execution in which the sound is produced by slighter briefer finger contact with the keys.

It is also useful to practice this Étude while introducing the same difficulties in the left hand. For instance:

In the same way one can recommend practising a left-hand part to the C major Étude, opus 10, No 7, as follows:

A similar exercise can also be devised for this A minor Étude, using contrary motion in the right and left hands – obviously not for the whole duration of the work, but for certain particular episodes. In view of this Étude's extreme difficulty, in order to rest the hand in the central episode, slight simplifications can be permitted by using the second finger and even the thumb for playing the chromatic passages. One should use more sparing, shallow pedal when the chromatic sequences lie in a higher register; in this way the pedal will be less noticeable. Totally impermissible, of course, is the pedalling indicated in Mikuli's edition, which metrically emphasizes each half-bar and unnecessarily weighs down the study, making it sound monotonous. A little pedal assistance is possible in those rare cases when an accompanimental chord is passed to the left hand for one of two beats in order to rest the right hand.

It is worthwhile learning the most difficult passages in the following groupings:

In discussing this Étude, it is essential to devote some space to a method of exercise often practised in Feinberg's class. He recommended basing each exercise on repetition of the same difficulty. Each link in the chain may have been mastered fairly well by the player, but the difficulty lies in maintaining uninterrupted movement of the whole passage. This concerns almost all forms of sequential passage, in which the movement has to be compressed into the shortest possible space of time. Some passages have to be practised using exercises in which the hand is taught to shape itself correctly at various points. One example is the flow of sixteenth notes in Chopin's G major Prelude:

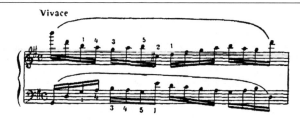

Here the right hand's sixteenth notes have also been written in for the left hand in contrary motion, since exercising with both hands is obviously more useful than with only one. Various links in this sequence can be pointed out, which, if performed uninterruptedly and very rapidly, will help players to master the difficulties of this passage. In this case other possible sequence links would be:

In this way the sequence can begin on any note in the passage. However, some sequences are more useful than others in studying this particular passage. It is best when the link begins on a weak beat of the bar. In this instance the most successful sequence is the first of the two. In the second example there is a slight fingering difficulty between the end of the link and the start of its repetition. If one can overcome this obstacle, and still achieve a clear and flowing execution, the slight awkwardness of fingering can be helpful in training the hand to take up position with speed and precision. Making intelligent use of this type of exercise, the pianist can choose the sequence that he finds most useful in overcoming any particular problem.

ÉTUDE IN C SHARP MINOR, OPUS 10, NO 4

In its texture, this Étude is one of the most typical of the genre. The left and right hand in alternation constantly have to negotiate the same type of difficulties. The rapid tempo of the piece is hardly ever interrupted. The placing of slurs also coincides exactly with hand and arm movements, and apart from a faultless finger technique, this Étude requires a virtuoso mastery of natural and essential turns of hand and arm while maintaining fluent finger movement. In the right hand this is especially necessary in passages such as:

A corresponding figuration for the left hand would be:

Although not all passages are executed only by these fingers, the pianist should strive wherever possible to retain the same fingering in all variants of this figure, particularly in the coda. Chopin is in general a master at combining precise finger technique with a unifying movement of the arm and hand corresponding to a phrase or slur mark. Whereas in its effort to develop strength and independence of fingers, the old pre-Chopin school tried to achieve this without movement of the whole arm and hand, it is typical of Chopin to coordinate finger movements with those of the hand as a whole.

The basic movement involved in this Étude is reminiscent of one in A major, opus 5, No 9, by Henselt, which can also be used as a preparatory exercise for mastering this pianistic figure.

One should point out the concealed part writing in certain passages of Chopin, for instance in bars 2, 8, and 11, and at several other points:

A frequent mistake to be avoided in playing this Étude is in allowing the light chords in the left-hand accompaniment (also similar passages in the right) to break the flow of sixteenth notes – if instead of moving in an unbroken stream, these break up into groups of four, the whole Étude will sound monotonous and mechanical.

Unlike the basic *leggiero* touch required for most of the Étude, some of the upbeats should be slightly (but only slightly) heavier, and are best played more *legato*. The octaves on the fourth beat of bars 16, 18, 26, and elsewhere, should be emphasized not as isolated *sforzandi*, thereby breaking the flow, but as the upbeat leading into the next phrase. The consistency of a slight *legato rinforzando* is felt particularly in bars 41-43:

A few bars excepted, this Étude requires a light touch throughout. Pedal should be sparing, and should be used to emphasize slightly the small *rin-forzandi*. In no way should the pedalling disturb the basic flow of the piece, particularly when this is maintained by the left hand.

'REVOLUTIONARY' ÉTUDE IN C MINOR, OPUS 10, NO 12

This Étude is full of revolutionary pathos and dramatic animation. The actual melody arises in original manner from the top notes – C, D, and E flat – in the storming left-hand part. Alternating *forte* and *piano* create an impression of gusting wind that carries the melody to the listener, sometimes rising, sometimes fading. Here, once again, one should point out the seeming contradiction between the 'artistic simplicity' of the piece and the difficult problems of its execution. The image of storm and revolutionary pathos is conveyed by Chopin with marvellous clarity, and this Étude will always remain a favourite of both pianists and listeners with its irresistible drama and blend of formal expressivity and content. This amalgam indeed demonstrates the highest form of simplicity, the achievement of a genius. Every note is made to count, there is nothing superfluous, yet nothing left unsaid. It is precisely this perfection that makes performing the piece so difficult, and any technical blemish immediately shows up as an artistic infelicity and distortion of musical image and idea.

Chopin is not a composer who cultivates imitative style. Usually in his work separate voices develop freely and independently. Particularly interesting therefore is the thematic interaction of melody and accompaniment in this Étude. In addition to the link between the first three melody notes and the left-hand passage, the following moments are also worth noting:

This phrase represents a toned-down version of the initial exclamatory out-bursts at the opening of the piece.

The figuration in the left hand in the central episode of the Étude is the first occurrence of sixteenth notes flowing in this form:

In this way one can see, at least in part, how Chopin achieves a sense of monolithic unity in his composition without resorting to imitation.

The *crescendo* and *diminuendo* markings in the left-hand passages should create a wave effect, and the *crescendo* should not reach the top note in such a way as to cut off the crest of the wave.

In bars 38 and 40 one should bring out the dramatic alternation of D flat and D natural by accenting these.

The tension wanes at the end of the work. The final *piano* recalls a similar onset of tranquillity in the coda of the first movement of Beethoven's Sonata, opus 111.

One of the Étude's greatest difficulties lies in playing the energetic *crescendo* up to the top notes of the left-hand passage in bar 9 and elsewhere. Various ways of practising can be tried in order to achieve the necessary force and precision of sonority. The most important thing is to shape the hand at the right moment for the movement it is required to make. It is useful to practise starting with the highest notes of the passage and use a particular phrasing:

There is little disagreement about the fingering to use in this study. The pedal should assist the wave-like motion of the left hand. In bars 38 and 40, the pedal should be used to give necessary duration to the chromatic change from D flat to D natural.

ÉTUDE IN E MINOR, OPUS 25, NO 5

The basic tempo and character of this piece are reminiscent of the lightness and the precise, piquant rhythm of some of Chopin's mazurkas. Here, as in the previous études, each successive phrase is stated in a manner slightly differing from the previous one. This is a special form of musical development built on constant variation, yet these changes in manner of statement do not lead to any structural breakdown.

Evidently the two styles of statement are similar. In both cases the grace-note falls on the beat and is probably equivalent to a sixteenth note. In the second example below, however, the upper note is to be more prominent.

The left-hand grace-notes in front of the notes D and B (bars 21-24 in the first part, and repeated in the reprise) are presumably weaker and are played before the beat; this is indicated by the stress mark over the half note

However the execution of the grace-note moving from weak to strong beat contrasts with the basic rhythmic flow of the Étude. This adds further variety to the treatment, emphasizing the middle voice against the delayed auxiliary notes in the other parts. The grace-notes have the effect of restraining the basic tempo, which then picks up again in the following bars and returns us to the original beat. In the Étude there is a general tendency to make an imperceptible *accelerando* in those episodes where the piquant dotted rhythm is replaced by flowing eighth notes.

The central episode of the Étude has a left-hand melody accompanied by right-hand figuration that has an unforgettably lovely, melting, poetic quality. This is another example of figuration that contains concealed melodic strata and echo effects. Although the statement first occurs in eighth notes, followed by a variation using sixteenth notes, a concealed melodic voice can be heard running throughout. Chopin himself provides a polyphonic resolution of it in bar 87:

The E major episode of the Étude should thus not be oversimplified and viewed merely as a left-hand melody with empty figuration in the right. In bars 3-4 of the central episode, the melody notes are already echoed in the right-hand figuration, and this should be pointed up lightly in performance. And in general one should pay attention to the main melody's frequent concessions to the other voice or voices. Thus, for instance, in the Étude's middle section, starting on the third quarter note of bar 58, the left hand loses its melodic priority and takes up the normal function of a bass part, while the right hand seems to continue the melody, offering variations on the main theme of the Étude. The textural layout here shows this similarity between the right hand and the opening of the Étude. The episode starting in the right hand at bar 61 should also not be regarded as mere accompaniment. On the contrary, the melody concealed within the figuration is far more interesting and expressive than the bass line, and it could be written out as follows:

ÉTUDE IN A MINOR, OPUS 25, NO 11

This Etude is one of Chopin's most important compositions. Despite the greater popularity of the C minor Étude, opus 10, this work has no equal among the other études in the grandeur of its conception and thematic material, and in the richness of its expressive resources.

The work has a four-bar introduction. The main theme is first stated *piano* by one voice. Bars 3-4 more or less repeat the same phrase with accompaniment. On the last quarter notes of this introduction it is essential to make a small *crescendo* in order that the start of the Étude proper does not sound too sudden.

The first phrase, starting in bar 5, is triumphantly assertive. The second (at the lower octave with the third omitted from the triad) is slightly more restrained.

The voice writing should be carefully observed. The left-hand part in fact consists of two voice parts:

This two-part writing is important, and the left hand should not be played as though it consisted one single thematic line.

At bar 41, the theme is passed for a short time to the right hand. Played at this higher register, it acquires even greater urgency and power.

The whole Étude should be played with full tone, *plena voce*. In order that the climactic moment is properly prepared and sounds even more expressive and significant, one can make a slight reduction in tone in bars 47-8. When working on this Étude, it is very useful to try transferring the same technical difficulties to the left hand.

The Étude requires skilful pedalling. It is important to use the pedal in order to point up the middle voice that carries the melody, separating it out from the bass accompaniment. At the same time one must watch that the chromatic upper voice and figuration sound clearly and without smudging, especially at those points where the right-hand part lies in the lower register. This is because in bar 8 the bass has a *tenuto* and is written out as a long note. The same occurs also in bar 16:

The brilliance and power of the right-hand part is achieved not only with finger strength, but using a technique characteristic of Chopin and combining finger movement and *tremolo* motion of the wrist and hand. The work demands great exertion and stamina from the performer, and an ability to bring off the pathos and heroics of the main theme combined with the figurative passagework in the right hand.

YAKOV FLIER

Reflections on Chopin's Fourth Ballade

Anton Rubinstein once maintained that 'no composer up to the present day has surpassed the poetry and magic of Chopin, that master who truly became the "soul of the pianoforte"... Songster, rhapsodist, spirit and soul of his instrument – that is Chopin.' Today there is hardly a single pianist whose repertoire does not contain a few of Chopin's works – be it his great compositions in tragic vein, or else his poetic dithyrambs, elegiac lyrical works, or the passionate and impetuous Scherzi. In the Soviet Union young people are brought up on Chopin, and for this reason I have chosen to analyse and discuss the F minor Ballade, opus 52, in the pages that follow. I have frequently performed this work in public, and have worked through it even more often with various pupils. In my view it is a true masterpiece of pianoforte literature, and it brings together and distils all the most important traits of Chopin's style.

In the main Chopin limited himself almost exclusively to works for the piano. As an eminent and unique performer himself, he discovered new and unprecedented expressive powers in his instrument. He enriched music with a wealth of new images, moods and ideas, and also prepared the way for previously unknown piano sonorities, expanding the scope of piano technique and firmly establishing a series of new musical genres created during the Romantic era. Foremost among these are the four Ballades. All of them are overwhelmingly confessional works: all four Ballades were written between 1835 and 1843, while Chopin was in exile. His music of that period was filled with a sense of love and yearning for his country, and with the possible exception of the Third Ballade, all these works exude an air of inexpressible grief. According to Robert Schumann and Chopin's own testimony, the Ballades were evidently prompted by his reading of poems by the Polish poet Mickiewicz.

Chopin left no detailed comment on the subject of his Ballades. He disliked talking about his works and never wrote about them. But thanks to their evocative pictorial quality, their striking themes and poetic colour, Chopin's Ballades are as easily comprehended as any actual work of programme music.

The nineteenth century saw the rise of a whole series of works deriving from, or associated with, literary narrative models. These included ballades, novelettes, legends, fairytales, and so forth. Prime examples include the Ballades of Chopin, Brahms and Grieg, the *Légendes* of Liszt, and Schumann's Novelettes. Such quasi-narrative compositions are all based on a combination of three elements - the epic, the lyric, and the dramatic. An epic quality emerges in the narrative gesture, especially in the works' opening themes, which are marked by an even, balanced melodic and rhythmic movement, corresponding maybe to the flow of human speech.

Structurally, the opening themes of Chopin's Ballades are distinguished from others of their type by their pronounced repetitive features and their strong element of variation that in some ways recalls the strophic construction of a poetic ballade text. The opening sections of all four Ballades are fashioned broadly and with great variety. They are based on a strong contrast between the narrative, or epic, main theme and a lyrical second subject that seems to exemplify a different world of visions and dreams. The one exception here is the Second Ballade, in which the themes are like two contrasting pictures, diametrically opposed in mood – an initial lyrical 'blossom' that is then swept away by the storm. The development and reprise sections of the Ballades show a continuous sequence of growing dynamic tension leading, as in many literary ballades, to a tragic finale. Chopin's Ballades are four musical poetic tales, four variously fashioned artistic forms, and their unusual conception prompted the introduction of a whole series of new and finely poised expressive pianistic devices whose subtlety and boldness evoked the admiration of Schumann and many contemporaries.

The Fourth Ballade is perhaps the most profound and intense of Chopin's works in this genre. It stands out from the rest by its graphic vividness, emotional concentration, and directness. It is difficult to talk here of any historical, legendary, or fairytale subject matter. This Ballade is a lyrical confession, an acute psychological drama that seems to hint at the final downfall of life's ideals. It has a peculiar spiritual poetry and a rare sublimity that mark both its melodic line and harmony. There is, too, a deep sense of sorrow culminating in genuine tragedy in the final coda. The Fourth Ballade thus stands alongside Chopin's most dramatic works, together with the B flat minor Sonata, the F minor Fantasy, the Polonaises in F sharp minor and E flat minor, the B minor Scherzo, the C minor Nocturne, and the Mazurkas of opus 44, Nos.1 and 2, opus 46, No 3, and opus 56, No 3.

Let me now offer a few specific ideas on Chopin's Fourth Ballade, opus 52, and try to explain my own views on its interpretation. The Ballade opens with a short but highly significant introduction that is lucent, contemplative, and at the same time elegiac in tone. One thinks of Pushkin's lines, 'Bright is my sorrow...' To convey this on the piano, the player needs to discover and bring out the various sonorities of his instrument: the tenderest *pianissimo* in the right hand, rising up almost from nowhere, gradually and imperceptibly moving to a *mezzo piano*. In the left hand meanwhile, the most striking note should be the first E natural, followed immediately by a *diminuendo*. There are thus two planes of sound – a steady and gentle *crescendo* in the upper voice, and a fine smooth *diminuendo* in the lower one:

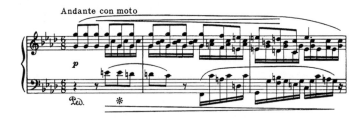

This introductory motif is heard twice, the second time in slightly altered form and requiring a fuller and more assertive tone.

I recommend playing the start of the Ballade with absolutely loose arm, using the hand to sink, without forcing, into the octaves. The upper G in the right hand should be a little brighter than the lower one, and the arm should therefore incline slightly toward the fifth finger.

The first five octave eighth-notes should be taken on one pedal, after which there should be a gentle and almost imperceptible pedal change on almost every eighth note. This should help create the impression of a radiant but suffused aura of light. The main theme in itself already reveals a variety of feeling seen in the transition from elegiac reflection to the brighter mood in bars 11 and 12, followed by a subsequent increase in anguish. This is largely underlined by the persistently repeating C in the melody. The whole of the first subject moves along in a free and improvisatory fashion:

a tempo [Andante con moto]

There is a particular problem with the correct choice of tempo for this Ballade. If the pace is held back unnecessarily, the natural line of musical discourse will be lost. On the other hand, even a slight increase over the prescribed 'Andante con moto' may introduce an incongruous waltz-like effect that would be quite out of place.

The structure of the theme with its many repetitions can also mislead the inexperienced pianist into thinking in terms only of one-bar phrases with, again, a consequent loss of overall coherence. To overcome this risk, when working on the theme one should try to achieve a songlike tone, with a sense of animated improvisation, sensitive pedalling, and thinking in long breaths or phrases. To avoid unwanted fragmentation of the theme, students should also be warned against making any *ritardando* at the end of each bar – even at those moments when only the left-hand accompaniment is sounding. The restatement of the theme, in A flat major, requires a new and brighter colouration and timbre. Thereafter each key change should be underlined, both tonally and with a smooth *rubato*. Still, however, no seams should be allowed to show in the musical fabric, and there should be no breaks in the general melodic development.

The listener should be made clearly aware of all three components: the sound of the melody, the sustained bass notes, and the accompaniment in the middle voices. In shaping the bass line, the pedal should be depressed fairly deeply, and with so-called half-pedal on each ensuing melody note. When the bass rises up an octave and thus reduces the distance between it and the middle voices, it should be sustained for the duration of a dotted quarter note, while the pedal should be changed with each melody note.

The still more animated restatement of the main theme (in my view, one of the composer's sincerest and heartfelt laments) leads to another episode of contrasting content:

I would emphasize that the contrast is here one of actual content. Very often musical contrasts are more ones of tone or dynamics – in many sonatas by Scarlatti or Haydn, for example. It is only when one pictures and experiences this sudden mysterious stillness, a benumbed sensation following some deeply felt revelation, that one can begin to depict this in musical terms. First of all, this is a place where the soft pedal is called for, and not simply because of the marking 'pianissimo'. The pianist must discover a completely different perspective of sound, use a different palette, with a new tone colour, hushed and mysterious. One must strive also for an absolute *legato*, a sense of 'creeping' in the bass octaves, and of course an absolute evenness of touch. It is no use here relying simply on the sustaining pedal – it too is obviously essential, but it must at the same time remain transparent and 'breathe'.

Here it is extremely useful to practise the legato octaves without help from the sustaining pedal. One must strive to ensure a perfect continuity between the third, fourth and fifth fingers, and at least try for an approximation to *legato* with the thumb as it works its own way through the part. All this can be achieved, though, by keeping the fingers as close as possible to the keys. It should be said, incidentally, that it is enormously important for a pianist to have a complete mastery of *legato* octaves. Without this it would be impossible to play properly several entrancing and important episodes in piano literature, for instance at the start of the second piece in Schumann's *Kreisleriana*:

or the following passage from the second movement of Brahms's Second Piano Concerto:

Mastery of legato octave technique is also a fundamental requirement for the whole of Chopin's B minor Etude, opus 25, especially in its central cantilena episode:

One could readily add to this list of examples. Returning, though, to the passage in question in Chopin's Fourth Ballade, I should also emphasize how important it is to achieve absolute synchronization and tonal equality in playing the chill harmonies in those right-hand chords. Here is one passage where one need not follow the standard practice of always underlining the top notes!

After this, the modified and more animated principal theme returns with new expressive force. One should not be shy about pursuing the climax through to the end, even thought the melody is eventually left hanging without any harmonic support.

This is yet another example of the astonishing boldness and originality of

Chopin's writing.

The third statement of the main theme (bars 58 and following) hardly requires any special commentary. The sinewy, compact writing, saturated with expressive supporting parts, has a sonority typical of Chopin and it automatically requires a different set of dynamics for its performance. The emotional tension rises steeply and it must move *consistently* toward the dramatic climax of this first episode. Working with students, I have often observed them trying to deal with this passage, as it were, *en passant*, and I have had to explain to them the development of this episode and point out why they have wrongly gauged the dynamic line. Too heavy treatment of the texture in this passage can end up by spoiling its most attractive and precious feature – the reappearance of the theme enriched by new polyphonic elements. A true musician must be able to perceive and bring out the tonal proportions of a passage such as this, making it part of the overall conception of the work as a whole.

The third statement of the theme with its stronger internal animation and tension leads to the subdominant, B flat major, and its sublime and splendidly radiant second subject. I picture this passage in terms of a silvery mountain stream flowing into a still and majestic lake. Such a poetic parallel here seems apposite in view of the barcarolle rhythm of the second subject, which is, incidentally, typical of several lyrical themes by Chopin:

This passage is also reminiscent of an episode in the same composer's *Barcarolle*, opus 60:

Also in the Second Ballade in F major:

This untroubled, guileless melody in B flat requires from the pianist a crystal clear tone and an ability to savour each harmony. It brings to an end the first section, or exposition, of the Fourth Ballade.

Serenity and equilibrium are short-lived however. The first notes of the development section, starting in bar 100, introduce and atmosphere of alarm and unrest. The brightness and poise of the second subject give way to hectic impetuosity. Typical of this section is its unstable tonality, and in the kaleidoscope of key changes G minor and A minor are juxtaposed amid an aura of lacy figuration. The main theme is then reworked and inflected with more and more decisiveness, and the commanding intonations of the introductory theme now also intrude on the dialogue. After a subtle modulation to A major at bar 129 the dreamily contemplative introductory theme is heard again, this time even more tranquil than before. Then everything fades and dissolves in a cadenza that recalls the rustle of some light breeze. Here the pianist must conjure forth the most delicate aquarelle tones, the fingers must be almost weightless and slightly extended, 'caressing' the keys, and there should be an illusion of barely perceptible movement. Then, once again, from a single note the main theme re-germinates and gently starts to unfold:

But the emphasis has now completely changed. The theme now sounds uncertain and unstable as it emerges almost gropingly from a distant labyrinth. The solo melody is joined by a second and then a third voice in a strange form of imitation. The voices roam around, following one another in ghostly fashion as though seeking some escape from their brooding. Finally, though, they return to the original idea. Even for Chopin this whole episode is exceptional in its subtlety and inspiration. Only a superb ear and sophisticated tone control can help in recreating these fine nuances from the keyboard. I would suggest the following dynamic scheme for performing the main theme at the start of the reprise: the first emergence of the theme at bar 135 – *pianissimo*; the second statement starting at bar 147 – *mezzo piano*; and the third, at bar 156 and following – *mezzo forte*.

In the F minor Ballade it is the main theme that undergoes most development. Starting with its first appearance in the exposition and moving through to the reprise, this theme appears several times in a series of variations that constantly add further nuances. The particularly fine and airily decorated variations in the reprise show a multitude of caesuras in the melodic line, that becomes progressively more expressive and increasingly appears to speak and breathe. The dynamics also develop and move toward the main climax of the work. Interestingly, many players seem to suggest that the reprise is intended to be much faster moving than the exposition. But this is not the case. The pace of the reprise still remains 'Andante con moto'. It is simply that whereas the exposition basically moved in eighth notes, the reprise tends to move along in sixteenths, which are sometimes grouped in triplets, so that compared with the original exposition the total number of notes in any measure is much greater.

I am convinced that maintaining an overall inner pulse rate is a most important factor in giving this work a formal unity and consistency. This must be felt and conveyed by the interpreter; only then will the Ballade emerge as an integrated and inspired piece of musical narrative.

A striking feature of the Ballade's reprise is the extent of improvisatory elements in the general variation development of the main theme. And paradoxical though it may at first seem, the actual performance of the work must be fairly precise and disciplined. Otherwise the improvisatory element written into the text, multiplied by the same factor in performance, can produce a sense of total chaos. Special attention should be paid to the numerous pauses in the upper voice that creates a feeling of breathlessness and unrest.

Here a sovereign pedal technique and perfect legato are indispensable. These assist in bringing out the melodic contours of the theme and are a guarantee against self-indulgent virtuosity, which would run counter to the whole spirit of the piece.

The appearance and development of the second subject in the reprise carry a quite different accent from the exposition. After the original mood, the romantic drama is now intensified and brought into line with the urgent dramatic tone of the whole work. A gigantic build-up leads to the climax of the Ballade – a calamity expressed in an avalanche of chords that spreads and expands outwards in opposite directions as it accelerates:

After this the formidable interjection that appears to bring the whole movement to a standstill seems like some triumph of evil:

Here on no account should there be any *ritenuto* on the last three chords, although so many pianists seem incapable of resisting this temptation. The basic effect should surely depend on the unprecedented suddenness of this menace. But the episode reaches no conclusion and it breaks off abruptly on the brink of the abyss.

After this fearful break, the composer might have been expected to plunge headlong into the final whirl of the dramatic epilogue. But before the coda, quite unexpectedly, comes a solemn, still, chorale-like colonnade of chordal 'stalactites':

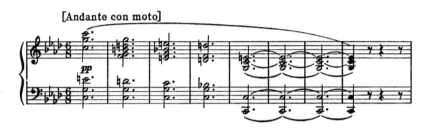

Chopin here sets two moods in contrast – the cold, tomb-like stillness of the chordal episode and the storming tragic urgency of the coda. Why this sudden freezing of all movement? What is conveyed by this sudden calm? Perhaps after the preceding fearful outburst of feeling, this is a momentary inability to proceed with the final tragic summing-up? Perhaps this is a final musing, a desire to hearken one last time to the stillness of nature before the final storm that will sweep everything away?

As we said earlier, the Ballade has no concrete programme, and I have no desire to limit the interpreter's fantasy with my own interpretations. A few final practical hints for performing the coda: The first section, starting at bar 211, is full of new melodic developments and rapidly shifting harmonies, and it does not call for an excessively fast tempo. There should be time and space in which to demonstrate the power and tragic sequence of events. The main essential in playing all this music, in fact, is *maximum expressiveness*.

Particular difficulty is caused by the two right-hand passages of successive rising perfect and diminished fifths. For ease of performance and in order to achieve a firm tone, I suggest leaving only the chords of the fifth to the right hand, and the single notes between each chordal pair should be taken with the left hand:

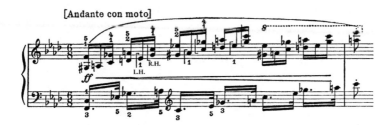

[Andante con moto]

This swarm of rising fifths should in my opinion begin more correctly on an E flat in the upper voice, despite the fact that most editions (as here) have an F natural at this point. In my view, a final confirmation of the tonic F minor is not yet meant to occur in this passage. The concluding *accelerando* should be played strictly according to Chopin's instructions – beginning in bar 227 and continuing through to the end in a single breath.

It is hard to describe music in words – even harder to demonstrate a work without the help of a piano, and to provide a complete account of one of the great masterpieces of piano literature. Unfortunately, no words can adequately convey the sound of this miracle of Romantic writing. When words fail, music alone can speak. But I shall feel adequately rewarded if my ideas on performing Chopin's Fourth Ballade are able to stimulate players or teachers in their own artistic explorations of this masterpiece.

ALEXANDER GOLDENWEISER

Notes on Chopin's Ballade in F Minor

The opening of this Ballade is more difficult to perform than appears at first sight. Before starting to play, one should concentrate for two or three seconds and imagine the basic pulse of the work in order that the very first notes one plays form part of this rhythmic flow, instead of having to search around for the right tempo once having started. I well remember Rakhmaninov often talking about this when he and I played two-piano music together. This sense of the 'time flow' of a work is very important – it is something that is there before the first notes sound, and it still continues after the last note has died away. Beethoven for instance, often placed a *fermata* over the final rest at the end of his pieces.

The left-hand theme should be played expressively from the very outset (example 1), whereas the repeated G octaves in the right hand are there initially only in order to set the rhythm. They should be played quite simply, like an echo, and only on the second note of bar 2 do they become part of an actual theme, where the left hand plays its final C. The pedal should be changed on each eighth note of this passage. On the broken chord of a 10th (E-G) in the right hand, the lower note should coincide with the bass note C (example 2):

The sixteenth notes in example 3 should be played without pedal – also elsewhere in similar passages. In example 4, the left-hand chords should be gentle and not sound too thick:

There should be breathing spaces between separate episodes of the Ballade, and they should not be run together by use of the pedal.

In the motif quoted in example 5, the final note is extremely important. Here it is a quarter note, elsewhere it is an eighth note. Sometimes it is held, sometimes cut short. All these details should be carefully noted and observed when playing.

The octaves (example 6) should not be played as if they represented some totally new idea, but they should flow out of what went before. The pedal should be changed on each eighth note:

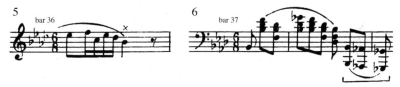

The entire passage that starts as in example 7 should be played evenly, *pianissimo*, *legatissimo*, with the soft pedal depressed, and without any undue 'expression'. The D flat in example 8 should be clearly audible.

Many modern pianists have lost all sense of the purity of a melodic line. In fact, though, this is not so much a recent habit; it is bound up with the style cultivated by composers and performers of the Impressionist period. The merging of different timbres that is typical of Debussy, Ravel, and the late Scriabin often produces some lovely tone colours and interesting sonorities, but this should not replace an attempt to achieve clean melodic lines, which are so vital in conveying the sense of a musical work.

The imitations in example 9 should be clearly heard: first the upper voice, then the middle, then again the upper. After which both parts should sound out with equal strength. The main notes here in each motif are the top ones: B flat, E flat, A flat, et cetera, and not the sixteenth notes that are nevertheless frequently allowed greater prominence.

At bar 54 (example 10) one should feel the end of the phrase, then make a fresh start on the next one:

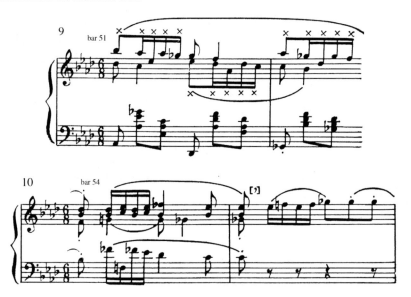

In the next episode with its thicker texture, it is not uncommon for players to start off already with a *forte*, but it is better to begin *piano* and fairly calmly, and then gradually work things up.

The second subject in B flat should have the character of a placid narration – this contrasts with its later statement in D flat major, which has a more dramatic quality. The calmer one's hand position in this first statement, however, the smoother it will sound.

In example 11, the first D natural begins the phrase:

Here, in example 12, lift everything off in order to register the eighth note rest.

The middle voice part in example 13 is an interpolated phrase; it should sound extremely calm and gentle.

On the E flat chord (example 14) it is sometimes useful when practising to pause and listen whether anything else is sounding on besides the notes of this chord.

Here again, in example 15 (bar 99), clear everything before starting the new phrase. The left hand notes (example 16) should sound significant. Similarly in the next bar also.

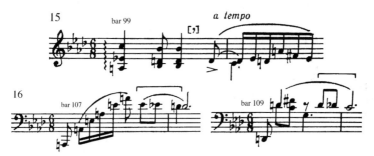

At bar 112 (example 17) take off the pedal on the third eighth note. The D flat in the left hand (example 18) should draw some attention to itself.

In example 19 one should be careful that the F sharp does not stand out too prominently.

When I have eventually shuffled off this mortal coil, I hope that my students will continue preaching my message about how important it is in music to have a sense of rhetoric. For me this is of utmost significance. A lot of people, however, regard this as mere pedantry on my part, and they play, as it were, without any 'punctuation marks'. The result is the same as if you were reading aloud and stopped in the middle of a word, or ran one word into the next, or else placed the stress wrongly – in short, it sounds as if someone were reading in a language they do not understand. But if the reader, or player, makes no logical emphases and pauses, the result is total nonsense.

It is essential that the imitative exchanges be clearly heard in the first and second soprano voices (example 20):

Then bring out the top part again, and in the next bar the upper set of sixteenth notes (example 21). The middle voice of bar 125 (example 22) should also be slightly pointed up. Similarly later on also.

When this theme (example 23) comes again, there should now be a sense of forward impetus. The player should not appear to be simply sitting there and nonchalantly strumming away!

The C in the left hand at this point (example 24) is part of a new entry and should be played with appropriate meaning. Also. later on, the E flat at bar 143.

The left hand in bar 152 and following (example 25) should be played absolutely evenly without any sense of leaping around. At points such as in example 26 and subsequently, do not dismiss this as mere passagework and decoration. It is all melodic material and should be played accordingly.

At bars 213 and following, the passagework should convey a sense of culmination, as though a peak of excitement has been reached and we now all tensely await what lies in store. It should not merely sound as if the pianist has finished playing his melody and is now whiling away the time with a few casual arpeggios! In the next passages of upward rushing unison make sure to take the pedal off in good time, otherwise the ends of the phrases will sound muddy.

In the coda (example 27) it is better to play E flat rather than F. I much prefer this as it further increases the tension, rather than prematurely releasing it.

not:

The three accents (example 28), on D flat, F and F, were placed there by Chopin, and they should be observed:

KONSTANTIN IGMUNOV

Chopin's Fourth Ballade in F Minor

(A verbatim account of a master class, following a student's performance)

Everything you do is perfectly correct. Your use of pedal was good, although maybe you change it almost too often. All the same, everything was splendidly clean and clear. I also agree with your choice of tempi.

With this Ballade there is a constant danger with the choice of tempo. People often play it too slowly, which produces a sort of nocturne effect. But this is, after all, a ballade, and even Chopin's slower tempo markings are not quite so slow as some people think. For instance, according to the author's metronome marking, the C sharp minor Étude, opus 25, No 7, should be faster than people play it nowadays. The D flat major Nocturne, opus 27, No 2, is also usually performed very slowly, whereas according to Chopin's marking it should be *animato*. Why should this be so? Perhaps partly because on Chopin's grand piano the sound was less sustained than on a modern instrument, but maybe part of the fault also lies with modern performers...

The Ballade in F minor is marked '*Andante con moto*', and it should therefore not be too slow. It also has some really animated passages, and if these are played too slowly the piece will tend to fall apart.

In Russia they keep reprinting the Klindworth edition. This is a pity, because Klindworth introduces a lot of things that the author never intended, and his fingerings are also too individualistic.

Let us start the Ballade from the beginning again. I found your introductory phrases too 'whispered', and this made them sound rather insignificant. They should have more emphatic meaning, because later on they are going to be repeated again, and more than once. In fact they form a sort of opening proposition, or an epigraph placed at the head of the Ballade. The first phrase should be started *piano*, with a climax on the G at the fourth eighth note in bar 2:

In this introduction there should also not be too much *ritenuto*. I think that initially there should be none at all. Otherwise the whole episode falls to pieces and sounds monotonous. In the two continuous phrases there should also not be absolutely identical *rubato*: if you slow down and accelerate at the same point in each phrase, this will sound too uniform. Repetitive *rubato* does not breath life into a performance but simply breaks it up. It is good to spread your *rubato* not over two bars, but over a broader phrase, even over the whole episode. This avoids any sense of fragmentation, and you can vary the bars and avoid having the same thing each time. If, say, you play the phrase straightforwardly the first time and the second time make a slight *accelerando* followed by a *ritardando*, the effect will be to combine everything and make a complete whole. There is nothing in the text to indicate a *ritenuto* in the first or second statements of the phrase; in the text the *ritenuto* comes only in bars 6-7.

The left-hand part in bars 1-2 should form a complete phrase, with a diminuendo from the D down to C. And you should also find a suitable tone quality for this phrase.

The note C in bars 7-8 should not be played on the previous pedal. You might touch the pedal again slightly, but it should not be kept down fully for the whole bar. One should also be aware of the counterpoint in bar 5 (in the middle voices), but it is not necessary to bring it out especially.

What about the left-hand accompaniment starting in bar 8? Remember that these chords in the left hand should be kept separated. Chopin has neither slurs nor *staccato* marks. There is nothing to be gained by playing the chords *legato*.

In the phrase in bars 8-9 the *mezza voce* marking might seem curious, but it should be strictly followed. Do not hold the B natural in bar 8 for too long – try to preserve a single continuing line. The difficulty in playing this theme lies in its repetitive phrasing. If we throw in all our expressive resources at the very outset, it will be difficult to maintain interest toward the end without lapsing into some sort of artificial, arbitrary 'expressiveness'. Initially, when the theme is still fresh, it should be played as simply as possible without major fluctuations. Slight tempo variations are possible, but major rhythmic distortions should be avoided. As the piece progresses, though, the rhythmic complexity can increase. But the dynamics should be clearly and carefully graded. The first statement of the theme (bars 8-12) should be tranquil; the second episode (starting at bar 23) – more disturbed and expressive. The sixteenth notes at bar 10 should be neither pulled back nor rushed. Play them calmly and let them lead naturally up to the E flat. As regards the pedal, do not let it sound 'empty', and keep the pedal properly down. Chopin takes it off on the third eighth note, and most players usually do this, but not always. In bars 9-11, a *crescendo* and *diminuendo* are marked. It is often thought that after the *diminuendo* sign there should be a sudden falling away in volume, but this is mistaken; each note should contribute toward a gradual *diminuendo*.

Overall I would like to hear you play with fuller tone. It seems to me that you make excessive hand and arm movements that are getting in your way. I know that such movements are supposedly meant to free the arm of tension. But this should be possible without raising it in the air. And however you play the melody, the fingers should always be actively working. But if you raise your hand and arm, the fingers become passive. Basically the movements you make are maybe correct, but they are too expansive. If ever you hear a pianist's tone fail to sustain and die away in the air, you can be certain that he is making superfluous movements of this sort, and that he is not making proper use of the upper arm. If you do this, your fingers will turn to 'macaroni' and you cannot feel them. The melody is only felt properly when you can feel your own fingers. Here it is not a case of pressure. It is essential to feel the fingers glued to the keys, and feel the bedrock of the key, no matter how softly you are playing. There must be no excessive movement. The physical sensation of each single note is important.

Incidentally, in playing a cantilena, the fingers should move into position but should never actually strike the key. Hitting the key in my view never produces a proper *legato*. There should be complete calm and relaxation, with a perfectly calm hand. In piano playing our greatest enemies are the elbow and forearm. All that is harmful and negative comes from a tight elbow, an elbow that is afraid to move away from the body. One must try every means to free up the elbow. The elbow is there only as a helm that turns the hand and arm in the right direction. But no good can come from having a cramped elbow.

Piano tone depends not only on one's approach to the instrument, but also on proper use of the pedal. The pedal not only sustains the harmony, but also gives the melody its full sonority. This is very important. I can tell you from experience that when the pedal is kept absolutely and completely crystal clear, not only does it not help the melody to sound, but it can also create an empty void. Because if I release the dampers every second, all the overtones disappear and only the bare fundamentals are left. You should bear this in mind and not raise the pedal without good reason; use half-pedal so that only the unwanted sounds disappear. In addition, the accompaniment should be supporting the melody. If it is not sufficiently full-bodied, then the melody itself will not resonate. All these chords provide harmonies and tone colour that add to the melody itself.

Here, in bar 10, you need not take off the pedal. This might cause a slight blur, but on the next change of pedal you can clean everything up. I personally think that it is sometimes permissible to use a fairly 'thick' pedal. Even if two harmonies come quickly one after another on the same pedal, so long as you can hear where they are leading to, this will not create a muddy effect. On the other hand, if you change the pedal too often, you will cause the strings to buzz or twang, and this can sound unpleasant.

A fault often found in students when they come to the conservatoire is poor placing of the feet on the pedals. It is very important to get this right. They often press the pedal with the whole of the foot, whereas in fact this should be done only with the toe. Women who play in high heels hardly ever pedal well. The pedal should be released in such a way that the foot never actually leaves it.

On the subject of delayed pedalling: in a slow-moving piece the pedal can be delayed by a sixteenth or eighth note time span. But in rapid tempo it is sometimes delayed by as much as a quarter note. What is the right approach? Sometimes you may want to retain the bass note. In that case depress the pedal slightly earlier than necessary and then immediately use a half-pedal on the next quarter note so as to shed the excess sound. That is one way to go about it. The other way is to hold down the harmony notes with the hand.

This is a frequently used ploy. When you want to retain some part of the harmony and when you cannot keep the pedal down, then use either the right or left hand to sustain the notes. You are thus left with a background of sound, just as an orchestral chord is held by one group of instruments while others play some figuration.

Returning to the F minor Ballade, in bar 38 the bass notes should be full of expression. They should be played very *legato* and *piano*, while the melody is held and continues to sound on. The pedal should be taken off not on the left-hand E flat octave, but on B flat, the last eighth note in the bar:

Starting in bar 58, the tone should be steadily built up to a climax without any falling away.

In bar 72 it is better to take off the pedal on the third eighth note. Here we come to the second subject with its highly interesting rhythmic structure.

The G minor theme you played correctly and cleanly. All the same, it could be made even simpler. It is best to begin without any pedal, then use it in bar 101, and take it off gradually toward the end of the bar. This phrase should sound *piano* the first time round, in G minor, then *mezzo forte* in its A minor statement. At first it is calm, then the mood becomes more disturbed and agitated.

Then comes the sequential passage starting at bar 114. It is good to make sure that the left hand speaks here. Prior to this the emotional temperature was allowed to rise, but there is nothing of that here. Play the passage *piano*, bringing out the left hand part. I would not take the pedal off before bar 119. Leave a generous lake or pool of sound.

The upper and lower voices in the next episode are of equal importance. Play the middle voice more with the fingers alone, to prevent it from 'shouting'. I play this middle voice part *leggiero*, and almost *legato* in order not to drown out the upper voice:

I would not make too much *rubato* here. This should sound like a voice of reason and calm exhortation.

In the fugato episode, the tonality keeps changing constantly. It is like wandering in the shadows till the moment when you arrive back in the main key and, as it were, recover your confidence.

In the reprise there is a shift in the rhythm pattern, and one should show this. There is an impression here of a succession of phrases like lapping waves. There is *rubato* in the right hand, which remains almost independent of the left. Chopin always produces his *rubato* with the left hand in steady tempo while the right hand is free to ebb and flow. It is important to remember this here.

In bar 153 bring out the notes A flat, G, F, and E natural in the melody, and make the bass notes in the left hand clear. Keep a quiet thumb; the left arm moves round in a circle.

In bars 167-8 one would like to hear a little more 'rumble' in the descending chromatic scale.

In the following passage take the right hand off each time in front of the slur. Here it is not only important to delay the change of pedal, but also to clear the pedal later in order not to leave the sound unsupported:

I take the pedal off here on the second quarter note. Best of all is if you remove your hand with a sideways motion.

Moving on to the 'chorale' passage at bar 204, do not cultivate the effect constantly heard with so many pianists – playing the dotted half notes on the previous pedal. The pedal should be released completely with the previous abrupt *fortissimo* chord, after which there is a pause. This is very important. Chopin loves such effects of utter and total calamity, and at this point everything should be allowed to fall in ruins. The chorale should be started on a new pedal and should be sustained *piano* throughout:

The coda in general should not be played too quickly – only slightly faster than the tempo at the start of the piece. In the coda you should ensure that there is a good sense of melodic figuration in the right-hand part. We want to hear that. The pedal should be sparse – almost none at all. And bring out the *crescendi* in the left hand.

The end of bar 216 should be played without pedal in order that the resolution from dominant to tonic is clear. In the left hand clearly bring out the tenths. Bar 222 should be without any pedal. In bar 226 there is no need to play the left hand *legato*. In bar 231 the right-hand figuration should be delivered slightly more broadly. Make the left hand in bar 233 more significant. The final chords should be detached from one another.

NINA LELCHUK AND ELENA DOLINSKAYA

Lessons with Yakov Flier

(Liszt's Mephisto Waltz No 1 and Prokofiev's Sonata No 3)

The celebrated Soviet pianist Yakov Vladimirovich Flier has for many years performed with success both in the Soviet Union and abroad. In addition he has made a name for himself as a teacher, developing and continuing the best traditions of the Moscow school of pianism.

Like other members of the Moscow Conservatoire pianoforte school, Flier focuses most attention on clear and faithful presentation of a composition, concentrating on artistic realization of the composer's intentions. His approach is a personal one and it highlights his artistic views and principles as a teacher. Relating compositional form and content, conveying the logical development and rhythmic structure, cultivating a tasteful use of tone colour – all these problems are approached by Flier in a manner epitomizing his personality as an artist.

For Flier, detailed painstaking work on an embryonic student performance begins only when the student concerned has absorbed and understood his teacher's basic requirements. How far a student can then actually 'penetrate' and project the work in question, and the extent to which he acquires professional performing habits, depends largely on his ability to absorb and apply what he has been taught. Flier requires young musicians to start work with an integrated view of the whole composition, a sense of its basic idea and dramatic outline. At the very outset, even if students are initially unable to convey all this in their own playing, Flier emphasizes the need to 'read' a work, following as closely as possible the composer's intention, trying to grasp its underlying sense and appreciate the vividness of its impact.

Following this comes study of separate fragments, grappling with technical and tonal problems, careful listening and cultivation of particular elements in a musical texture. All this is probably the most vital and searching part of the operation. Only after this comes the emergence of a full-fledged artistic performance, the final 'synthesis' (although of course any notion of finality in the performing arts is somewhat arbitrary).

Flier's ability to develop and direct pupils' abilities and instill fine artistic taste in them while still preserving their individuality marks him out as a great teacher. As he teaches, he in effect acts as a musical 'stage manager' or producer, eliciting a personal performance from each pupil who comes to him for instruction.

In his work with students, Flier uses a whole series of compositions that concentrate the basic principles of his teaching method and artistic philosophy. In the main these are works by Bach, Beethoven, Mozart, Chopin, Schumann, Liszt, Rakhmaninov, Scriabin, Prokofiev, Shostakovich and Bartók. What follows is a verbatim account of Flier's comments and statements during his lessons on a handful of such works, in particular Liszt's *Mephisto Waltz* No 1 and Prokofiev's Third Sonata.

FRANZ LISZT: MEPHISTO WALTZ NO.1

Any excessive concern with this work's merely technical and virtuoso qualities shows a failure to understand properly Liszt's colourful range of poetic and philosophical ideas. The work's technical aspect is obviously based on a deeper underlay of idea and emotion. The *Mephisto Waltz* is in fact unique in pianoforte literature. Although still a fairly small-scale concert piece, it brings together and distils many of Liszt's ideas and presents several motifs that typify his whole oeuvre – a combination of romantic yearning and Mephistophelian sarcasm, languid and dreaming lyricism, acerbity and impetuosity.

The work is composed as though in a single breath, a continuous sweep that leads up to a tragic climax. In performing it is thus vital that pianists learn to husband their emotional and physical reserves. The progression from *Allegro vivace* through *piu mosso* and *presto* to a final *prestissimo* has to be finely calculated. The first section, preceding the lyrical central episode, should not reach such incandescent emotional heat as the later sections. The first part should therefore retain a certain piquancy and dance-like quality, and only the work's concluding section should turn into a storming demonic whirlwind.

The characteristic lilt of the first waltz theme is maintained through all sections preceding the central climax. The player should all the time clearly feel this waltz rhythm.

The lyrical central episode contrasts sharply with the outer sections of the work. The main difficulty here lies in phrasing the theme with its unusual emphasis on the weak third beat of the bar. Unconsciously this can lead one to think in terms separate isolated notes rather than complete phrases. When starting the lyrical section, bear in mind how the theme eventually develops (even the famous 'leaps' later on are derived from it, and for this reason they should not be played as a mere virtuoso display passage). Similarly in the final coda, the left-hand part is merely a version of the second element in this central lyrical theme.

In order to better understand the imagery behind this composition it is essential to read and immerse oneself in the world of Liszt's original literary source – the *Faust* poem by Nikolaus Lenau. In fact, much of Liszt's work contains hints of such Faustian and Mephistophelian imagery, questing for life's ultimate meaning, agonies of love and happiness. Examples include his *Faust Symphony*, the B minor Sonata, the 'Dante' Sonata, *Les Préludes, Tasso,* and other works.

It is worth noting that there are in fact two versions of the *Mephisto Waltz* – one for piano and another for orchestra – and this is a rare instance where both variants are of equal quality. Any pianist starting to learn the piece would thus do well to familiarize himself with the orchestral score and be aware of its wealth of detail and instrumental colour. The opening bars of the work in fact sound like an orchestra tuning up. But this is a highly organized tuning process: the rhythm of the waltz breaks in immediately and without preamble, and we should sense its sharp electric pulse from the very first notes:

For ease of performance and to achieve an even tone, it is best to play the *ac-ciaccatura* D sharp and A sharp with the left hand and to use the right hand for everything else up to bar 9. The fifths in bar 9 should be taken with the left hand so as to avoid an awkward leap in the right hand. The character of these opening bare fifths is enhanced by the clash of superimposed ninths in the next few bars – suggesting perhaps a Mephistophelian sneer and a tension that emotionally infect the whole composition. This effect gains in brilliance and relief if very slight pedal is added. Those elements of the main theme that have a sarcastic exclamatory character should be especially brought out:

On its appearance the main theme also has an emphatic dance-like quality. It is preferable to play it without too much bravura and slightly deliberately and ponderously, but still emphasizing the waltz element. This theme requires a keen and springy rhythm, and its tempo is slightly slower compared with the opening bars of the piece.

As a rule, Liszt's works are laid out in a manner that is pianistically extremely convenient. Occasionally, though, a few slight improvements in distribution of the keyboard parts are possible. One such example occurs in this passage:

Here a large jump in the left hand between the second and third measure can be obviated by *starting* the *acciaccatura* eighth note passage with the *left* hand rather than the right. In the following passage it is essential to articulate *martellato* and with great accuracy. And on the whole, when performing the entire first section of the *Mephisto Waltz* (up to the central lyrical episode) one should strive for absolute rhythmic precision and pungency. The one exception is the lead-up and statement of the theme in left-hand octaves, which should be taken at slightly reduced tempo – this makes it easier to give due emphasis to this motif:

To avoid miscalculation of the tone here, the theme should be played as close as possible to the keys and with a compact hand, although naturally the fingers themselves should be active and alive.

Gradually the emotional heat increases. A Mephistophelian trait comes through particularly strongly in the menacing octaves descending in duplets, while the ebullient octave outbursts between them should be played with growing impetuosity. (Incidentally, the harmonic logic of this passage suggests to me that the middle voice in bar 2 of this example should play E flat rather than E natural; this may well be an error in notation.)

In the final statement of the main theme before the central episode, I recommend transferring the fifth from the right hand to the left, leaving simply the C sharp and A for the right to play. This trick helps in achieving greater brilliance, precision, and a well defined *martellato*:

The transition from the stormy jubilation of the dance to the exquisite lyricism of the second subject is bound up with Lenau's poetic image of Mephistopheles, who seizes a fiddle from one of the village musicians and embarks on an act of 'musical seduction'. Here I never cease to marvel at Liszt's mastery in slowing the tempo of his twirling waltz, and at the way in which he contrives to preserve the original basic dance rhythm while serving up a new theme full of sensuousness, dreaminess, and languor:

Performers should here observe the composer's tempo marking: *Un poco meno mosso (ma poco)*. There are two inferences to be made from this. First, the new theme should not become lost in a lake of sentimental tranquility, since the taut rhythm of the waltz still continues. Secondly, though, it means that the opening section of the work should not be taken at too hectic a pace (despite a recent vogue for this type of treatment, especially among younger players).

The lyrical theme consists of two elements – a question and answer, as it were: which are present in all the varying presentations of this theme:

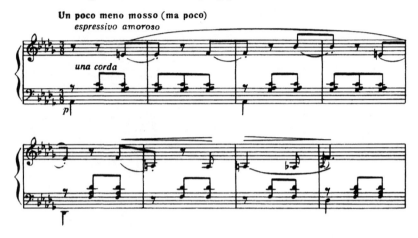

Here it is very important to vary the articulation of the theme. The 'question' motif rises as though on a short, light 'up-bow'; the descending intonation of the 'answer' should have a slightly more plummy tone. In playing all this section, the pianist has a chance to show his imagination and resourcefulness, since each return of the theme can be given slightly differing tone colouration. One of the problems is to overcome the theme's rather 'foursquare' structure and its movement in eight-bar phrases. One should therefore resist a temptation to slow down at the end of each phrase. Try to bear in mind the development of this central episode as a whole and its unity of movement. At the same time, though, the treatment should not be rigidly metronomic – that is, there should be some *rubato*.

In the *dolce appassionato* section, I would draw special attention to the falling intervals of a second in the right-hand octaves. This phrase is a leitmotif of the whole work.

I would recommend a slight 'settling' into the first of each of these pairs of octaves. The emotional temper of this section seems in some ways to anticipate the music of Scriabin while at the same time showing an awareness of Wagnerian harmony. I advise pupils to play the basic unadorned version without the decorative rising *fioriture* – this, incidentally, corresponds to the orchestral version.

The next episode, marked *presto*, conjures up a picture of diabolical laughter, suggesting Mephistopheles the eternal sceptic mocking at humanity's weakness and delusions that have always led to catastrophe (see the examples below). I am much opposed to displays of empty virtuosity in this passage, and also dislike any heavy accent on the first beat of the bar. This creates the effect of a nervous spasm, and many pianists fail to cope with the passage precisely because they make this accent. The important thing here is precision, lightness, and airiness. The hand and arm should be free, and the fingers should not be raised, but held as close as possible to the key surface, independent and unencumbered. The *staccato* eighth notes should be played from the wrist, not from the elbow.

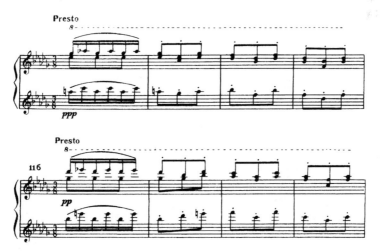

Next comes an expansion and development of the main lyrical theme, marked 'poco allegretto e rubato':

Here the music should move quite freely, with a flexible rhythm. It is vital not to follow the rhythmic notation too slavishly. In the last two bars the two hands should be completely independent. The right-hand passage should be played airily, lightly and slightly capriciously. The left meanwhile preserves its rhythmic definition.

Although played più animato as a whole, the episode set out on three clefs is marked 'un poco meno mosso' and should preserve its different strata of sound. While bringing out the theme with the thumb of the left hand, one should at the same time hear clearly the echoes of the theme in the right hand. It should all sound tremulous and excited above its foundation in the bass.

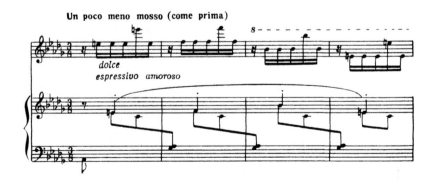

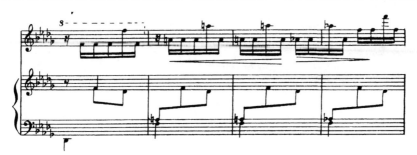

From the *Più mosso* episode through to the end of the piece there is a rapid build-up and a stormy whirl of events that lead to a shattering climax. For this we require not just enormous inner tension but also a masterly ability to grade the build-up of forces. Mephisto's furious dance is made up of new transformations of the initial waltz theme. The tone colour of the right-hand part I imagine as being slightly nasal, while the left-hand tremolo should pulsate with nervous energy:

Now there is a sharp collision of the two motifs. Don't be too absorbed with the right-hand part. The main events are in the left hand, which is based on the two elements making up the central lyrical theme; all one needs to do meanwhile is convey the upward surge of the right hand:

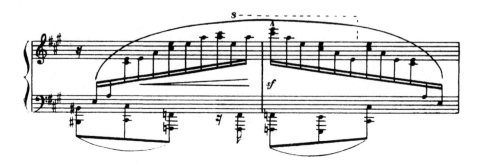

The growing excitement leads eventually to a desperate episode marked 'Presto':

I should emphasize again, however, that this *Presto* episode loses in effect if played too fast. Remember that it is really nothing more than a new transformation of elements from the lyrical theme. This is music at once profoundly expressive and agitated, and it should be played meaningfully, emphasizing the interval of a falling second, as before:

Finally, the famous 'leaps': Try and forget that they *are* leaps – first and foremost, they are a further reworking of the lyrical theme. The main aim should be to demonstrate this point and to convey its lightness, impulsiveness, and sequined brilliance. It is best to jump off from the thumb rather than the second finger. This has the psychological advantage of reducing the interval from two octaves, apparently, down to one:

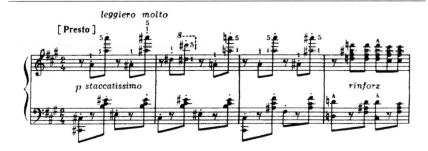

It is very useful to practise these leaps using just the thumb while keeping the hand in its octave stretch position. More complicated are the leaps in the left hand. These should be rhythmically precise, and the eighth note rest should not be shortened, even though we are in 2/4 time. It is essential to emphasize the triple-time rhythmic pulse. The problem lies in playing the third eighth note of each left-hand group as short as possible.

Another technical problem arises in the repeated chords in both hands of the next section:

Here I should warn against the error made by many pianists, who tend to settle on the first of the repeated chords. The result is that their hands, which are tired by now, tend to 'stick' in the keys. It is in fact rare to hear a completely impeccable performance of this passage. My advice is to try and free the hand and arm of all tension. The sensation should be that of trying to shake something from one's sleeve. The first two sixteenth notes must not be played too heavily; instead make a *crescendo* toward the third chord of the group.

Now comes the climax. If I find that I cannot draw enough sonority from the instrument I am playing, I often rearrange the melody slightly: the left hand plays an octave lower while the right, instead of resting, doubles up the D-C sharp figure. This helps achieve a more 'orchestral' sound:

In the final section the various ideas are presented with even greater prominence and striking impact. This is the moment of final catastrophe, where everything seems to crash into the abyss. For a deep, bell-like sonority I sometimes transfer the *fortissimo* chord an octave lower:

The subsequent cadenza passage is best split between the two hands. This is especially effective for pianists blessed with a good and accurate *martellato*:

The episode immediately preceding the coda has a mysterious, poetic quality, suggesting perhaps a state of bemusement in the wake of disaster, and it seems to reflect a passage with similar atmosphere in the literary text of Lenau's *Faust*:

When working on a programmatic work of this sort, I always warn pupils against looking for too much fussy illustrative detail. Nevertheless, in order to show a complete understanding of the composer's intent, one should certainly try and convey clearly the main outline of the 'programme'.

The stormy, headlong coda that sweeps away everything in its path can be played with flamboyance and virtuosity. The image is that of quickly ringing down the curtain on the tragedy that has just been played out.

In the above remarks and commentaries it is apparent that Yakov Flier concentrates prime attention on the artistic image or poetic content of the composition. It is this that prompts all his suggestions for such things as tone production, pedalling, use of convenient fingering, et cetera. Obviously, though, the above record of just one lesson on a single composition cannot illustrate all aspects of his teaching method. Below is an account of another of his lessons on a work of different style and form.

SERGEI PROKOFIEV: SONATA NO. 3

For Prokofiev composition and performance were closely linked activities. Several of his personal traits as a pianist influence the basic features of his compositions for the piano – their emphatic toccata-like quality, their elemental force, relentless spirit and élan, and their steely rhythms and orchestral tone colours. At the same time Prokofiev's writing is inextricably bound up with the Russian song tradition, and there is a deeply felt lyrical quality in many of his works.

The Third Sonata is marked by youthful zest, springy rhythm, *martellato* and *toccata* writing, precision and laconism of expression. Written in a condensed one-movement form, it lasted a mere six minutes in the composer's own performance. The work opens with a stormy whirlpool of triplets on the dominant that inject a rhythmic charge into the whole composition. But it is a tightly organized whirlpool. Total precision and bouncing toccata rhythms set the pace:

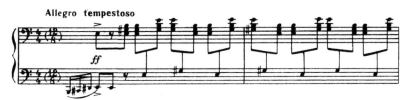

Despite the *fortissimo* marking at the beginning one should not overload the tone in the first couple of bars, since the actual introductory theme comes only in bar 3 and must have the effect of a triumphant call on the solo trumpet (see first example below). Its second statement should sound even more intense, like two trumpets calling in duet (second example):

Then the whirling triplets on the dominant enter again. But now the storm abates and prepares the way for the soaring main theme, which is airy and slightly capricious:

It is important to observe the supporting inner voices notated in quarter notes and played by the thumbs of either hand. The tone colour here has to be quite different: the implied instrumentation of the introductory theme recalled the proud ring of brass instruments, although here there is more of a hint of woodwind.

The bridge passage requires special precision of tone and rhythm. To achieve the proper effect, one needs the faintest possible accent on the first note of the right-hand triplets:

Here almost all young pianists unconsciously tend to 'settle' on the second eighth note however, which distorts the character of this important episode. (Its importance is in fact confirmed when Prokofiev uses all this material again in the reprise in place of the main first subject.)

One last but important reminder à propos of the first section of the exposition: despite their differing character, all the themes should be held rigidly together in the same iron rhythmic framework. If they are not, the entire section can easily fall apart.

An important moment is the short chromatic episode leading to the lyrical second subject:

The rising bass part is suddenly slowed in its tracks ('*poco rit*'). It comes to rest on a low G sharp and then re-emerges in a new, mysterious chromatic guise that foreshadows the heartfelt sincerity of the second subject. It is like a fine, fragile chain linking two contrasting themes – the stormy tension of the first subject relieved by the rapt tranquillity of the second. In the bridge passage the right hand must be played with impeccable *legato* and evenness. Avoid any artificial 'expressiveness'. The remarkable thing about this episode is its complete absence of dynamics – following it, the C major second subject should ring out with special warmth and sincerity. (It is striking how often Prokofiev turns to a glowing C major at moments when he needs to express elevated feeling, a love of life, nature and humanity. His affection for C major can be traced through from the works of his youth to his final compositions. Some notable examples occur in the third movement of the Sixth Sonata, the orchestral introduction to the Third Piano Concerto, and also of course in the 'love theme' from the ballet *Romeo and Juliet*.)

The second subject is close in character to traditional Russian folksong:

In striving for bright, clear tone colours here, it is important not to ignore the polyphonic element. The theme appears first in the right-hand lower voice and is then imitated in the upper voice:

Like a good conductor aware of all his instruments, the pianist must listen carefully to the entire musical fabric. One must clearly hear the bass with its wind instrument timbre, and every note of it must be gently 'pressed home' with the fifth finger. The chromatic movement of the middle voice, in the left hand, should be played *legatissimo* and without dynamic variation, i.e. like some continuation of the bridge passage. The second subject consequently raises a problem: four quite separate strands of sound are present here, each of which has to be heard independently, yet in such a way that none of them disturb the sense of a balanced ensemble (see second example on p 188). To achieve this, I would recommend playing the upper voice brightly, and the bass somewhat more heavily, while the middle voice in the left hand should, as it were, crawl along from note to note in a stealthy, mysterious manner. The thematic imitation in the right-hand lower voice should meanwhile be especially expressive.

Moving on, it is important to follow the second subject's development, its successive variations and tone colours. I imagine the sound quality as follows: the first statement of the theme in the middle register should be bright and clear (see above); its second statement in the lower register (first example at foot of p 188) is more muffled, with a slightly nasal twang; the third statement, in the upper register (second example), is gentle, barely audible, and recedes into the distance.

The closing section rounds off the exposition. In the first few bars it has an obvious dance-like quality, as evidenced by the syncopated bass and actual lines of the melody:

But from bar 5 another songful element comes into play. In order to maintain the general lyrical mood therefore, try not to over-emphasize the dance element. In fact, one should tone down both the syncopated bass and the right-hand melodic manner, especially the *acciaccatura* and chord.

In the last eight bars of the exposition, the broad melody of the upper voice blends with the lower supporting part, and this juxtaposition forms a passage of unusual beauty:

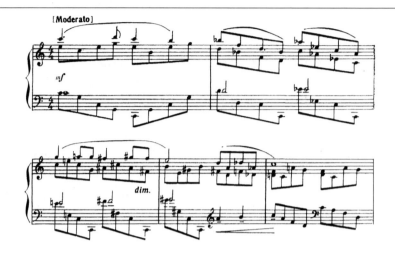

Initially the voices are two octaves apart (middle C and the C two octaves higher). They then gradually converge, tone by tone, and flow together calmly on the intermediary C. This effect has to be both 'seen' and clearly heard. (There is a similar device in Prokofiev's opera *The Fiery Angel*: at the very end, in the concluding measures, a converging sequence of harmonies emerges from the chaos and settled forlornly on the interval of a third.)

The development is marked '*Allegro tempestuoso. Feroce*'. What better description? Storm and fury ensue. One imagines a flood smashing down all the sluice gates. Cries for help are heard (*precipitoso*), and the crashing waves of a force nine gale, and a sudden unleashing of the elements – elemental nature and elemental feeling. It is a passage of brilliant tonal character. Not content with a *marcato*, the composer calls for '*marcatissimo*'. The tension built up in this development section is stupendous. (A perhaps even more extreme example of Prokofiev in this mood comes in the famous cadenza of the Second Piano Concerto.) Despite this emotional avalanche, the player must keep himself in check. Above all, he must bring out the thematic substance of this passage in which the two main themes of the sonata are set in stark conflict. Only the lyrical second subject is left aside for a time, although in due course it too will be allowed to weigh in.

The rhythmic aspect of the development section causes problems. In the exposition, it was triplet rhythm patterns that predominated (in the main subject and bridge passage material); in the second subject duple time was uppermost. In the development section, however, there are rapid shifts between duple and triple rhythms. In performance this creates a risk of rhythmic disintegration, and one therefore has to be persistent and purposefully 'play into' the complex rhythm changes in order to bring out their effect.

In the sonorous bass *marcatissimo*, the second subject 'exclamations' (bars 117 and following) now appear transformed. They must be well defined and not allowed to drown amidst the other raging elements. The upper voice in flickering triple rhythm does fade slightly to a *mezzo forte*, but this also leads to a new collision of opposing forces. A rapid deceleration (half a bar of *ritenuto*) leads to a now unchallenged domination of the second subject. But it no longer sounds as it did in the exposition. Earlier, the crawling eighth notes in the middle voice helped weave a mood of calm. Here, though, the background is different: the intermittent left-hand triplets inject a sense of tender palpitation.

At *piu animato* the appearance of a duet between the second subject (in the bass) and the closing section motif comes as a surprising piece of fantasy:

This extreme contrast of high and low registers creates a combined sense of profundity and caprice. The newly transformed lyrical theme seems to come floating in from some watery kingdom and proceeds to spread itself out over an amazing five and a half octaves. Here one has to grade the increasing sonority with perfect control. Tenderly mysterious tones must gradually turn into brilliant rhetorical exclamation. Then, broadening out in the last bar, we reach the sonata's gigantic culmination. Note that this is the only point where Prokofiev actually writes '*fff*'. It is important not to let the heavy 'trombone' progression of bass notes drown out the pulsing upper part:

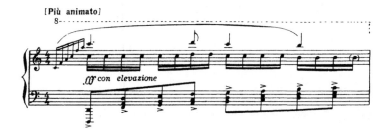

The climax comes with crushing force. Hold on to the *fermata* and then suddenly snatch away the hands and take off the pedal in the same instant, leaving the E to sound on alone. Listen carefully as it dies away:

Only when it has died down to the faintest *pianissimo* should you gradually, and barely audibly, begin winding your way into the recapitulation.

The reprise is highly condensed. None of the exposition's themes are fully unfolded. The whole section has a playful, skittish character. The character of the second subject has changed amazingly: now it is airborne and moves in sketchy, scherzo-like manner. In order to convey its glittering flight one needs a perfectly light, soft and elegant touch, although occasional 'stings' in the theme must not be ignored. The coda uses the closing section material to bring the work to a brilliant and fiery conclusion. It begins barely audibly, but quickly starts to roar with increasing ferocity. The galloping bass has more and more menace, and the supporting voice of a jubilant trumpet must be brought out with absolute precision:

One imagines the scene of a hunt moving at full gallop, sweeping ahead and drawing everything after it. At the end of the coda the second subject sounds out once again in a joyous fanfare. In the final measures I suggest the following fingering that produces a good trumpet sound:

The Third Sonata is unique in its coherence, impetus, emotional tension, and in the invincible power of its creator's optimism.

In the above discussions of works by Liszt and Prokofiev it is evident that Yakov Flier demands of his pupils both technical mastery and an ability to convey the musical content of these pieces using richly varied sonority and a sense of the works' formal cohesion. Pupils are thus simultaneously faced with a set of highly demanding tasks. Furthermore, Flier is no narrow professional. He keeps a constant watch on the balanced growth of his pupils and on their spiritual and intellectual development, concerning himself both with their artistic outlook and also with their general literary and cultural knowledge. Nevertheless, the prime consideration remains his students' musical erudition and their knowledge of both classical and modern music.

Without trying to cover every aspect of Flier's teaching, we shall now try and examine a few special principles of his – in particular his emphasis on pupils' mastering each work as a whole, his attention to matters of tone, fingering, and cultivation of interpretative freedom, et cetera.

There are many ways of approaching a new composition. At his first lessons with more independent students, Flier tends to work on a few details of the text that they have failed to understand or bring off successfully. Less self-reliant students have to begin with an analysis of the work, noting its principal thematic and structural links, special harmonic and melodic features, et cetera. If Flier's own view of a work disagrees with a student's already formed approach, he usually adopts an attitude of 'friendly neutrality', helping the student sort out his own ideas and advising on the best way to realize them. Having once expounded his own approach, he gives pupils time to absorb and make sense of it, in order that they work up their own plan for a performance, bearing in mind his advice. In such cases he usually instructs them simply to go home, think things out and then begin work, and he is happy if his own comments provide stimulus and interest.

Flier has never tired of pointing out that pupils should constantly check and listen to themselves when practising at home. They are not supposed ever to pass over wrong or smudged notes, or ever to practise in a mechanical fashion without total commitment. It is better to work less than to work un-productively. Flier regards an ability to work on a piece independently as the main sign of a pupil's maturity. The more attentively students work at home in private, the better their chances of success. Conversely, anything studied in an inert, mechanical manner is liable to produce only a dull performance.

In presenting these records of Flier's lessons, we have tried to stress his view that the overall artistic conception of a work should dictate the manner of working on its component elements. The one flows out of the other and is bound up with it. Flier has often said how wrong it is to regard technical devices as an end in themselves. This is particularly true of piano tone pro-duction. Before a pupil begins to play a work, he must clearly understand its tonal colouration. He has to know in advance what to strive for, otherwise random searching around will be a waste of time. Flier has often repeated the words of Konstantin Igumnov, who always insisted that 'everything, ab-solutely everything is reducible to one main principle: listening carefully to oneself – in one way or another everything else is bound up with this.'

Igumnov's legacy also probably explains Flier's desire to achieve effects on the piano approximating as closely as possible to the human voice. Ways of tone production are as many as there are tone colours and timbres. Here everything is determined by fantasy, imagination, and sensitive hearing. Working with pupils on the cultivation of tone, Flier follows a few firm and abiding principles:

1) Even the quietest tone must always be heard. Even in a *pianissimo* there-fore one must feel the 'bed' of the keys.

2) One should avoid using extreme *fortissimo* or *pianissimo* (many musicians err in this respect, not just young pianists but also particularly singers and violinists.

3) One should learn to 'sing' on the piano. One must hear longer notes for their full duration, and the notes that follow should be played as though at the volume level at which the previous one faded. It is important, too, to be able to convey an illusion of *crescendo* on a long held note. There is no doubt that some piano composers had this in mind. For instance, in the four-bar introduction to Chopin's B flat minor sonata, the 'secret' lies in being able to imagine a *crescendo* on the left-hand octave E, and the result is a single

complete phrase whose climax comes midway through the third bar:

In his classes Flier has often commented on the pianoforte's main fault as being the short duration and rapid fading of each note. He requires that every pupil devote special effort to cultivating a good *legato*. At the same time, though, the piano has specific advantages over other instruments. Its richness of touch and tonal variety enable it to imitate the timbre of orchestral instruments to a certain extent, and even the human voice. In addition to a tonal range from the deepest bass to the highest coloratura, the piano has a colossal dynamic range – from *pianissimo* to *fortissimo* – and all this means that it can be regarded not so much as one instrument, but as a whole orchestra with a great variety of different tone colours.

Hence Flier's remarks comparing piano sound to that of an orchestra, and his requiring pupils to try and produce orchestral effects. On one occasion he is recorded as saying that a certain passage should be played 'with full breath, in one long stroke of the bow'. Or, at the start of the second movement of Beethoven's A flat sonata, opus 110: 'In this movement it is important to observe exactly all the articulation marks; imagine how a string quartet would play it, and try to achieve the same sonority.' This is why Flier requires pupils to be able to 'orchestrate' the work they are performing. They have to be like a conductor with a score, listening to the complete musical texture and hearing its main lines, supporting parts, et cetera.

Another of Flier's basic requirements is to develop his pupils' sense of artistic freedom. Success here depends on total contact between teacher and pupil, and on their work together as a team. It depends, too, on the teacher's ability to approach his pupil as an individual and find the key to his particular gifts. Flier is of course well able to unfold the artistic potential of all his pupils. Furthermore, he usually derives most satisfaction when a pupil shows personal artistic initiative, even if this does not closely reflect his own views.

In brief, what Flier aims for is to treat a young pianist's own artistic leanings with due care, and at the same time to develop his all-round musicianship. This also of course dictates a choice of repertoire that includes works designed to bring out pupils' own individuality to the full, while building up experience, knowledge, and artistry.

Going through records of Flier's lessons, one realizes what an important part in these is played by correct choice of fingering. Here, for instance, are some further examples of his suggestions for special fingerings. As a rule, it is not just a matter of what is most convenient, but what is required in order to achieve a particular tone colour or phrasing. Furthermore, by intelligent rethinking, many complex passages can be made more easily accessible. The following episode from Chopin's F minor *Fantasy* is a good instance of this:

For greater security in playing the small cadenza near the start of the first movement of Tchaikovsky's B flat minor Concerto, the final notes are more conveniently played by the right hand alone, rather than splitting them between both hands as the score suggests:

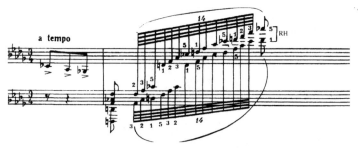

Pupils often also have trouble with part of the middle section of the second movement, because they deliberately speed up the tempo and fail to appreciate the succession of tritones that are best played with the following fingering:

In another episode in the finale, in order to achieve absolute evenness, Flier recommends the following fingering that simultaneously places both the left and right hands in a similar position:

Sometimes a difficulty is overcome by transferring notes from one hand to another. For instance, in the same movement, by taking the last sixteenth note of the bar with the left hand, an awkward upward leap can be avoided in the right:

In the Liszt B minor Sonata the fanfare effects in the fugato section are best played with both hands:

To increase the dramatic fervour of another episode in Liszt's Sonata, the texture can be thickened slightly by playing a *gruppetto* in octaves instead of the usually notated triplet:

Choice of fingering is certainly bound up with artistic considerations, but it is also essential to consider the peculiarities of individual hands, their size, elasticity, and span between the fingers. For smaller hands Flier recommends more frequent changes of finger, allowing, for example, the use of the fifth finger on black notes when playing octaves. In finer technical passages he advises more frequent use of fingers 1, 2 and 3, rather than 4 and 5, and has no qualms about tucking under the thumb. To develop thumb dexterity, Flier advocates practising scales of C major in both directions using only the thumb and second finger.

The achievement of brilliant orchestral sonority also largely depends on choice of particular fingering. Here artistic aims might well override normal fingering habits. To suggest the sound of solo trombone or French horn, one might use the thumb on black keys. One example occurs in the reprise of Rakhmaninov's *Étude-Tableau* in E flat minor, opus 39, No 5. By using the left-hand thumb here the theme can be made to stand out with special prominence. The same holds true in the climactic passage in Chopin's *Barcarolle*:

Another example occurs in the Ravel Concerto for Left Hand, where in the first statement of the theme it is helpful to finish the descending passages using the thumb on the black keys. In the Schumann *Toccata*, too, the rising thirds immediately before the closing section should be played with just fingers 2 and 4; this helps obtain an even and dry *staccato*.

Flier spends a lot of time in his classes teaching pupils to use finger and wrist *staccato*, as well as *staccato* involving the whole arm. As a rule, newly enrolled students often have only mastered this latter type. Yet an ability to use all three forms of *staccato* is an essential piece of the pianist's equipment. To assist in acquiring a wrist *staccato*, Flier recommends repetition of one and the same note or chord using exaggerated upward movements of the wrist, first gradually increasing the tempo, then reducing the number of repetitions and returning to the prescribed notation and tempo. Wrist *staccato* often occurs in left-hand parts, for instance in the *Gnomenreigen* of Liszt, in Chopin's waltzes, Schumann's *Toccata*, in Rakhmaninov's arrangement of the Scherzo from Mendelssohn's music to *A Midsummer Night's Dream*, and elsewhere.

If his pupil is working on a concerto with orchestra, Flier does his best to familiarize him with the orchestral part. Knowing well how orchestras play certain passages, Flier prepares his pupil for this. It is well known, for example, that because of the thick orchestration it is often hard for the piano to be heard at the start of Rakhmaninov's Second Piano Concerto. Flier therefore recommends special fingerings that make maximum use of the more powerful first, second and third fingers. The climax of this concerto's first and last movements requires brilliant tone from the soloist, which can be obtained only by using the full weight of a free and unrestricted arm, reinforced by the weight of the shoulder and the whole body.

In the B flat minor variation of the same composer's *Rhapsody on a Theme of Paganini*, the clarinetist usually tends to draw out his statement of the main theme. Any pupil about to play this work with orchestra for the first time is warned by Flier to listen out at this moment and wait for the clarinet and avoid rushing. And in the 'Dies irae' variation, when the piano has its descending chromatic scale, there must be a touch of *sostenuto*, otherwise the solo and orchestral parts can come adrift, since the trombones tend to play their part in a ponderous manner and at slightly slower tempo.

An inexperienced pupil, accustomed only to the accompaniment on a second piano, may find it hard to get used to the new timbre of orchestral instruments. On his own against the orchestra, he might well feel uncertain of himself, and this can immediately affect the orchestra. To avoid such failings, Flier recommends thoroughgoing study of the orchestral score, bearing clearly in mind not just the piano part, but the sound of the music as a whole. Some knowledge of the acoustic properties of certain concert halls can also be of considerable importance.

To sum up Flier as a teacher, one could say that he sees his prime task as teaching students to think independently and to work in a true professional manner. He seeks also to inspire in them a love of music, to help them discover their own artistic personality and leave a personal imprint on the works that they perform. Yakov Flier has produced a whole constellation of successful performing artists, and their endeavours and achievements form a notable chapter in the biography of this remarkable artist and teacher.

OLGA STUPAKOVA & GENRIETTA MIRVIS

Yakov Zak as Teacher

The scale and seriousness of the problems that Yakov Zak sets himself both as pianist and teacher organically reflect the richness of his own spiritual world. It is no coincidence that some of his greatest achievements have included performances of the most challenging masterpieces of piano literature such as Beethoven's *Diabelli Variations* and *Hammerklavier* Sonata, both the concertos of Brahms, Prokofiev's Second and Third Concertos, Medtner's Second, and most of the Prokofiev sonatas. A fondness for Chopin has also been apparent throughout Zak's career. In addition he is also a brilliant interpreter of Rakhmaninov's piano concertos and solo works, while at the same time showing a warm concern for Mozart and Schubert, whose sonatas and other works regularly figure in his programmes.

Teaching method is of course indivisible from the personality of the teacher, and Yakov Zak's own love of music and his vital awareness of the moral functions of art are something he tries to instill and educate in his own pupils. His lessons and the whole of his teaching thus amount to more than the mere passing on of professional expertise. Indeed, routine conversations with his pupils are a veritable school of life in which human and artistic qualities are nurtured.

Usually many students sit in on Professor Zak's classes, listening to colleagues playing and profiting from their teacher's comments and explanations, which are usually accompanied by demonstration on a second piano. Students also find themselves drawn into discussion with him on a variety of subjects – maybe a new work by some young composer, a recent symphonic concert, a new programme played by the Beethoven Quartet, publication of sketches by Sergei Eisenstein, new verse published by some contemporary poet, or other events in the artistic life of Moscow.

Concerts given by students from Yakov Zak's classes take place not only in

Moscow, but also in Leningrad, Riga and other cities. Students recall with special pleasure a concert when they played recent or rarely heard works by contemporary Soviet and foreign composers. In preparing for this, they learned to create their own interpretation of these new musical works, and they were proudly aware of their own pioneering role in this. Another token of respect for Russian musical traditions was a class concert to honour the centenary of Leningrad Conservatoire at which works by Rubinstein, Liadov, Glazunov, Leonid Nikolayev and others were performed. This programme was later repeated in Leningrad itself.

The musical bond between Yakov Zak's students is not limited to their attendance at lessons. They are also actively involved in one another's development. Often Yakov Zak details students to go through some already familiar work with a friend, or else if two of them are studying the same piece, he has them jointly work in private on the suggestions and comments he provides at their official lessons.

In his student programmes, Yakov Zak regularly assigns works for piano duet or two pianos, such as Schubert's F minor Fantasia, works by Mozart, Bach concertos, and the *Symphonic Dances* and suites by Rakhmaninov. He also urges pupils to familiarize themselves with works of chamber music. Students are always struck by Zak's knowledge of the chamber repertoire, in particular the complete quartets of Beethoven, which are an object of his particular affection and admiration. Zak in fact regards these quartets as compulsory literature for his students, who study them not only by listening to records or concerts, but also via their own music-making in four-hand arrangements.

Yakov Zak's attitude toward his students is based on the principle of paying closest attention to those who work most assiduously, all of which leads to a healthy professional and artistic rivalry between the students themselves.

At lessons with his pupils, Zak is insatiably demanding, and his strictly cultivated tastes brook no compromise. On one occasion he expressed doubt over one student's use of an edition of Schumann's *Études Symphoniques* in which the theme contained a series of arpeggiated chords. His own verdict was that 'it is better to play all notes of the chords together; this edition maybe reflects the influence of the late nineteenth-century salon style of piano playing.' On another occasion, when working on the lyrical D major episode in the development of Liszt's Sonata, a pupil was told: 'We'll have no coquettishness, please. It should be played more simply.' One recalls many similar instances.

A striving for naturalness and a revulsion against any artificial embellishment go hand in hand with Yakov Zak's own poetic nature. All this is manifest in the wealth of association and imagery that he cites in order to reveal some elusive nuance or mood in a musical composition. The source of his remarks lies in a profound knowledge of other fields of art. Space forbids a complete account of this, but some typical examples are as follows. Once, when dissatisfied with the too 'fleshy' sound in one student's playing of Debussy, his comment was: 'Why is this all so succulent? This isn't Rubens after all!' And he reminded his student of various impressionist canvases that seemed woven together out of air and light. Meanwhile, in the reprise of the Liszt Sonata, the main thematic motif introduced in the bass, according to Zak, 'comes floating out of the darkness, like characters in the pictures of Rembrandt':

One also hears from Zak instructions such as 'Play this *dolce*, and as you do so remember the enchanting tenderness of outline and colour in Botticelli.'

'In your performance,' Zak told one student, 'the phrasing sounds grey and shallow. You've broken up the acoustic 'structure' of the entire work and left it lying there on one level. Above all, in every theme there is a melodic profile, or outline, which calls for dynamic expression. An even more complicated task is to appreciate how the composition as a whole is constructed, where the main centres of meaning are concentrated, and what is the dynamic relationship between smaller climaxes and the main culminating point in the piece. Once you find that highest peak, the centre of the structure, then it becomes easier to fashion the details around it.'

Zak is also a master at observing the features of nature relating to music, at finding some poetic element in any natural phenomenon. 'Have you ever looked through a frosted window on a winter evening and watched the sweep of a blizzard or the airy twirling of snowflakes?' he asked one pupil. This rhetorical question was in fact an answer to the question as to how the coda of the first movement in Rakhmaninov's Second Sonata should sound:

Poco accelerando

How does Zak begin work on a new piece with his students? One of his main tasks is to help shape his student's approach to a new composition, revealing its meaning through various stylistic devices that typify the composer's work. In working on Mozart, for instance, Zak does not fear to go against several old-fashioned ideas about the composer, which have still unfortunately not yet been laid to rest. Enthusing about the freshness, incomparable grace and gallantry typical of Mozart's genius, Zak insists on the masculinity and universality of experience captured in Mozart's work – from the most tender lyricism to expressions of profound suffering and torment, especially in his works in a minor key. This is the figure of Mozart depicted in Rodin's striking sculpture, which shows him not as a radiant youth but as the figure of a great man. And the problems of performing Mozart largely relate to this: there should be no smoothing over his angularity, no veiled emotion; on the contrary, but there should be unashamed contrasts, boldness and drama. Thus, after a student had played the second movement of Mozart's Sonata No 2 in F major, Zak's comment was: 'Pay attention here to the sharp switch between *forte* and *piano*, and don't be scared of the contrasts. They are part of the drama of this movement.'

In working on the E flat major second movement of Mozart's B flat major Concerto, K.595, Zak draws his students' attention to the melancholic, dreaming quality of this music, which requires that the whole texture be filled with song; there should not be a single note here that does not sing and is not deeply felt.

Zak pays much attention to realizing the character of both complete works and their separate episodes. Thus, for instance, in his words, the theme of Schumann's *Études Symphoniques* is filled with a mournful dignity, and one senses its concentrated progression throughout the piece. In the introit to Liszt's B minor Sonata, following the mysterious pizzicato octaves, comes the cautious 'procession' of the descending scale theme – as if moving in the dark. Often, though, in Zak's lessons there is talk of more detailed interpretative tasks. In the eleventh of the *Études Symphoniques*, for instance, 'the rustling of thirty-second notes in the left hand should create an atmosphere in which the melody comes floating in':

In the exposition of Liszt's Sonata, just before the second subject appears, the 'solo' phrases in the left hand should have an alarmed and cautiously insinuating quality:

Yakov Zak frequently alludes to concrete images in order to illustrate a point. Thus in Chopin's G sharp minor Étude in thirds, opus 25, No 6, one should picture an endless forlorn roadway steadily receding into the distance to the tinkling sound of little bells. Then, in the F major lyrical episode marked '*dolce con grazia*' in the exposition of Liszt's Sonata (bars 20-23, following the '*Grandioso*') we hear the 'plaint of Francesca'.

In all these instances, the association is designed to stimulate the imagination and serve as a pretext for seeking out the right tonal characteristics of a musical passage.

The touching image of the 'flute that lost its way' in the coda of Rakhmaninov's arrangement of the Mendelssohn Scherzo helps to reshape a student's thinking, to get him away from over-concern with his fingers, and helps him to hear and convey the splendour and poetry of the flute's mysterious musings. The same is true of the Chopin A minor Étude, opus 10, No 2, where Zak suggests that the student pretend to watch the flight of a falling autumn leaf and follow the sad and capricious pattern of its movement. By contrast, in the second movement of Bartók's Third Piano Concerto, we encounter what Zak calls 'sonorous tombstones' – a metaphor designed to make one listen harder to those long and dispassionate sounding chords and discover in them a peculiar noble enchantment.

How does Yakov Zak pursue further work on a composition? For all the variety of methods and devices at his disposal, Zak always follows methods designed to get as close as possible to the essence of the music and to achieve the right sonority. He is an outspoken opponent of so-called 'prepared' musical material, believing that technical difficulties should be overcome while focusing clearly on the idea behind a particular musical work. Without this, technical experiment becomes purely arbitrary and lacks any firm grounding. The following are some examples:

If a technical difficulty is hampering and slowing down one's pace, Zak maintains, one should mentally divide the passage concerned into convenient segments each of which can be played without difficulty. Thus, in the *Études Symphoniques*, one can group the chord sequences in Étude No 9 into the following:

The same can be done with the eighth variation of Rakhmaninov's *Paganini Rhapsody*:

Also, in Chopin's F minor *Fantasy*, after the second subject comes an episode that is difficult especially for small hands. In this case Zak suggests a mental rearrangement of the passagework and chord sequences in such a way that they lie more conveniently:

In working through Chopin's *Fantasy*, technical problems often arise in spanning broad intervals while playing *piano*. This is particularly true of the left-hand passagework in the second subject, where wide intervals interfere with the continuity of sound. Zak's advice here is: 'Learn this in a non-mechanical way at a moderate tempo, listening to the melody and all the time making the whole of the left-hand part fit the melodic outline in the right hand. Call your imagination to help in overcoming these wide intervals. Imagine to yourself that you have a gigantic hand and that you can easily cover this wide interval without effort. You will then succeed in spanning this large space in a free and flexible manner.'

In working on the ninth of the *Études Symphoniques*, mentioned above already, Zak's advice is 'Forget about the skip, and don't jump. There should be no sense of any convulsed leaping around, instead there should be free and rapid transference of the hand. When once you can smooth over these 'seams', you will be able to create the illusion of a *legato*. The pedalling is very important in this étude. Use light pedal without either fully depressing or completely releasing it. This helps to preserve the 'harmonic atmosphere', and the slightly 'smudged' harmonies will very quickly fade.' A similar requirement – namely, playing 'along' the keyboard with totally free hand and arm, and without thinking of any leaps – will also help in negotiating the difficulties in the final variation of Rakhmaninov's *Paganini Rhapsody*.

Various methods devised by Yakov Zak for dealing with rhythmic problems in the *Paganini Rhapsody* also spring to mind. In the fourteenth variation the triplet chord sequences when played by students often tend to 'stick together' and turn into an acoustic porridge because young players fail to observe the important pause on the first eighth note of each right-hand group. If you actively raise the hand on these pauses, as a conductor might give an up-beat, the rhythmic pulse will become clearly audible:

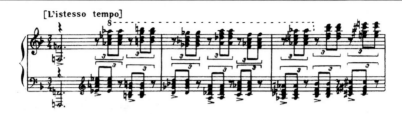

In the tenth variation, the combination of syncopated eighth and sixteenth notes sometimes causes problems for students. In such cases Yakov Zak suggests hearing each rest as the start of a group of four, in order to prevent the syncopation from 'hanging in the air'. He maintains that things usually go wrong first of all in the player's head rather his fingers. Zak is also an expert at identifying passages in a pupil's playing that show some rhythmic or dynamic unevenness, and once these passages are isolated he suggests taking this group of notes and examining it under the 'magnifying glass' of one's own hearing. To increase a pupil's self-control in passages that are unclear, it is necessary to control the articulation of every single sixteenth note, playing through and listening to the whole figuration like some living melody (this is especially relevant in the works of Chopin). This form of deliberate articulation assists in perfecting the performance of those episodes where a lack of clarity in articulation is apparent.

When a pupil brought two Chopin études to a lesson – the F major Étude, opus 10, No 8, and the one in C minor, opus 25, No 12 – Zak's comment was: 'In the C minor etude you are accenting the thumbs. You should hear a single flow of eight sixteenth notes. And what about smoothing and evening out the passagework in the Étude, opus 10, No 8? You must be conscious of the structure of the passage, get a sense of its "topography". Your wrist should follow your fingers. Then, in order to smoothen out those "rough" first fingers, it is useful to "iron out the seams" on the turns, gradually adding one note at a time on either side of the thumb and playing exaggeratedly *legato*. In order to get rid of accents on the first note in a group, mentally think of the passage as starting not on the first note, but on the second, as though covering the joints by a slur.'

This psychological refashioning of phrases with slurs often helps students to overcome technical difficulties with ease, turning apparently difficult passages into meaningful phrases.

Yakov Zak is categorically opposed to practising by hammering out notes, and he regards this as devoid of sense, and often actually harmful. As he says, this activity dulls and coarsens one's hearing, and a musician's hearing is like the eyes of an artist. All those methods that students often use for learning passages by playing *staccato*, or by altering the rhythm, et cetera, are maybe useful in working on instructional drills by Moszkowski, Czerny, Clementi and others, but they are quite inadmissible in working on a musical work of art. These devices are no help in achieving any artistic aim. They even distract one from it, especially if you need to achieve a *legato* when playing softly. A hand trained to play *forte* is forced to relax when playing *piano*, and then all the work on practising at *forte* level is wasted. Or else the result will be *marcato*, rather than *legato* and *piano*. Thus, for instance, in working on Chopin's F minor Étude, opus 25, No 2, Zak's advice is: 'Learn the étude at *piano* level, but with active fingers and a wrist that follows the fingers, haunting them like a ghost. One has to hear the melodic pattern, like a cantilena, so play with expression and meaning. As you increase the tempo, the finger sweep decreases, and at rapid tempo the fingers should be in maximum contact with the keyboard, while still preserving a sense of independence in each finger.' And half-jokingly, he adds: 'The final aim should be to play this étude *legatissimo*, *pianissimo*, and *leggierissimo*.' Advice of this sort is given also in dealing with the problems of variation fifteen in Rakhmaninov's *Paganini Rhapsody*.

In more complex examples, such as the Chopin Étude, opus 25, No 6, Professor Zak suggests imagining the right-hand part in thirds as a piece of two-part counterpoint, in which each voice should be studied separately, using the correct fingering and carefully following the melodic outline, until one has a sense of total freedom in each voice. The same principle operates as a basis for working on flexibility and plasticity of phrasing, where the player is forced to use 'uncomfortable' fingering of a sort often encountered in polyphonic works.

Thus, for example, in the development section of Liszt's Sonata one has to use the left-hand thumb to play an expressive phrase where *legato* playing is absolutely essential:

Yakov Zak regards it as essential to study separately this part played by the thumb, playing it smoothly with horizontal sliding movement from one key to the next. And only when one is used to the feel of playing this sort of *legato*, then one can add the other voice.

A routine mistake with students is that their *forte* playing is coarse, while their *piano* sounds feeble. Yet this often contradicts the sense of the actual music (in such pieces, say, as Bach's Fugue in C sharp minor from Book II of *The Well-Tempered Clavier*, or the separate Fugue in A minor, and others). Yakov Zak's requirement is that there should always be a sense of 'nervous engagement': one should learn to play energetically even at *piano* level.

Zak is also an opponent of using simplified fingerings, referring to them as a form of parasitism. Each and every change of the composer's prescribed fingering should be artistically justified. Examples of such justified changes occur in Zak's fingerings for a number of variations in the *Paganini Rhapsody*. In variation six, the rapid upward flights of melody in thirds and the piquancy of rhythm are well reflected in the following suggested re-fingering:

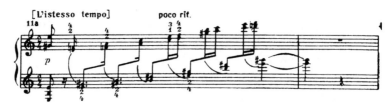

instead of the standard version:

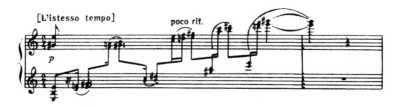

In order to achieve an insistent pulsing crescendo at the end of variation eleven, the left hand is used in playing the sequence:

And finally, the redistribution of eighth notes between the hands in variation nineteen enables one to achieve rhythmic evenness and a uniform rendering of the whole passage, as if played *pizzicato*:

instead of the usual:

One feature of Yakov Zak's method, most typical of him, is his training of 'polyphonic thinking' and an ability to discern concealed polyphony in episodes that at first sight seem quite non-polyphonic. 'In the first of the *Études Symphoniques*, the counterpoint set against the main theme defines the character of the whole étude,' was one of Zak's remarks. 'It has to be performed strictly, with no smudging of the rhythmic outline':

In the finale of Schumann's *Études Symphoniques*, in the episodes with *ostinato* dotted rhythm, one should hear the 'little drums' separately. They should be played *piano*, clearly, but not fussily, so that this pattern accompanying the whole episode sounds like a rhythmic leitmotif:

[Allegro brillante]

This meaningful interpretation of all the lines in a texture is combined with work on distributing them in 'acoustic space', creating a sense of stereophonic sound. To avoid details being perceived by the ear as if on the same plane, Yakov Zak makes a point of establishing the registers in both chordal and linear episodes. He starts with considerations dictated by the characteristics of various registers. In order that the upper register make itself felt above the rumble of lower tones, it should sound out keenly, and if a melody or figuration moves toward the upper register, then its sonority (though not its volume) and intensity of tone should increase. And the higher it moves, the greater its sonority (and in this high tessitura one can permit oneself more generous pedal).

In works that embrace a large space of sound, such as Chopin's Études of opus 10, No 8, and opus 25, No 12, Zak always reminds pupils of this so-called 'exploration of the registers', i.e. the need to create a rounded perspective in terms of sound. This is achieved, in particular, by a higher lifting and a more energetic and rapid depression of the fingers in the upper octaves and a closer (though in no way lighter) contact with the keys in lower registers.

In pieces with dense harmonic texture, and in general in chordal and octave episodes, Zak lays great stress on the tone produced by the fifth finger – this is, as it were, the pianist's first violin section, which is always under rude pressure from the thumb, especially in octave passages. Once, half-jokingly and half in earnest, Zak remarked on 'What does each of our fingers express when we play? The fifth finger is the soul, and the thumb is the body.'

Plenty of attention in Yakov Zak's classes is allocated to work on accompaniments, especially in the classical repertoire. The fact is that an inability to play a sequence of equal eighth notes as part of an accompaniment – especially if the figure begins on the second eighth note – is one of the most widespread 'ailments' among junior students. Equalization in timbre and rhythm, control over each note, and activation of the fingers – these are the only way to achieve mastery and control over each finger. And then, when once the pupil feels himself firmly held in a rhythmic framework, he can achieve a new and higher level of freedom: he feels himself free to play in a relaxed fashion, yet also strictly and with a proper sense of shape and proportion.

Yakov Zak lays great stress on the artistic realization of an accompaniment. One recalls his work on one of the Mozart concertos. 'Pay special attention to the 'pulse, the rhythm,' he insisted. 'The accompaniment in the left hand is one of the fundamental traits of this composition. Mere formal precision is not enough here. The rhythm should not dominate or seize the music in its grip, but it should have a youthful pliability and come alive.'

Usually, when students bring to a lesson such works as Chopin's Études, opus 10, Nos 5 and 8, or opus 25, Nos 6 and 11, and play the right-hand parts with jaunty fluency but without giving equal prominence to the left hand, Professor Zak is highly displeased. 'But it is a study in thirds after all,' the student objects, and Zak's rejoinder is usually: 'Yes, you've certainly made it a study in thirds. But the leading part here should be that of the left hand, which has its own expressive pattern. It is the left hand that provides the mainstay of the piece's character and imagery.' Similarly in the other Études mentioned, Zak suggests that the left-hand part should be practised for a long time as a separate musical work in itself, and that one should strive to convey its independent logic and completeness.

Yakov Zak spends a lot of time working with students on producing various timbre and phrasing. In polyphonic works, and in episodes that can be treated contrapuntally, he often uses expressions such as 'voices in disputation', 'contradiction', 'parrying' and so on, in order to stimulate students' active response to polyphony and its characteristic expression. Voice parts that often at first strike the student as disconnected then seem to enter into a living dialogue. Thus, for example, in the fourth variation of Rakhmaninov's *Paganini Rhapsody*, Zak sees the exchange of sixteenth note phrases between hands not as a single continuum but as a disputation, and he gets students to play the entry of each hand in decisive fashion:

Similarly, at the start of the development section of Liszt's Sonata, Zak insists that there be no let-up in the syncopated interruptions of the left-hand chords:

Continuing with the same work: 'In the fugato of this Sonata, where the theme collides with its own mirror inversion, the theme is set out in compact chords, as if played by the brass section, and it is contrasted sharply with its own one-voice inverted image. Here one ought to emphasize the relentless upward surge of the triplets':

In unfurling moments of conflict and tension in the text (rhythmic in the form of syncopations and polyrhythms; melodic in the sharp and angular sequences; and harmonic in unexpected modulations and unusual chords), Zak tries to get his pupils to appreciate the mechanism by which artistic images are built up, and to follow the development of the work as if it were a sequence of live events.

In one episode in the exposition of Liszt's Sonata, where an element of the main subject is being worked out, Zak emphasizes that 'the left-hand entry must sound as if it is "arguing" with the right'. Here he insists on pointing up the sharp contrast between duple and triplet rhythms:

In Zak's view a similar active 'interpolation' should be felt in the left hand's sudden drop of an octave (in the exposition episode marked *incalzando*); this is treated as the start of a new phrase that charges and further intensifies the atmosphere:

Yakov Zak's skill as a teacher enables him to undertake a survey of details in a composition while at the same time preserving a view of the work as a whole. Perhaps this is one of the most enlightening parts of his work. Another interesting aspect of his method lies in forcing pupils to consider the work they do with him in class as a preparation for performance on stage, working out various criteria concerning tone, timing, and pedalling, and allowing for various different types of concert hall.

Zak sets great store on having a conductor's view, as it were, of the composer's text. Pupils, he maintains, must 'know the score like a conductor'. He himself knows by heart every strand and chord of the works that he studies in class, and he helps develop students' ability to work with their own 'orchestra' (that is, to listen to themselves, as it were, at one remove). His advice on 'educating one's own orchestra' essentially applies the same methods that a professional teacher of conducting would use.

Just as the conductor carefully thinks through his score, so the pianist should first of all go through a composition and form a complete general conception of it, assimilating its ideas and general plan. Then he should ascertain the place of all its component parts and details and work their tonal, dynamic and emotional characteristics into the general scheme, obtaining the right sonorities from various 'instrumental sections' which are necessary for achieving an overall balanced 'orchestral' sound. One of Zak's favourite methods is working with these 'sections' – assisting the achievement of a strict ensemble in chord playing, overcoming any inequality of sounds within the chord (a chord played, as it were, by a single group of instruments), and the testing of unisons in various lines that move in parallel.

This imaginary conductor's work stimulates the pianist's own activity and willpower, organizes his thoughts, and forces him to undertake a detailed analysis of the work under study as if it were a conductor's score. There are a few instances where, for example, it becomes necessary to establish what beat to conduct. Much depends on this, and some things may need to be altered in light of it. For example, if a student draws out a slow movement unnecessarily, it may be useful to point out that it should be conducted in 2/4 and not in 4/8 time. On the other hand, if the pupil rushes matters and fails to hold dotted notes for their full value, then he should try for a time to conduct mentally in smaller measures. (The second movement of Beethoven's Sonata, opus 2, No 3 might serve as an example of this.)

When changing to a slower tempo between movements or separate episodes of a work, and especially when there is a *ritardando*, Professor Zak may well ask a pupil to 'conduct' that bar in shorter units. This form of 'breaking up the bar' constantly occurs in an orchestral conductor's work, and it prevents a passage in broader tempo from falling apart, holding it firmly under the player's control and maintaining *ritardandi* within a rhythmic frame, while at the same time permitting a measure of freedom. This device of breaking up the bar is used, for instance, in working on the rhythm of the following sequence from Liszt's Sonata, in which Zak recommends that the final two quarter notes be 'conducted' in 4/8 time:

Another important element in Zak's teaching is his requirement that 'sectional rehearsals' be held. This is of assistance in obtaining the required sonority in passages with many layers of sound, such as in the development section of the finale of Prokofiev's Third Concerto. It is not sufficient here to play with separate hands; it is important that the theme should not change timbre as it moves from one hand to another, and that the dense chord sequences in the right hand sound like an orchestral section of three instruments. To achieve this, Zak recommends repeatedly playing over individual chords and the theme, using the requisite fingering.

Some further examples of this are the following:

In the fifteenth variation of the *Paganini Rhapsody*, a student may well play the sixteenth notes hastily and unevenly, in which case Zak's suggestion is to 'learn separately the part that plays against the sixteenth notes. It is distributed between the two hands, but despite this it should be played and sound as a single whole, strictly marked and keenly phrased. Once you have this mastered, it will serve as an organizing feature for the sixteenth notes,' which can then be added.

Such 'sectional rehearsals' that assist in bringing together material divided between the two hands can also be conducted with Liszt's Sonata (for instance, the first subject in the exposition). Here it is useful to learn separately the part in sixteenth notes and the main theme which are passed between the hands:

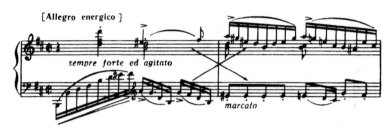

In the first subject of Ravel's *Sonatine* it is hard to secure a light and even tone in the middle voice, since a series of accents occurs as a result of the fingering. The theme itself is indeed hard to play *legato* and in a single breath. In this situation, a 'sectional rehearsal' can again be of benefit.

In the second of the *Études Symphoniques*, too, it is of help in achieving the right sound if one first works up the thematic duet separately, only later adding the chords of the accompaniment. Another variant of 'sectional rehearsal' is implied in Zak's recommendation to 'learn the upper voice part in Chopin's Étude, opus 10, No 2, first of all without the chords, striving for maximum legato and flexibility on the turns. The wrist and hand should closely follow and "guard" the fingers.'

Orchestral phrasing and other similar expressions are often used at Zak's classes, and students are required to 'orchestrate' separate episodes, trying to achieve the tone or some particular instrument. All these are methods of helping students find the right tonal characteristics for whatever they play. Zak frequently uses such terms as: *détaché*, *spiccato*, 'with a separate (or single) bow', *vibrato*, *pizzicato*, or 'played on gut strings'. 'You have no sense of the finger-board,' another student was told who failed to maintain close contact with the keys and who preferred to 'hedge-hop', skating over the surface of the keyboard.

As an example of the effectiveness of using 'bowing marks', one could take Bach's two fugues in D sharp minor – the one from Book II of the *Well-Tempered Clavier*, and the other that exists as a separate composition. In both of these it is difficult to get all the sixteenth notes to speak clearly, and to achieve an even rhythm and an energetic, flexible sound that is not too heavy. However, when Yakov Zak asks for these fugues to be played with each note detached and 'on a separate short bow' with equal attention to each sixteenth note, students quickly achieve the right sound quality. One should add that what is implied here is not just the stroke of some purely imaginary bow, since the hand of the pianist also makes a 'stroke' which enhances the activity of the fingers with the flexible, elastic movement of a free wrist.

When working to achieve some particular tone colour – for example, a flute in Chopin's Étude, opus 10, No 2, or the 'forlorn trombones' in the reprise of Liszt's Sonata, or else a dull bassoon tone in Chopin's Third Scherzo – Zak suggests various devices for various types of tone production. The tone of brass instruments is produced by playing with almost straight, firm fingers but with an active wrist; flute tones are obtained with the free flight of one's fingers; the bassoon is imitated with flat fingers accompanied by slight movement from the elbow, and so forth:

Despite what has been said above, it would be wrong to think that Yakov Zak regarded pianoforte tone merely as a pale reflection of the orchestra's palette of tone colour. The richness and variety of piano sound and its own unique splendour and attraction always remained at the centre of his attention. Not for nothing do we find that one of the special features of Zak's own pianism is his remarkable mastery of the most varied shades of purely piano sonority.

He also devotes a good deal of time in class to working on his pupils' tone production. This takes two directions – he both encourages pupils with associations and images that suggest the necessary approach and forces them into finding the right sound and phrasing, while he himself provides demonstration of various technical devices.

For obtaining the right touch, Yakov Zak often appeals to the pupil's imagination, asking him to play with 'nervous', or 'evil' fingers, or to pretend that he has a tiny diamond mounted in each fingertip so as to elicit a precise and intense tone quality. In some cases the fingers have to be 'subtle', and draw with a 'fine quill', with less area of contact with the keyboard; in other cases the fingers have to be 'flat' – something that is usually beyond most younger students, who play with fingers always in the same position and thus deprive themselves of some finer gradations of tone that can be achieved only by using the sensitive cushion at the tip of each finger.

In the development section of Liszt's Sonata there is one point where, in order to obtain a feather-light rustling of sixteenth notes, Zak requires that pupils play with a low wrist, very close to the key, and with flat fingers and the entire first phalanges of the fingers in contact with the keys:

By contrast, in the twenty-second variation of the *Paganini Rhapsody*, marked 'Marziale', he suggests playing with almost straight and hard fingers, even at *piano* level. This manner of playing creates a concentrated and severe tone quality.

'Play *espressivo* and *vibrato*, with alert fingertips, but sing with your own voice and without shouting!' is another of Zak's warnings designed to cool the fire of pupils who are inclined to thunder at the keyboard. 'A banging percussive sound is inadmissible in a cantilena – there should be a sensation not of striking, but of pressing down with the bow.'

On the other hand, Zak also works to counter the opposite extreme – a tendency to deprive the tone of all breath, starving it of flesh and blood. This type of tone Zak describes variously as 'dusty', 'milk and water', or 'colourless' – all designed to convey a sense of the pupil's lifeless tone. Elsewhere the word 'grimacing' evokes an image that helps a student sharpen his tone in order to characterize some grotesque episode (in Prokofiev's *Suggestion diabolique*, for instance). Other such similar expressions used by Zak include 'razor-like rhythms', and 'on devil's hooves' (describing the fugato passage in Liszt's Sonata).

When playing the figuration in variation twenty-two of the *Paganini Rhapsody*, a pupil may hear the order to play with 'stern fingers', 'kneading the harmonic dough', and in the first episode of Ravel's G major Concerto never to release the 'shifting harmony' from underneath one's fingers – all these images are designed to suggest the requisite technical approach and assist the player in achieving the acoustic effect he is aiming for.

Working on piano tone, Yakov Zak observes a general principle of playing 'close to the keys'. He calls for playing more 'into the keys' – even in *staccato*, which might otherwise emerge as empty and lacking in body. But just as often pupils may hear the warning that 'playing into the keys does not mean playing heavily or ponderously'. Thus in the eighth variation of the *Paganini Rhapsody*, Zak asks for elastic, youthful playing. And in the fourteenth variation, after the *tutti*, the chords should be made to sound 'ecstatic', as if on springs.

The idea of active fingers is most important for Zak. Even *staccato* in certain instances is regarded as a finger technique (for instance in the nineteenth and twenty-first variations of the *Paganini Rhapsody*, where '*piano*' is marked). In Zak's own words, the fingers should be 'mining' or 'extracting' the sound. This also concerns the playing of chords that are often treated polyphonically.

We have talked already about some of Yakov Zak's demands regarding use of the pedal. With him the question of pedalling is also usually treated in a concrete manner, in connection with some artistic problem. And even if the pupil knows the school rule about the pedal being used for just one harmony, artistic use of the pedal often involves breaking this rule. In those cases where an actual melodic line has to be heard, Zak suggests using half-pedal to prevent the melody notes from congealing into chords. This is the case, for instance, in the C sharp minor Prelude from Book II of *The Well-Tempered Clavier*. In other instances, too, the pedal recommended for sequences moving in seconds but in a high register is used to support a *crescendo* made with the fingers.

Zak suggests playing the sixth variation of the *Paganini Rhapsody* without pedal, in order to bring out the melodic figuration:

Conversely, in the subsequent phrases, he finds it necessary to use half-pedal in order to create a melting and dissolving sonority. The same sort of 'dissolving pedal' should be used in the Liszt Sonata, in bars 45-48 following the *Grandioso* episode. In the same Sonata, before the final *Andante sostenuto*, Zak's instruction is: 'Don't take off the pedal too early, together with the final chord. We first have to hear the whole stream of notes collected together on the pedal, and only then should we take it off.'

Music of course develops and unfolds through time, like some living organism. And the performer must have a sense of time and use it in fleshing out his artistic ideas. Concrete problems arise, such as defining the tempo of the work one is performing, the tempo relationships between various episodes, and the distribution of time within a single episode.

À propos of this one recalls Yakov Zak's work on the third movement of Beethoven's B flat major sonata, the *Hammerklavier*. It is well known how difficult it is to pace this superb *Adagio* movement, and to obtain a sense of integral wholeness over the large span of time that it occupies. Its sublime and courageous sorrow is reinforced by the sense of its measured pace. The rhythmic pulse is here the anchor and unifying element. The pauses and *fermata* markings placed there by Beethoven do not strike us as at all formal or arbitrary, but they are filled with living breath and are perceived as unique and essential because they are animated by an inner rhythm. The sense of movement within them never ceases, and the music seems as it were to continue sounding.

In other works, when the melody seems to demand freer treatment, or *rubato*, Zak recommends imagining it as if it were one's own personal improvisation. He also suggests playing the cadenza in variation eleven of the *Paganini Rhapsody* in this way.

However freely a melody is performed, interruptions of the general rhythmic flow are inadmissible. At one lesson, Yakov Zak was especially infuriated at one *rubato* that a pupil permitted himself in the chord accompaniment to the second subject section (*Grandioso*) in Liszt's Sonata. 'These chords should sound unshakeable, like the expression of some law, but you make them sound like a rather dubious accompaniment.' Zak insists that the character of any *ritardando* be decided depending on the character of the episode where it occurs. In his view, there is an enormous gradation of possible *ritardandi*, sometimes leading to a general dissolving of the rhythm (as in the Liszt Sonata, see example on p 216), sometimes expressing caution, as at the end of Variation eleven of the *Paganini Rhapsody*, where Zak wants pupils to retain the piquant rhythmic figuration and make a *ritenuto* by increasing the pauses between phrases – each one following slightly later and more insinuatingly than its predecessor:

Yakov Zak lays great stress on the meaning of various pauses. Thus, in the Liszt Sonata (see example on p 205), 'the pauses,' he maintains, 'should be filled with agitated expectation. After all, the pregnant meaning of these pauses requires plenty of time.' In another episode a change of emotional state seems to occur in the course of these pauses. 'But,' Zak objected to one pupil, 'you just keep on playing and don't give yourself time for any inner change of feeling...'

Students who feel inhibited in the ecstatic *precipitato* episode of Liszt's Sonata, just before the second subject's appearance in the reprise, and who cannot hear and theatrically maintain the following pauses, are told by Zak that 'Here you have to knock the sound off the edge of a precipice and keep gazing down and watching for a long time...'

However, the general pause just before the E flat major chord in the first subject of this Sonata, has a somewhat different character. According to Zak, it occurs as at were at a moment of weighty decision, and naturally one hears the insistent demand: 'Don't hurry. Don't rush the decision!'

Very often Yakov Zak directs students' attention to a broadening of tempo associated with the embracement of an increasing sound space. One example occurs in the six measures that prepare the climax at the end of the development in Prokofiev's Third Sonata: 'Here the culmination is something that has almost to be conquered and won. You have to calculate the expansion depending on the space you have to occupy and combine this with a reckoning of the dynamic expansion too.' Very often, along the way to some culminating point obstacles arise in the form of syncopations, gigantic leaps, or, for instance, in the following episode in the development section of the Liszt Sonata:

To overcome these obstacles requires energy, willpower, and considerable restraint with the tempo. This regulation of the tempo and dynamic relationships in preparing the climactic points, the reprise, and the limits of each episode is an architectural measure of this whole work.

This article sets out to introduce readers to a few features of Yakov Zak's teaching methods. His own main aim is to teach students to listen to themselves critically, to arouse and develop their powers of imagination, and to give direction and impetus to their own artistic ambition. Nevertheless, no matter how effective and attractive these methods may be, they are not a recipe for dealing with all of life's situations. In Yakov Zak's daily work, none of his views and comments ever degrade into mere dogma or stereotype thinking. And in this, probably, lies the secret of his great achievement as a teacher.

BIBLIOGRAPHY

MAIN SOURCES

Pianisty rasskazyvayut, ed M.G. Sokolov, No 1, 2nd edition. Moscow: 'Muzyka', 1990 [PR]

Voprosy fortepiannogo ispolnitel´stva, ocherki, stat´i, vospominaniya, ed M.G.Sokolov, No 1, Moscow: 'Muzyka', 1965 [VFI-1]

Voprosy fortepiannogo ispolnitel´stva, No 2, Moscow: 'Muzyka', 1968 [VFI-2]

Voprosy fortepiannogo ispolnitel´stva, No 3, Moscow: 'Muzyka', 1973 [VFI-3]

INDIVIDUAL ARTICLES

A.Gol´denveizer, 'Sovety pedagoga-pianista' [PR, 119-32]

S.Rikhter, 'Tri otveta na voprosy o sonate Betkhovena op 57 ('Appassionata')' [PR, 102-4]

K.Igumnov, 'O rabote nad balladoi Shopena f-moll' [PR, 113-18]

G.Neigauz, 'O rabote nad sonatoi Betkhovena No.28 op.101' [PR, 133-49]

S.Feinberg, 'Put´ k masterstvu' [VFI-1, 78-127]

S.Feinberg, 'Ispolnitel´skii kommentarii k "Appassionate" Betkhovena' [VFI-3, 73-83]

M.Eshchenko, 'Etyudy Shopena (ispolnitel´skii analiz v klasse prof. S.E.Feinberga)' [VFI-3, 120-37]

G.Ginzburg, 'Zametki o masterstve' [VFI-2, 61-70]

L.Oborin, 'O nekotorykh printsipakh fortepiannoi tekhniki' [VFI-2, 71-80]

Ya.Flier, 'Razdum´ya o Chetvertoi ballade Shopena' [VFI-2, 100-112]

O.Stupakova and G.Mirvis, 'Pedagogicheskie vzglyady Ya.I.Zaka' [VFI-2, 228-251]

N.Lel´chuk and E.Dolinskaya, 'Na urokakh Ya.V.Fliera' [VFI-2, 252-282]

'K.Igumnov o tvorcheskom puti i ispolnitel´skom iskusstve pianista. Iz besed s psikhologami' [VFI-3, 11-72]

A.Gol´denveizer, discussion of Chopin's Fourth Ballade in the section 'Razbor proizvedenii' in V klasse A.B.Gol´denveizera, edited by D.D.Blagoi and E.I.Gol´denveizer, Moscow: 'Muzyka', 1986, 105-12

INDEX OF PIANISTS, COMPOSERS & WORKS

Numbers in bold indicate pages where substantive interpretive or technical discussion is offered

ALEXEYEV, ALEXANDER / 34, 52n

ARENSKY, ANTON / 79

ASHKENAZY, VLADIMIR / ix, xx

BACH, J.S. / xi, xii, xiv, xvii, 39, 41, 49, 53, 108, 173
  Concerti / 202
  Fugue in A Minor / 210
  Fugue in D sharp minor / **218**
  The Well-Tempered Clavier, Book II,
    Prelude and Fugue in C sharp mi /
    210, **220**

BALAKIREV, MILII / 38

BARTÓK, BÉLA / 173
  Concerto No 3 for Piano and
    Orchestra / 206

BASHKIROV, DMITRII / xix

BELINSKY, VISSARION / 42, 52n

BEETHOVEN, LUDWIG VAN / xii, xiii, xv, xvi, xvii, 9, 31, 32, 39, 49, 60, 87, 97, 117, 121, 131, 132, 173

Sonata No 3 in C ma, op 2, No 3 / 107
Sonata No 7 in D ma, op 10, No 3 / 107
Sonata No 8 in C mi (Pathétique),
  op 13 / 107
Sonata No 11 in B flat ma, op 22 / 107
Sonata No 15 in D ma, op 28 / 104
Sonata No 17 in D mi, op 31, No2 /
  xiii, 92, 106, 114
Sonata No 21 in C ma (Waldstein),
  op 53 / 105
Sonata No 23 in F mi (Appassionata),
  op 57 / xii, xiii, **23-4, 34-5**, 89, **97-109**
Sonata No 28 in A ma, op 101 / xii, 60,
  110-28
Sonata No 29 B flat ma
  (Hammerklavier), op 106 / 201, 221-2
Sonata No 31 in A flat ma, op 110 / 195
Sonata No 32 in C mi, op 111 / 141
33 Variations on a Waltz of Diabelli,
  opus 120 / 201
Concerto No 5 for Piano and
  Orchestra / 103
Symphony No 3 / 103
Quartets / 202

BERMAN, LAZAR / xix

BLAGOI, DMITRII / xiii, 53, 109

BLUMENFELD, FELIX / xi, xviii

BORODIN, ALEXANDER / xiii, 86, 94n

BRAHMS, JOHANNES / 31, 69, 11, 147
   Concerto No 1 for Piano and
      Orchestra / 201
   Concerto No 2 for Piano and
      Orchestra / 151, 201

BRUMBERG, LEONID / xx

BÜLOW, HANS VON /118, 125, 128n

BUSONI, FERUCCIO / x, xvi, 39, 54, 80

CHALIAPIN, FYODOR / 6

CHOPIN, FRYDERYK / xii, xiv, xvii, 31,
   51, 60, 0, 89, 108, 129ff, 173, 208
   as pianist / 73, 81, 129ff
   Ballades / 146-7
   Ballade No 1 in G mi / 23, 132
   Ballade No 2 in F ma / 153
   Ballade No 3 in A flat ma / 146
   Ballade No 4 in F mi / xii, **146-71**
   Barcarolle / 152-3, **198**
   Études, op 10, No 2 in A mi / **135-7**,
      205-6, **217**, 218
   No 4 in C sharp mi / **137-40**
   No 5 in G flat ma / **213**
   No 7 in C ma / **135-6**
   No 8 in F ma / **208-9, 212, 213**
   No 9 in F mi / 132, 134
   No 10 in A flat ma / 132
   No 12 in C mi ('Revolutionary') / 134,
      140-41

Études, op 25, No 1 in A flat ma / 132
   No 2 in F mi / **209**
   No 5 in E mi / 132, **141-3**
   No 6 in G sharp mi / 205, **209, 213**
   No 7 in C sharp mi / 134, 165
   No 10 in B mi / 151
   No 11 in A mi ('Winter Wind') / 133,
      139, **143-5, 213**
   No 12 in C mi / 117, **208, 212**
   Étude in A flat ma / 132
   Fantasy in F minor / 148, **196, 206-7**
   Mazurkas / 142
   Mazurkas op 44, Nos 1 & 2, op 46,
      No 3, op 56, No 3 / 148
   Nocturne in D flat ma, op 27, No 2 /
      75-6, 165
   Nocturne in C mi, op 48, No 1 / 148
   Polonaise No 1 in C sharp mi / 134
   Polonaise No 2 in E flat mi / 148
   Polonaise No 5 in F sharp mi / 148
   Prelude No 3 in G major / **35-6**, 134,
      136-7
   Prelude No 14 in E flat mi / 129, 134
   Prelude No 24 in D mi / 134
   Scherzo No 1 in B mi / 148
   Scherzo No 3 in C sharp mi / 134, **218**
   Scherzo No 4 in E ma / **13-14**
   Sonatas for Piano / 109
   Sonata No 2 in B flat mi / 20, 89, 129,
   131, 134, 14, 194-5
   Waltzes / **199**

CLEMENTI, MUZIO / xiv, 209
   Gradus ad Parnassum / 81

CORTOT, ALFRED / 130

CZERNY, CARL / xv, xvi, 209

DEBUSSY, CLAUDE / 51, 159, 203

DOOR, ANTON / xvi

DREYSCHOCK, ALEXANDER / xvi

DUBUQUE, ALEXANDER / xvi

DVOŘÁK, ANTONIN
Piano Concerto in G mi / 108

EISENSTEIN, SERGEI / 201

ESHCHENKO, MARIA / xii

ESIPOVA, ANNA / xv

FEINBERG, SAMUIL / x, xi, xii, xiii,
xix, 3ff, 53, 97, 100, 103, 106, 129

FIELD, JOHN / xiv, xvi, xvii

FLIER, YAKOV / x, xi, xii, xix, 172-200

FISCHER, EDWIN / x

GABRILOWITSCH, OSIP / xv

GAVRILOV, ANDREI / xi

GERKE, ANTON / xiv, xv

GIESEKING, WALTER / x

GILELS, EMIL / ix, xi, xviii, xx

GINZBURG, GRIGORII / x, xiii, xix,
84ff

GLAZUNOV, ALEXANDER / xiii, 202

GLINKA, MIKHAIL / xiv

GOLDENWEISER, ALEXANDER / x, xi,
xii, xvi, xviii, xix, 53, 58-9, 60, 67,
82,84-5, 105

GORNOSTAYEVA, VERA / xx

GRIEG, EDVARD / 14

GRINBERG, MARIA / xix

HANDEL, GEORGE FREDERICK / 54

HANON, CHARLES / xvi, xix, 35, 52n, 69

HÄSSLER, JOHANN / xiv

HAYDN, FRANZ JOSEPH / 49

HENDERSON, WIGHT / xx

HENSELT, ADOLF VON / xvi, 138

HOFMANN, JOSEF / ix, x, 22, 39

HUMMEL, JOHANN NEPOMUK / xiv,
xvi, xvii

IGUMNOV, KONSTANTIN / x, xii, xv,
xvi, xix, 69, 78, 94n, 194

IPPOLITOV-IVANOV, MIKHAIL / 82n

JOSEFFY, RAFAEL / xvi, 69

KABALEVSKY, DMITRII / xix

KALKBRENNER, FRIEDRICH / xiv, xvi

KAMENSKY, ALEXANDER / 50

KANT, IMMANUEL / 66

KAPLAN, ARNOLD / xix

KAPP, KARL / xvi, 49-50

KASHIN, DANIEL / xiv

KINGSLEY, COLIN / xx

KISSIN, EVGENY / ix

KLINDWORTH, KARL / xvi, 165

KOGAN, LEONID / ix

KONDRASHIN, KIRILL / ix

KRAINEV, VLADIMIR / xx

KULLAK, THEODOR / xvi, xvii, 52n

LANDOWSKA, WANDA / 41

LEIMER, KARL / x

LENAU, NIKOLAUS / xii, 174, 177, 184

LERMONTOV, MIKHAIL / 42, 52n

LESCHETIZKY, THEODOR / x, xv

LHÉVINNE, JOSEF / ix, x, xi, xvi

LHÉVINNE, ROSINA / ix

LIADOV, ANATOLII / 202

LIAPUNOV, SERGEI / xvi

LISZT, FRANZ / xii, xiii, xiv, xv, xvi, xvii,
    31, 52n, 70, 89, 125, 128n, 133, 199
  as Pianist / 82, 86
  Faust Symphony / 174
  Gnomenreigen / 199
  Légendes / 147
  Les Préludes / 174
  Mephisto Waltz No 1 / **173-85**
  Sonata in B mi / 31, 174, **197-8**, 202,
    203, 204, **205, 209-10, 213-15, 216,
    217-19, 221, 222-4**
  Sonata 'Après une Lecture
    de Dante' / 31, 174
  Tasso / 174
  See also under Schubert

LITOLFF, HENRI / xvii

LUPU, RADU / xx

LYUBIMOV, ALEXEI / xx

MAHLER, GUSTAV / 109

MALININ, EVGENY / xx

MAXIMENKOV, LEONID / xx

MEDTNER, NIKOLAI / xi, xvi, xx, 9, 38,
    117
  as pianist / 39, 89
  Concerto No 2 in G ma for Piano and
    Orchestra / 201

MENDELSSOHN, FELIX / xvii

MENDELSSOHN-RAKHMANINOV
  Scherzo from A Midsummer Night's
  Dream / 199, 205

MICKIEWICZ, ADAM / 146

MIKULI, KARL / 136

MILSTEIN, YAKOV / xi, xix

MOGILEVSKY, EVGENY / xx

MOSCHELES, IGNAZ / x, xvi

MOSZKOWSKI, MORITZ / 209

MOTTA, JOSÉ VIANNA DA / 125, 128n

MOZART, WOLFGANG AMADEUS / xiii,
    xiv, 9, 19-20, 24, 31, 39, 54, 89, 201,
    204, 213
  Concerto in B flat ma, K 595 / **204**
  Sonata No 2 in F major, K 280 / **204**

MRAVINSKY, EVGENY / ix

MUSSORGSKY, MODEST / xiv, xvi, 52n

NASEDKIN, ALEXEI / xx

NEMENOVA-LUNTZ, MARIA / 115, 128n

NEUHAUS, HEINRICH, (GENRIKH NEIGAUZ) / x, xi, xii, xviii, xix, xxin, 53, 108, 110-28

NEIGAUZ, STANISLAV / xix-xx

NIKOLAYEV, LEONID / 202

NIKOLAYEVA, TATYANA / xix

OBORIN, LEV / x, xii, xix, 68-77

OISTRAKH, DAVID / ix, xviii

ORLOV, NIKOLAI / xix

PABST, PAVEL (PAUL) / xvi, xix

PALMER, PHYLLIS / xx

PAPERNO, DMITRII / xix

PAVLOV, IVAN / 94

PETRI, EGON / 58, 75

PLETNEV, MIKHAIL / ix

POGORELICH, IVO / xx

PROKOFIEV, GRIGORII / 67, 78-82

PROKOFIEV, SERGEI / 9, 39, 49, 173, xi, xii
Concerto No 2 for Piano and Orchestra / 190, 201
Concerto No 3 for Piano and Orchestra / 50-51, 188, 201, **216**
Romeo and Juliet / 188
Sonatas for Piano / 201

Sonata No 3 / **185-93, 223**
Sonata No 6 / 188
Suggestion diabolique / 220
The Fiery Angel / 190

PUSHKIN, ALEXANDER / 19-20, 51n, 121, 148

RAKHMANINOV, SERGEI / xvi, xix, 49, 108, 133, 173
as pianist / 20-21, 38, 39, 59, 84-5, 94n
Concertos / 201
Concerto No 2 in C mi for Piano and Orchestra / 84-5, **199**
Études-Tableaux / 51
Étude-Tableau in E flat mi, op 39, No 5 / **198**
Rhapsody on a Theme of Paganini / **199, 206, 207-8, 209, 210-11, 213, 216-17, 219, 220-21, 222**
Sonata No 2 in B flat minor / **203-4**
Suites / 202
Symphonic Dances / 202
See also under Mendelssohn

RAVEL, MAURICE / 159
Concerto in G for Piano and Orchestra / 220
Concerto for Piano Left Hand and Orchestra / 198

REINECKE, CARL / xvi

RICHTER, SVIATOSLAV / ix, x, xi, xii, xiii, xviii, xx, 107-9

RIES, FERDINAND / xiv, xvi

ROIZMAN, LEONID / xix

ROSTROPOVICH, MSTISLAV / ix

ROZHDESTVENSKY, GENNADII / ix

RUBINSTEIN, ANTON / ix, xiii, xv, xvi, 80, 82, 83n, 85, 94n, 146, 202

RUBINSTEIN, ARTUR / 65, 117

RUBINSTEIN, NIKOLAI / xiii, xvi, xvii, 80, 83n

SAFONOV, VASILII / xi, xv, xvi-xvii, xix, 80, 115

SALIERI, ANTONIO / 19-20

SANDOR, GYÖRGY / x

SAUER, EMIL VON / xiii, xx

SCARLATTI, DOMENICO / xi

SCHARWENKA, XAVER / 128n

SCHLOEZER, PAVEL (PAUL) / 20, 52n

SCHNABEL, ARTUR / 89, 114, 128n

SCHUBERT, FRANZ / 201
    Fantasia in F minor for Piano
        Duet / 202
    Schubert-Liszt, Serenade / xvii, 62

SCHUMANN, CLARA / xiv

SCHUMANN, ROBERT / xv, xvi, xvii, 24, 31, 45, 49, 65, 108, 146
    Études Symphoniques / 202, **204-5**, **206, 207, 211-12**
    Fantasy in C major / 60
    Kreisleriana / 150
    Novelettes / 147
    Toccata in C major / **198, 199**

SCRIABIN, ALEXANDER / xvi, 9, 31, 38, 39, 41, 51, 108, 115, 128n, 133, 159, 173, 179
    as pianist / 65

SHAKESPEARE, WILLIAM / xiii, 10-8, 121

SHATSKAYA, VALENTINA / 115, 128n

SHOSTAKOVICH, DMITRII / xi, 173
    24 Preludes, op 34 / 88-9
    Prelude in E flat mi / 89-90

SILOTI, ALEXANDER / xiii, xvi, xxin

SLOBODYANIK, ALEXANDER / xx

SOFRONITSKY, VLADIMIR / xviii

STANISLAVSKY, KONSTANTIN / 84, 94n

STARKMAN, NAUM / xix

STASOV, VLADIMIR / 85, 94n, xvi

STEIBELT, DANIEL / xiv

STEINHAUSEN, FRIEDRICH ADOLF / 27, 52n, 66

TAMARKINA, ROZA / xix

TANEYEV, SERGEI / 65

TAUSIG, CARL / xvi, 69, 81

TCHAIKOVSKY, PIOTR / xiv, xvi, 38, 40 49, 52, 92, 94
    Concerto No 1 in B flat mi for Piano and Orchestra / **36-7, 197**
    Francesca da Rimini / 43

TEICHMÜLLER, ROBERT / x

THALBERG, SIGISMUND / xiv

TORADZE, ALEXANDER / *xx*

TOMÁSCHEK, JOHANN / *xvi*

VENGEROVA, ISABELLE / *ix*

VILLOING, ALEXANDER / *xv, 80, 83n*

VITSINSKY, ALEXANDER / *44-5, 52n*

VOLODOS, ARCADI / *ix*

WAGNER, RICHARD / *17*

WEBER, CARL MARIA VON / *xvii*
   Perpetuum mobile / *89*

YUDINA, MARIA / *xviii*

ZAK, YAKOV / *x, xi, xii, xviii, xx, 201-24*

ZHUKOV, IGOR / *xx*

ZVEREV, NIKOLAI / *xvi*

INDEX OF PIANO PLAYING TERMS

Numbers in italics indicate passages giving detailed treatment to particular technical questions. References prior to page 97 are to specific technical problems discussed in Part One. References to pages 97 and following relate to technical problems in the context of specific compositions.

arm movement / *9*, 76, **80-83**

arm weight / **73-4, 78**

arpeggios / 80 (*see also* thumb movement)

authenticity (*see also* style) / **40-42**

cantabile / **14-15**, 18, 43-4, 56-7, 81

chords / 64, 82-3, 206, 212

double notes / 62, 209

exercises / **25-7, 27-37**, 136-7

finger technique / **8-9**, 32, **68-77, 78-83**, 135-7, 138, **167**, 179, 220

fingering / **36-7**, 62, 138, 156-7, 192-3, 196-8, 199, 210-11

forte / 12-13, 16

freedom (*see* position at the piano) 12, *3*, 70-71, 79, 117, 118, **168**, 179, 183

gesture / 7-8, **9-12**, 16-17, 114

hand position and weight, / 61, 64, **71-3**

hand movement / 9-10, **76**, 79-83, 138, 145

leaps / *33*, **64, 182-3, 207**

left hand (technique, action, vis-à-vis r.h. etc) / **35-7**, 135, 137, 140-41, 144, 207, 213

legato / 12-15, **75-6**, 139, 150-1, 209-10

leggiero (vis-à-vis *tenuto*) / **75-6**, 135, 139, 170

memorizing / 22-4

movement (physical) / **12**, 61-2, 114, 167, 168,

musical erudition / 110, 202

octaves / **61, 62, 79, 150-51**, 212

pedal (damper/sustaining pedal) / 5, **60**, **88-90**, 106,136, 168 9, 207

performance in public / 10-12, 18-19, **49-51**, 64-5, 199

phrasing / **59-60**, 76-7, 85-6, 162

physical movement (*see* freedom, gesture, *and* position at the piano)

pianissimo / **18**, 57, 209

piano (dynamic level; see also *pianissimo*) / 18, 74, 167, 194

pianoforte mechanism / 3-4, 6, 14-15

position at the piano / 72, 79, 82

practising / **20-27**, **44-9**, 63

practising away from the piano / **92-4**

repertoire / 48-9

rhythm / **57-9**, 216, 221-14

scales / 62, 77 (*see also* thumb movement)

staccato / 62, 179, **198-9**

style in performance / 37, 53-5

tempo / **84-8**, 108-9, 131-2, 223-4

tenuto (vis-à-vis *leggiero*) / **75-6**, 139

thumb (movement) / 62, 77, 80, 82, 198, 210

thumb (tucking under) / 31-2, 62, 77

tone production / 7, 15-16, 44-5, 55-7, 61, **194**

tone colour / 3-6, 17, 75-6, 194, 195, 198, 218-20

touch (*see* hand position *and* finger technique)

tremolando / 62

vibrato / 7, 114

Other interesting piano titles published by Kahn & Averill:

The Art of Piano Playing by Heinrich Neuhaus

Great Pianists and Pedagogues in conversation with Carola Grindea

Lipatti by Dragos Tanasescu & Grigore Bargauanu

Alkan – The Man, The Music by Ronald Smith

French Pianism by Charles Timbrell

The Pianist's Talent by Harold Taylor

Pianists at Play by Dean Elder

The Classical Piano Sonata by Michael Davidson

Chopin: A Graded Practical Guide by Eleanor Bailie

Haydn: A Graded Practical Guide by Eleanor Bailie

At the Piano with Fauré by Marguerite Long

Mozart and the Pianist by Michael Davidson

Piano by Louis Kentner (Yehudi Menuhin Music Guide)

All available from www.kahnandaverill.co.uk